OSTRICH CHRISTIANITY

Self-Deception in
Popular Christianity

Van B. Weigel

UNIVERSITY
PRESS OF
AMERICA

LANHAM • NEW YORK • LONDON

Copyright © 1986 by

University Press of America,® Inc.

4720 Boston Way
Lanham, MD 20706

3 Henrietta Street
London WC2E 8LU England

Library of Congress Cataloging in Publication Data

Weigel, Van B., 1954-
    Ostrich Christianity.

    Bibliography: p.
    1. Christianity—Essence, genius, nature.   2. Self-
deception—Religious aspects—Christianity.   3. Bible—
Evidences, authority, etc.   I. Title.
BT60.W45   1986   230'.044   85.17981
ISBN 0-8191-4974-8 (alk. paper)
ISBN 0-8191-4975-6 (pbk. : alk. paper)

TO MY PARENTS . . . WHO TAUGHT ME

THAT LOVE FOR GOD AND INDEPENDENT

THOUGHT ARE NOT MUTUALLY EXCLUSIVE

All quotations from the Bible are taken
from the Revised Standard Version unless
otherwise noted.

iii.

"Nothing is easier than self-deceit. For what each man wishes, that he also believes to be true."

> --Demosthenes (c. 384-322 BCE)
> Third Olynthiac, section 19

"To escape detection, chicks as well as adults may lie on the ground with neck out-stretched; a habit that may have given rise to the legend that the ostrich buries its head in the sand when danger threatens."

> --The Encyclopedia Britannica,
> 15th edition

TABLE OF CONTENTS

ix.

x.

PREFACE

The guardians of traditional religious beliefs are often torn between the aims of preserving orthodoxy and articulating their sacred tenets in a credible framework for a new generation. On the one hand, if loyalty to the past is sacrificed to an inordinate infatuation with the present, a religious movement forfeits its distinctive identity. On the other hand, if devotion to the past is not continually redefined by an authentic appreciation of the present, the strength of a religious movement is diminished. As long as the creative tension between loyalty to the past and openness to the present can be sustained, a religious movement has ample potential to reproduce itself.

This book represents an attempt to summon conservative Protestant Christianity to the arduous but rewarding task of recovering this essential tension between the claims of tradition and the challenges of modernity. Admittedly much of the book is highly critical of several popular conservative beliefs, a fact which may lead some readers to conclude that I am advocating the demise of evangelical Christianity, instead of its renewal. However, it must be remembered that just as true patriotism is founded on the will to criticize, authentic religious commitment is born in an environment of risk, introspection and inquiry. Nothing compliments the truth and strength of Christianity more than the courage to question.

In the midst of the critical portions of the book, I emphasize that self-deception seriously undermines the integrity of the Christian proclamation and severely restricts the scope of the church's mission. I argue that it is both unnecessary and undesirable for Christians to indulge in self-deception, as the essential truths of Christianity shine brightly in the harsh light of reality and self-deception can only subvert the best intentions of those who unwittingly practice it.

The occasion for writing the book was a welcome lull between my doctoral exams and dissertation. Like any author, I am profoundly aware of the debt I owe to others who have challenged my thinking, affirmed my confidence and enriched my understanding of the Christian faith. Among those friends and teachers who assisted me in my quest for understanding, the following people deserve special acknowledgment: Clayton Barnes, Marion and Yvonne McQuigg, Kathleen Sarpen, Ronald Kirstein, Karen Hadley-Dike, Joseph Finley, Carmine Colasante, Ann Montaney, Miriam Nolte, Carmen Beals, Culbert Rutenber and Thomas McDaniel.

In more ways than I can recount here, I owe a great debt of gratitude to William French, especially for our many discussions on self-deception in relation to ethical theory, which provided the immediate inspiration for the approach taken here. I am also grateful to Christina Jackson and Ann Maher for their helpful editorial advice, and to Leila Cardwell and Alberta Kirk who worked long hours in typing drafts of the manuscript. Moreover I appreciate the many helpful suggestions which Thomas McDaniel offered upon reading the manuscript. Special thanks are also due to Victor and Valerie Dalosto who provided me with many inspirational moments on the slopes of the Cascade Mountains while writing the manuscript.

Finally, I am grateful for my parents and their unwavering support, to whom this book is dedicated.

CHAPTER 1

THE DILEMMA OF POPULARITY

THE RESPONSIBILITY OF AMBASSADORSHIP

This book is about the misrepresentation of the Christian faith. Ironically this distortion of the truth is not the product of malicious intent or religious hostility. It is the work of devout Christians themselves. Because millions of Christians have unwittingly indulged in self-deception, contemporary Christianity faces a crisis of credibility . . . a crisis of authority.

It is cause for profound sadness that well-meaning Christians have subverted the credibility of their religious beliefs by adhering to counter-factual claims about reality, particularly in view of their high calling to be "ambassadors for Christ" (II Cor. 5:20).

The notion that Jesus' followers are "ambassadors" is a powerful image. It suggests not only that Christians are trustees of the liberating message of the Gospel, but also that they are obligated to represent the message of Jesus accurately and competently.

Unfortunately 'ambassadorship' is a dying art within the Christian community. Too often the art of persuasion is valued far more than the art of inquiry. Consequently, the message of Jesus is modified in order to maximize its market appeal, and what survives of his radical proclamation amounts to little more than a muted, 'respectable' rendition of Jesus as we wish him to be.

Whereas the Jesus of the Gospels understood the Kingdom of God as an integral social reality which involved both the transformation of individuals and political structures, many contemporary Christians

1

preach a compartmentalized version of the Gospel which only touches the heart, leaving the world at large unscathed. Whereas the one from Nazareth had the audacity to count despised Samaritans and irreligious Gentiles as heirs of God's Kingdom, too often the contemporary Christian community is characterized by a kind of religious tribalism, where great energy is expended on proving the doctrinal purity of one denomination over another. Whereas the Jesus of history displayed a profound confidence that no segment of everyday life was beyond the redemptive touch of God's love, not a few contemporary Christians prefer eschatological despair over constructive social transformation, reclining on Armageddon's bleachers to await the 'big event'.

Ultimately, the responsibility of ambassadorship amounts to nothing less than the challenge to penetrate the comforting illusions which mask the essence of what it means to be a Christian. Unfortunately comforting illusions die hard, and a true apprehension of reality as it is, not as we want it to be, is often cause for profound discomfort.

THE PRICE OF POPULARITY

Popularity exacts its price. Once a set of beliefs has gained mass acceptance, something happens to those beliefs--they are codified, institutionalized and altered to suit individual purposes.

The process occurs time and time again. The innovative, nuanced teachings of a religious or social leader are entrusted to a group of disciples who, lacking the imagination and subtlety of their founder, either alter the teachings of the leader in some way or find themselves preoccupied with 'digging foxholes'.

Fortunately, for their own sake, most founders of major social or religious movements do not have to witness the denigration of their teachings at the hands of professed disciples. The historical Jesus would have been appalled by the greed and corruption of Medieval Christendom, and Marx was long dead before Joseph Stalin instituted his reign of terror against the Soviet people in the name of the working class. Sometimes, though, as in the case of St. Francis of Assisi, a great leader greets death with the bitter realization that his followers have poisoned the values he held so dear.

THE LOSS OF VISION

The driving force behind any movement of social transformation is a vision . . . a glimpse of a better tomorrow that guides the actions of today. The great religious and social leaders of history were able to bequeath to their followers some segment of their vision. But, with the death of these leaders, invariably the vision grows dim or, perhaps, dies altogether.

Max Weber, a noted German social theorist, identified this process as the "routinization of charisma." Weber understood charisma as "a certain quality of an individual personality by virtue of which he is set apart from ordinary men and treated as endowed with supernatural, superhuman, or at least specifically exceptional qualities."[1] He went on to claim that charisma is "the greatest revolutionary force" in traditional societies.[2]

The 'home' of this great revolutionary force is the 'charismatic leader' himself. This leader might be a great warlord, prophet or king who stirred his followers to devotion to his peculiar mission.

Weber observed from his historical studies that the innovative force of charisma soon dissipated after the death of the charismatic leader, and was supplanted by either traditional or rational authority. He called this process "the routinization of charisma." Because charismatic authority is highly volatile and unstable, Weber believed[3] that this process of routinization was inevitable.

Of course, the routinization of charisma can be very positive, as the charismatic dimension of the leader is translated into the practical sphere

---

[1] Max Weber, On Charisma and Institution Building, ed. by S. N. Eisenstadt (Chicago: University of Chicago Press, 1968), p. 48.

[2] Ibid., p. 53.

[3] Ibid., pp. 54-61.

of everyday life. Often, though, the routinization of charisma has a negative consequence: the progressive, creative vision of a founder is reduced at the hands of his followers to rigid, unimaginative dogmas and lifeless, stratified institutions.[4]

It is quite easy to see how the normal process of routinization always creates some reality-distortion, where the purity and impulse of a founder's teachings are concerned. For instance, one cross-cultural investigation of fifteen religious founders (including Jesus, Luther and Calvin) discovered that these primary leaders differed from their "second leaders" (i.e., the disciple who became the movement's primary leader after the founder's death) in three

---

[4]Subsequent investigations have significantly modified and broadened Weber's concept of charisma. Perhaps the most important discovery is that the charismatic leader does not need to stand outside conventional social institutions, as Weber had thought, but can arise from within those institutions [Peter Berger, "Charisma and Religious Innovation: the Social Location of Israelite Prophecy" (American Sociological Review 28/6:940-50, 1963); cp. Joachim Wach, Sociology of Religion (Chicago: University of Chicago Press, 1944), pp. 173ff.]. Also Weber's use of the term 'charisma' was applied too narrowly to describe the relationship between an authoritative, gifted leader and his followers. Hence Weber did not realize how charisma could be the possession of the followers themselves [Dorothy Emmet, Function, Purposes, and Powers (London: Macmillan, 1958), pp. 233-35; Luther Gerlach and Virginia Hine, People, Power, Change (Indianapolis: Bobbs-Merrill, 1970), pp. 38-41] or an attribute "diffused" throughout a culture [Bryan Wilson, The Noble Savages: The Primitive Origins of Charisma and Its Contemporary Survival (Berkeley: University of California Press, 1975), pp. 95, 119ff.] Finally it must be emphasized that the routinization or institutionalization of charisma may itself bear the imprint of the charismatic leader, so that we may speak of "a latent form of charisma" that underlies formalized roles or ideologies and legitimates periodic innovations within that formalized structure [Michael Hill, A Sociology of Religion (New York: Basic Books, 1973), p. 172; Michael Harrison, "The Maintenance of Enthusiasm: Involvement in a New Religious Movement" (Sociological Analysis 36:150-160, 1975)].

significant respects. First, unlike the founder, the teachings of the second leader were usually uninnovative. Second, whereas the founders viewed dominant religious symbols as socially-constructed and capable of manipulation (e.g., "You have heard it said . . . but I tell you"), the second leaders perceived such symbols as fixed, absolute and inalterable. Third, all of the second leaders had an institutional office (hence a vested interest to conserve tradition) in contrast to most of the founders.[5]

THE LOSS OF NUANCE

In addition to the distortion of a founder's vision by the process of routinization, another factor leads to the misrepresentation of a founder's teachings and the distortion of reality in general. This factor is a popular movement's need for a well-defined belief system.

The investigations of recent popular movements conducted by Gerlach and Hine have yielded a fascinating conclusion. They discovered that movements as diverse as Pentecostalism, the Black Power movement and the Ecology movement share a common, five-fold structure.

One common denominator of these movements is that they offer their adherents a well-defined, codified belief system which, among other things, creates an aura of certitude, demands intense personal involvement, confers a sense of personal power, and clearly identifies 'the opposition'.[6]

Although we must be careful about generalizing

---

[5]Douglas Barnes, "Charisma and Religious Leadership: An Historical Analysis" (Journal for the Scientific Study of Religion 17/1:1-18, 1978).

[6]Luther Gerlach and Virginia Hine, "Five Factors Crucial to the Growth and Spread of a Modern Religious Movement" (Journal for the Scientific Study of Religion 7:23-40, 1968); _____, Lifeway Leap: The Dynamics of Change in America (Minneapolis: University of Minnesota Press, 1973), pp. 174-179; _____, People, Power, Change: Movements of Social Transformation, 159-182.

upon this limited sample of social movements, it seems plausible that any popular movement must proffer a well-defined belief system or 'party line' in order to sustain a program of personal or social transformation. The corollary of such a well-defined belief system is the loss of nuance. Consequently we might expect that some degree of reality-distortion is inherent in any mass movement, due to the loss of nuance in the movement's official ideology.

DISTORTION BY SELF-DECEPTION

The price of popularity is the <u>loss of creative vision</u> (due to the routinization of charisma) and <u>the loss of nuance</u> (due to the need to define a 'party line').

The price is high. Vision and nuance are hardly peripheral virtues where Christianity is concerned. Christians need vision to expand the parameters of Christian mission; they need discernment to articulate the Gospel responsibly.

The dilemma of popularity, then, is this: What level of reality-distortion is an acceptable price to pay for the growth of a religious or social movement, specifically Christianity? Assuming that some degree of reality-distortion is inevitable in any popular movement, it seems obvious that Christians should aim at minimizing such distortion, instead of exacerbating it by their own participation in self-deception.

To explain why millions of sincere, well-meaning Christians have unintentionally subverted the credibility of their own religious beliefs, I found it necessary to develop a theory of self-deception. What I call "Self-Deception Analysis," is a helpful tool for critical reflection which provides many opportunities for constructive criticism, fresh insight and renewed direction. The concept of self-deception will be discussed in Chapter 2.

Chapters 3, 4 and 5 concern the impact of self-deception upon dominant Christian beliefs about God's participation in human history. Three settings for God's involvement in human life are discussed: (1) God's participation in everyday, ordinary existence (Chapter 3); (2) God's involvement in moments of crisis

6

(Chapter 4); and (3) God's participation in humanity's future (Chapter 5).

Chapter 6 considers the influence of self-deception on dominant perceptions of 'Christian lifestyle' and 'Christian growth'.

Finally Chapter 7 takes up the controversial issue of biblical authority and argues that the popular notion of the Bible's inerrancy has been perpetuated by self-deception.

The book concludes on a positive note with a chapter on "The Possibilities of Frankness." In that chapter key aspects of Jesus' proclamation of the Kingdom of God are discussed in relation to a pivotal question of the book: What is the essence of Christianity?

A salient theme which runs throughout the discussion is that authentic Christian commitment enables one to face reality squarely, with a vision unclouded by the need to fabricate comforting illusions. It is fitting that contemporary disciples of Jesus should strive to reproduce the penetrating frankness and probing honesty of Christianity's founder. Authentic Christianity never prefers psychic well-being to an accurate perception of the truth.

WHAT IS POPULAR CHRISTIANITY?

Anyone who has seriously studied American Christianity appreciates its vast diversity. One cannot speak of American Christianity as a unified, homogenous entity. Religious groups in the United States differ markedly in terms of their theological tenets, institutional structures, and religious behavior.

Moreover, beyond the overt institutional sphere of American Christianity, there is a noninstitutional form of Christianity which is latent throughout American society . . . hidden from sight . . . but extremely significant nonetheless.[7] This noninstitutional facet of American Christianity inhabits our social and

---

[7] See Robert Bellah, The Broken Covenant (New York: Seabury Press, 1975); _____, "Civil Religion in America," in Beyond Belief (New York: Harper and

political institutions, penetrating to the bedrock of America's fundamental core of values.

An example of the pervasive presence of noninstitutional Christianity in American culture is found in the general public's view of the Bible's origins. A recent Gallup Poll indicates that eight out of ten Americans believe that the Bible is divinely inspired. Of these, a full 37% take the conservative position that the Bible is literally the Word of God, from cover to cover, inspired word for word. These findings are extraordinary when one considers that only four in ten Americans attend a church or synagogue during a typical week.[8]

Throughout the book I refer to the term 'Popular Christianity'. The institutional referent of Popular Christianity is the conservative wing of American Protestantism. In its noninstitutional setting, Popular Christianity is manifest in the religious ideas of the stereotypical 'man on the street'. Assuming that a person considers himself 'religious' but does not have formal ties with a particular religious group, there is a strong likelihood that he will view the Bible as an inspired document, perhaps even as a dictated memorandum from God. Additionally we could expect that he will tend to rely upon God in times of crisis, believing that God will somehow turn a bad experience into something good. Moreover, in many situations, we could expect that he subscribes to some kind of divinely-sanctioned principle of reciprocity: "what you dole out to others will eventually come back upon yourself." Finally, even though our 'man on the street' may be unfamiliar with biblical prophecy or Popular Christian jargon like 'the rapture' or 'the second coming', he may feel a generalized anxiety that life, as we know it, is about to end, with the attendant hope that something better may emerge from the rubble.

Row, 1970), pp. 168-189; Robert Jewett, The Captain American Complex (Philadelphia: Westminster Press, 1973).

[8] George Gallup and Associates, Religion in America: The Gallup Report, Nos. 201-202 (June-July, 1982), pp. 42, 73-74.

In both its institutional and noninstitutional
settings, the amorphous entity which I call Popular
Christianity could be defined as the constellation
of religious ideas which are typically (but not necessarily) affirmed by the conservative wing of the Protestant religious public.

Popular Christianity is an expression of Christian
faith and practice with which I am intimately
acquainted. While my remarks are largely critical,
actually this book could be construed as a kind of
'vote of confidence' for this expression of Christianity. It is my conviction that much of the sincerity and enthusiasm of Popular Christianity has been
misdirected and wasted. This is particularly unfortunate, given the immense problems facing humanity and
in view of the tremendous transformative potential
that resides within the Christian Gospel.

A common retort among the defenders of Popular
Christianity against the critics is the argument that
the following of various television evangelists and
the growth of conservative Christianity indicates
that they must be doing something right. However
the argument is fallacious. There is no obvious connection between Nielsen ratings or the size of a church
and the correctness of a religious belief. Perhaps
if the Christian faith was a commodity bought and
sold on the open market, this type of argument would
have some validity.

Obviously the Christian faith is not such a traded
commodity. It is a religious tradition originating
from the life and teachings of its founder--Jesus
of Nazareth--and shaped by the beliefs and practices
of his followers--the Church--down through the ages.
The task of distinguishing valid Christian beliefs
from specious ones is not a matter of optimal performance on the market of religious ideas.

WHAT IS VALID CHRISTIAN BELIEF?

Are there meaningful ways of discerning valid
Christian beliefs from invalid ones? Are there some
objective criteria that can guide us in this task?
Obviously questions such as these raise difficult
issues.

Is the Bible the ultimate standard for true

Christian belief? Many readers would probably respond with an unequivocal 'yes'. But actually to pose the question in this way is misleading. A more precise restatement would be: What segment of the biblical tradition and which interpretation of those portions of scripture should be the criterion of true Christian belief?

Or perhaps the teachings of the Church should be our guide? But this prompts several other questions. Which period in the history of Christianity best articulated the Christian proclamation? Some would respond that the teachings of the early church are the most authoritative because of their chronological proximity to Jesus' life. But what does nearness in space and time have to do with discerning true Christian belief? Why is that relevant? In fact an excellent case could be made that we--nearly 2000 years distant from Jesus' era--are in a much better position to discern the nature and significance of his life and teachings.

If the teachings of the Church are to be our guide, what theologian or school of thought sufficiently integrated the subtleties of Christian belief with the timeless predicaments of human communities, so that their formulations remain authoritative to us today? What religious denomination or movement most faithfully embodied the ideals of Jesus? Is there any way of escaping the subjectivity of determining valid Christian belief simply on the basis of what each local church or denomination thinks?

Or should some moral principle, a particular theological concept or a philosophical system provide us with the ultimate criterion for correct Christian belief? Which moral principle? What theological concept should have priority? What system of philosophy? Is the search for objective criteria altogether in vain? Do such criteria of validity lie only within the conscience, 'spirit', experiences or feelings of each individual believer?

Surely it would be unacceptable to throw up our hands in exasperation at this seeming melee of ambiguity, declaring that there is no way to distinguish valid Christian beliefs from invalid ones. There ought to be something more we can say about the Christian faith than to report that person 'A' has this religious belief and person 'B' has another, group 'X' holds this view and group 'Y' adheres to another.

Certainly the Hebrew-Christian scriptures must play a pivotal role in our search for criteria of true Christian belief. Moreover to ignore the development of Christian thought and practice throughout different historical periods and across divergent cultures would be utterly foolish. Also the judgments of contemporary believers--who may face a fundamentally new set of issues--and their respective communions should, and inevitably will, play some role in the formulation of these criteria of valid Christian belief.

To carry the matter further would go far beyond the purposes of this book. The issue is raised, though, to make explicit one criterion of validity which is assumed throughout the book. I make the assumption that any belief that is falsifiable and has compelling evidence against its validity should not be regarded as a true Christian belief, no matter how many Christians of the past or present may cleave to it. More will be said about the condition of falsifiability in Chapter 2. The intuitive idea behind this criterion of validity is that, at the very least, Christian commitment should be reality-affirming instead of reality-evading.

THE PASSION FOR TRUTH

It is especially fitting that the Christian faith should be in the business of unmasking self-deception, in view of the life and teachings of its founder. Jesus' brief but epoch-making ministry exhibited a preoccupation for "speaking the truth in love" (Eph. 4:15). He adroitly penetrated the masks of false religion and made its hypocrisy and exploitation transparent to the unlearned. Stern and forceful with money changers in the Temple (Mk. 11:15-19) but kind and forthright with the Samaritan woman (Jn. 4:1ff.), we see a Jesus who went about disclosing truth and inaugurating the Kingdom of God.

Jesus' task did not permit many euphemisms. The Jesus of the Gospels irreverantly addressed King Herod as a "fox" (Lk. 13:32), and he vigorously decried the economic exploitation of the helpless and the poor (Mk. 12:40). Jesus unmasked the fraudulent piety of the scribes and priests by declaring that prostitutes and despised tax collectors stood a better

11

chance of entering the Kingdom of God than they did
(Mt. 12:28-32). He demonstrated a highly distasteful
disrespect for canons of politeness and proper
behavior. For instance, he associated with some con-
temptible types (Mt. 11:19; Mk. 2:13-17; Lk. 15:2);
he ignored important Sabbatical rules (Mk. 2:23-28,
3:1-6; Lk. 13:10-17; 14:1-6); and he even permitted
a prostitute to display her affection for him in public
(Lk. 7:36-39).

The pointed, radical character of Jesus' message
has become lost in our distance from his era. We
forget his obsession for the truth, courtesy of our
candy-coated versions of Christianity. Our familiarity
with the content of Jesus' teachings--removed from
the historical context in which they were articulated
--makes his message seem very orthodox to our ears.

In his day, though, things were different. Jesus'
words were so annoying that it took death on a cross
--an act of the state--to silence him. Jesus did
not retreat into comforting illusions. Instead he
courageously unmasked the self-deception of his age.

Contemporary disciples can be satisfied with
no less than appropriating his passion for truth.

CHAPTER 2

THE ANATOMY OF SELF-DECEPTION

THE TASK OF PERCEPTION

Reality. The ground under our feet, the sky above our heads, death, life, pain, joy, every human emotion imaginable, the most imperceptible sensory experience, and an abtruse philosophical thought--all of these can be labeled 'reality'.

The concept of reality is so broad that any definition of the word seems hopelessly tautological: reality is that which is real and is not that which is unreal. 'Reality' is a symbol which is used as a means of signaling others: "Listen, now I am telling you the way things are." We often hear about the 'real world' and constantly punctuate our speech with words like 'actually', 'valid', 'genuine', 'really' and 'in fact'.

Yet, curiously, despite our profuse usage of reality-language, most of the time reality is something to which we simply refer. Rarely do we pause to consider exactly what reality is in itself. Instead we tend to assume that reality is something self-evident to any normal person. In short, we take reality for granted.

The various mechanisms of the human body which receive, transmit and interpret the complex data of the physical senses work overtime at making sense of reality. This marvelous process is so commonplace and routine that we fail to appreciate it. We do not usually think of reality as a jumbled mass of sensory stimuli. Ordinary reality has enough coherence and constancy to create the illusion that it exists 'out there' and that we are simply passive receptors of it.

But the illusion of a reality 'out there' perishes when our reality becomes a little less ordinary, when we encounter what has been called a "critical situation."[1] The extreme conditions of a concentration camp, being marooned on a deserted isle, experiencing prolonged sensory deprivation, or suffering mild or acute schizophrenia--these can deny us of the stable norms and conditions which we call 'reality'. To a less extreme degree, when we encounter people of markedly different intellectual or moral perspectives, or when we travel to a foreign culture, sometimes our reality is shaken up.

Obviously reality is not 'out there'. We, along with others, create it (to some extent) and nourish it by the thousands of repeated practices or habits that make up our day-to-day existence. Children have routine ways of relating to parents, parents to children, teachers to students, employers to employees, and so forth. These repeated practices embody and reinforce standards or norms by which 'appropriate' conduct is encouraged and 'inappropriate' behavior is discouraged. People participate in dynamic patterns of belief, communication, cooperation and exploitation--reality is this and much more.

This means that the business of perceiving reality is a tricky task. Perception is an action word. We do not just passively 'see' the world around us. Our 'seeing' involves us personally. From the day of our birth we were thrust into a world of interpretation.

TWO ASPECTS OF PERCEPTION

What is perception? Perception, broadly speaking, can be thought of in terms of two processes: recognition and avowal.

Recognition refers to the way we receive and interpret data. The process of recognition can be

[1]Anthony Giddens, Central Problems in Social Theory (Berkeley: University of California Press, 1979), pp. 123ff. Giddens' "theory of structuration" has strongly influenced my thinking in this chapter.

roughly divided into four basic categories: (1) reception, (2) attention, (3) selection, and (4) classification.

Of these four aspects of recognition, <u>reception</u> mainly concerns the physiology of perception, that is, the biochemical complexities involved in the stimulation, transmission and organization of the millions of nerve impulses which translate into sense experience and thought. <u>Attention</u> refers to the motivational factors which affect the relative energy we devote to seeing, hearing, tasting, touching or smelling a 'perceptual field'. <u>Selection</u> involves the split-second, subtle process of filtering certain things out of a perceptual field, eliminating what is 'unnecessary' or unpleasant. <u>Classification</u> refers to the 'boxes' we use to file our sensory experiences, ranging from simple notions of space and time to more complex interpretive 'paradigms' or 'world views'.

<u>Avowal</u> refers to the attitude or posture we take toward the information we have recognized. It means that we acknowledge or 'own' something, instead of suppressing or avoiding it. To avow reality is to strive to minimize, to the best of our ability, the use of 'inappropriate' defense mechanisms as a means of evading threatening or unpleasant aspects of reality.

Those people who are proficient in the skill of avowal have adopted a stance toward life which I shall call 'ideological openness'. In essence, ideological openness simply means that we recognize that no one--including ourselves--has cornered the market on truth. It means that when we encounter data which challenge our beliefs in some respect, we neither run from the conflict nor abandon our own views prematurely.

It is important to distinguish between 'openness' and 'commitment'. A person can be genuinely open to new ideas and still remain committed to his or her own beliefs. In fact, it is difficult to see how a firm and secure commitment to any belief system can be built on a foundation other than that of openness. Otherwise one's commitment will always be subject to fleeting pangs of doubt which can never be explored, for fear that the very foundations of one's commitment may be undone.

There is certainly no inherent conflict between

15

commitment and openness. Yet, it is often the case that tolerant people are usually willing to take the risk of openness but less willing to take the risk of commitment. We are all familiar with people who are so eager to see 'all sides of the question' that they find making definitive commitments to be a painful experience.

Commitment injects us into the struggles of the real world; ideological openness provides us with the means to make commitments which are informed, intelligent and moral. Openness without commitment yields an emaciated form of tolerance; commitment without openness opens a Pandora's Box of mindless fanaticism and misguided utopianism.

Avowal, as a perceptual process, demands that we take a continual posture of openness, but the ethos of openness will never permeate human affairs unless it is matched with commitment.

THE CONCEPT OF PSYCHOLOGICAL DEFENSE

Psychologists speak of reality-evasion in terms of the theory of psychological defense. Defense mechanisms, as they are called, are the mind's equivalent of the external mechanisms of defense which are found in every sector of our society. Like locked doors, confidential records, police forces and elaborate preparations for national defense, the defense mechanisms of the mind attempt to create an aura of security in the midst of potentially threatening situations. But there is one significant qualification to this analogy. Psychological defenses are usually deployed in situations that appear threatening, when, in fact, they pose no real threat to our well-being.

We are indebted to Sigmund Freud for the first systematic theorization of the concept of psychological defense. Of course, the basic idea that human beings use various devices to evade reality is an ancient one. For instance, Jesus himself spoke of the defense mechanism of projection, that is, imputing rejected or disowned aspects of ourselves upon others (Mt. 7:3).

The full complement of defense mechanisms available to any would-be evader of reality is quite extensive. One psychiatrist has identified 22 major

16

mechanisms of defense and 26 minor ones.[2] Included in this list are the more familiar mechanisms of projection, denial, rationalization, repression and compensation. Other defense maneuvers are less known, such as dissociation, idealization, reaction formation, isolation, compromise formation and symbolization.

The idea that human beings have certain ways of evading intolerable or unpleasant aspects of reality seems straightforward and uncontroversial. The matter becomes somewhat complicated, though, when we assign a particular motivation or explanation to a defensive maneuver.

Any act of defense--whether physical or psychological--involves some type of motive or rationale that makes the action explicable. If we are defending ourselves against some form of external aggression, the motive for our defensive response is usually obvious and clearcut. We want to protect our property or our very lives!

But the motives for psychological defense are not quite as obvious. Classical psychoanalytical theory--formulated by Freud--held that all defense mechanisms were devices used by the 'ego' for the purpose of warding off instinctual desires which are socially unacceptable (i.e., as a means of resolving conflicts between the 'id' and 'superego').

Certainly the psychoanalytic theory of defense is still the 'received' theory on the 'how' and 'why' of defense mechanisms; although, subsequent theorists have voiced objections which qualify or limit the claims of psychoanalytical theory. For instance, some theorists claim that defense mechanisms are pressed into service for the purpose of protecting and enhancing our self-esteem.[3] Others, from the 'cognitive dissonance' school of thought, have suggested an alternate or supplemental explanation for defense mechanisms. They argue that these mechanisms function to reduce the amount of dissonance or 'noise' which two opposing thoughts create in our minds.

---

[2] Henry Laughlin, The Ego and Its Defense (New York: Appleton-Century-Crofts, 1970), p. 7.

[3] See Morris Rosenberg, Conceiving the Self (New York: Basic Books, 1979), pp. 55-57.

Hence defense mechanisms are a means[4] of turning down the blare of 'noise' within our minds.

The common denominator of all these explanations is that defensive reactions are a way of dealing with threatening situations and the anxieties which they generate.

THE PROS AND CONS OF DEFENSE

Are defensive maneuvers always a bad thing? Definitely not. Some psychologists have distinguished between "successful" and "unsuccessful" defense mechanisms, between those mechanisms which are "repressive" and "nonrepressive," or between defenses which are "normal" in contrast with those that are "pathological."[5] These kinds of distinctions are founded on the differing structural features of various defense mechanisms.

In speaking of good or bad defense mechanisms, it is important to identify whether 'goodness' is used as a technical term or as a moral term. In the technical sense of goodness, a defense mechanism is good if it is an effective means to some end. But if we speak of a defense maneuver as being 'good' in a moral sense, we mean that it promotes some aspect of human well-being, like mental health or self-respect. Moral goodness refers to the ends to which defense mechanisms are directed. Often the semantical difference between the technical and moral senses of 'good' is overlooked by those who distinguish between positive and negative defense mechanisms, an oversight that leads to needless confusion.

Throughout the book defense mechanisms will be evaluated in terms of the technical sense of their 'goodness' or 'badness'. I distinguish between two

---

[4]See Jack Brehm, and Arthur Cohen, Explorations in Cognitive Dissonance (New York: John Wiley, 1962), pp. 165ff.

[5]See Charles Eriksen, and Jan Pierce, "Defense Mechanisms," in Handbook of Personality Theory and Research, ed. by E. F. Borgatta and W. H. Lambert (Chicago: Rand McNally, 1968), p. 1008.

types of defense mechanisms: those that are appropriate in relation to a particular end and those that are inappropriate in relation to that end. It is a separate question as to whether that end or goal is 'good' or 'bad' in the moral sense of the term. For example, a young man who aspires to become a mafia 'hit-man' will find the defense mechanism of isolation (divorcing an idea or object from the emotional meaning that is normally attached to it) to be very compatible with his vocational goal. In a technical sense, then, isolation is a 'good' defense mechanism. Of course, it is an altogether different question as to whether this young man's career choice is 'good' from a moral point of view.

Whether or not a particular defense mechanism is 'inappropriate' will depend upon the values of the person in question. If a person is obsessed with the discovery of truth as an end in itself (to the extent that she is prepared to forego many pleasures and endure much hardship to find it), then probably nearly all defensive maneuvers would be incompatible with her personal values. On the other hand, the person who concerns himself only with functioning as a 'normal' person in society would probably approve of a wide range of defense mechanisms, as long as they promoted efficiency, success or self-confidence.

The distinction between appropriate and inappropriate defense mechanisms is important to the central objective of the book: to show how certain defensive responses are often practiced by Christians and why these reactions are incompatible with both their implicit aims and the essential features of the Christian faith.

Incompatible defense mechanisms have a way of foiling our true intentions and sidetracking us from our stated purposes and ultimate aims. They prompt us to reactionary modes of action, diminish our creativity, and pollute the sources of inspiration from which our ideals draw their sustenance. In short, inappropriate defense mechanisms are a thing to be avoided.

AWARENESS AND DEFENSIVE RESPONSES

Do mechanisms of defense operate within us unconsciously, or are we aware of them to some degree? Most psychologists would respond that defense mechanisms, to be true defensive maneuvers, must be "unconscious" or "preconscious" reactions. These psychologists may distinguish among "levels of unconsciousness," but still insist that the "automatic" or "effortless" quality of defense maneuvers implies that their sphere of operation is outside the realm of consciousness. However this assumption is now being questioned.

The criticism has mounted on at least two fronts: (1) the _philosophical_ question as to whether it is necessary to posit the condition of unconsciousness in order to develop a cogent theory of psychological defense;[6] and (2) the _empirical_ question as to whether the presence of an "automatic process" necessarily precludes the possibility of some degree of learning and awareness.[7]

What seems important to any theory of psychological defense is not the element of the unconscious _per se_, but the fact that the defensive reaction itself has a habitual or "automatic" quality about it. Certainly the notion of the "unconscious" or "subconscious" may play a critical role in explaining the _why_ of defensive maneuvers; but, it need not play a major role in explaining the _how_ of defense mechanisms.

We can point to other explanations of the 'automatic' quality of defense responses. For instance, all of us are familiar with certain habitual tasks or reactions which we seem to perform almost unconsciously. We may be completely unaware that these repeated behaviors are deeply ingrained habits. But the moment something happens to prevent us from accomplishing these routine tasks, we become acutely aware

---

[6]See Herbert Fingarette, _Self-Deception_ (London: Routledge and Kegan Paul, 1969), pp. 113ff.

[7]See Eriksen and Pierce, "Defense Mechanisms" (in _Handbook of Personality Theory and Research_), pp. 1031-1032.

of them and experience "de-routinization."[8]

Habitual or repetitive actions are commonplace in the thousands of practices or behaviors which make up our lives. We are certainly not always immediately conscious of what we are doing; yet, such practices could not exist apart from our willingness to reinstate or recreate them by our actions. As social theorist Anthony Giddens has argued, even though we may not be able to verbalize why we do what we do, we have a "practical consciousness" of these social practices: "tacit knowledge that is skillfully applied in the enactment of courses of conduct, but which a [social] actor is not able to formulate discursively."[9]

Giddens' notion of "practical consciousness" is an intermediate category between what he calls "discursive consciousness" (the ability to verbalize the how and why of action) and the classical notion of "the unconscious." He notes that many psychologists and sociologists have tended to assume that any bit of knowledge which cannot "be brought to and held in consciousness" belongs to the unconscious.[10]

Throughout the book it is assumed that some, not all, mechanisms of defense (including all those treated in this discussion) operate mainly within this intermediate sphere of 'practical consciousness'. This point may seem purely academic, but it is a crucial cornerstone for a theory of self-deception in two respects: (1) for self-deception to be a morally significant concept, it is necessary for a person to be responsible--to some degree--for the perpetuation of defensive reactions; and (2) for self-deception to be a strategically significant concept, it is necessary to identify the implied or reported intentions of a social actor for the purpose of demonstrating why defense maneuvers are malfitted for the goals toward which a person acts.

The first point emphasizes that people share some personal responsibility for their use of defense

---

[8]Giddens, Central Problems in Social Theory, pp. 220ff.

[9]Ibid., p. 57.

[10]Ibid., p. 25.

mechanisms. If defense mechanisms actually operate involuntarily, well beyond the region of consciousness, it would be impossible to develop a cogent theory of self-deception. If those patterns of perception which dim our intellectual, emotional, sensory and spiritual capabilities were controlled by forces outside the realm of decision (e.g., some genetic trait, a malevolent deity or social conditioning), we would be victims of cruel deception, having ample grounds for profound despair; but, we would not be self-deceived. Self-deception is a moral concept; hence it must be founded on a plausible basis of authentic personal freedom.

The second point emphasizes that defensive maneuvers are perpetuated with some purpose in mind--either a stated aim or an implied intention. Those purposes may be credible or ridiculous, healthy or unhealthy, meaningful or pointless. But whatever the purpose may be, it supplies a social actor with a rationale for his perpetuation of self-deception: a strategy. Defense responses which are incompatible with a stated set of objectives will not produce the desired bill of goods. The first line of criticism advanced in this book is that certain defensive reactions practiced by many Christians ultimately subvert the goals which they purport to achieve.

WHAT IS SELF-DECEPTION?

Deception. The word conjures up negative images: deceit, unfaithfulness, manipulation and betrayal. From fair-weather friends who betray us to governments that lie about true intentions, all of us are familiar with deception. It is an unsightly piece of furniture in the household we call life.

Self-deception is a special form of deception. Here the source of deception lies within ourselves, not in external forces beyond the realm of our control. Often we think of self-deception in such extreme terms that it is easy to exclude ourselves from the company of the self-deceived. A middle-aged family man who romances a 19 year old, a deluded stockboy who declares his intention to run for President, or a mother who persists in the belief that her thrice incarcerated son is actually a nice boy afterall--they may be self-deceived. But not us, of course. We face reality squarely.

22

Not necessarily. Our participation in self-deception begins where our ability to entertain the possibility that we ourselves are self-deceived leaves off. Self-deception and its cast of supporting characters cannot be vanquished in an instant. The job of accurately perceiving reality is a lifetime vocation.

I define self-deception as <u>the determined perpetuation of patterns of perception which obscure relevant aspects of reality</u>.

The definition emphasizes that self-deception is a willful, on-going process. To participate in self-deception is to <u>continue</u> in self-deception. If we are completely <u>oblivious</u> to poor perceptual habits, willing to make improvements when they are called to our attention, we are not self-deceived. By contrast, true self-deception induces a kind of self-imposed blindness by reinforcing resilient perceptual patterns that obscure reality and diminish our perspective. It perpetuates bad habits of perception that ultimately lead us down a road paved with defeat and disillusionment.

The crux of the definition is the phrase "relevant aspects of reality." At issue is the term 'relevant'. When is it correct to apply the concept of self-deception? I define 'relevant' in terms of three <u>necessary</u> criteria of relevancy. For the concept of self-deception to be applicable, both the 'self-deceived' and the 'non-deceived' must: (1) have access to the same basic sources of knowledge; (2) agree on the approximate meanings of their terms; and (3) disagree over a matter which is falsifiable. If any of these conditions are absent, then it is incorrect to invoke the concept of self-deception.

1. The first condition of relevancy holds that unless all parties have <u>real</u> access to the same "stocks of knowledge," we do not have a genuine case of self-deception. This qualification is especially important where differing personal backgrounds (relating to cultural, educational or historical factors) produce markedly divergent versions of reality.

For example, when ancient man saw lightning in the sky and heard thunder, he interpreted the event in religious terms--perhaps as the awesome display of the storm-god, as a sign of divine disapprobation, or as the aftermath of a war among the gods. Obviously the interpretation offered by modern science is much different. Lightning is explained in terms of such things as static electricity and the convergence of certain atmospheric conditions--concepts unknown to the ancients. It would clearly be inappropriate to say that observers in ancient times were self-deceived in their religious interpretation of lightning and thunder. They simply did not have access to the data available to us today.

2. The second condition of relevancy specifies that both the 'self-deceived' and the 'non-deceived' must agree on the approximate meanings of their terms. This point is obvious, but it should be mentioned nonetheless. A homely woman who genuinely believes her boyfriend when he exclaims--"You are beautiful!" --does not indulge in self-deception, that is, unless he adds: ". . . and I think you should enter the beauty contest." The term 'beauty' appropriately encompasses a broader range of meaning than the super-ficial sort of beauty proffered in a beauty pageant.

Similarly a woman who is unaware of her husband's many shortcomings (painfully apparent to everyone else), because of her love for him, may confirm the adage "love is blind," but she is not self-deceived. The woman's apparent 'blindness' is not the outcome of a reality disavowed, but illustrates how different perspectives or standpoints create differing versions of reality. To say that she is 'blind' is a kind of shorthand for: "I don't know what she sees in her husband, but she must see something"; or "she loves her husband so much that she is willing to over-look his idiosyncracies."

3. The third condition of relevancy is that both the self-deceived and the non-deceived must dis-agree over a matter that is falsifiable. To say that a statement is falsifiable means that it is capable of being proven false. Beliefs that are unfalsifiable (or not capable of being proven false) are not within the purview of self-deception.

This point is especially important when it comes to examining various religious beliefs in relation to self-deception. I make the assumption that self-deception analysis tells us little to nothing about the origins of religious belief--its ultimate causes. Sometimes it is tempting to ascribe religious beliefs to non-religious causes--human psychology, economic motivations or sociological determinants. But to treat religion as an epiphenomenon, a dependent variable with no autonomy of its own, is an unhelpful and biased way of approaching religious issues. In order to avoid this tendency (often referred to as "reductionism"), I will make a distinction between general religious beliefs (which are unfalsifiable) and particular articulations of those beliefs (which may be falsifiable).

General religious beliefs such as the belief in the existence of God, miracles or human spirituality are unfalsifiable. We are unable to prove that God does not exist, that miracles never occur or that an integral aspect of the human personality does not survive the grave. Yet while general religious beliefs are not falsifiable, specific articulations of those beliefs may be falsifiable. An absurd example would be the following. Suppose an angel appeared to me and categorically declared that God lives on the moon, in the midst of streets paved with gold and lush vegetation. Because of the unusual nature of my encounter with the angel, I chose to believe the lunar reality that he described. Hence I concluded that the reports of astronomers and astronauts must be wrong, because their observations contradict my theological beliefs. In this hypothetical case my belief in God is unfalsifiable, but my heartfelt conviction that God resides on the moon in an idyllic paradise is falsifiable.

SELF-DECEPTION ANALYSIS

What I call "Self-Deception Analysis" is the process of discerning and isolating instances of self-deception. In doing this, it is helpful to identify five separate components of a self-deception problem: (1) the deception; (2) the intended objective(s); (3) the primary defense mechanism(s); (4) factors which perpetuate self-deception; and (5) the unintended consequence(s).

1. THE DECEPTION. The first element of Self-Deception Analysis is the deception. This consists of a falsifiable assertion about reality which in fact, is untrue. To falsify a statement it is necessary to demonstrate that, in at least one case, the statement is false. The statement may be false because it entails some logical contradiction, or because it is disproven by convincing data or 'intersubjective'

25

observations.

2. THE INTENDED OBJECTIVE(S). The second component of Self-Deception Analysis is the intended objective. Obviously people usually have reasons for holding a particular belief about reality. That belief may turn out to be incorrect; but, in the mind of the person holding that belief, some aim or purpose is allegedly supported by that belief. The role of Self-Deception Analysis is to show how this intended objective is subverted, in some sense, by self-deception.

3. THE PRIMARY DEFENSE MECHANISM(S). The third element of Self-Deception Analysis concerns the identification of the primary defense mechanism(s) that supports one's belief in the deception. In a sense, defense mechanisms are 'windows' through which we can discern some plausible motives for our participation in self-deception. By looking for such mechanisms, we avail ourselves of an important opportunity to understand why well-meaning people perpetuate self-deception with relative ease and the best of intentions.

4. FACTORS WHICH PERPETUATE SELF-DECEPTION. The fourth aspect of Self-Deception Analysis attempts to isolate the root causes behind self-deception. While defense mechanisms explain the 'how' or the 'mechanics' of self-deception, they cannot supply the motive which prompted the defensive maneuver in the first place--the 'why' of self-deception. In speculating about the motivations behind beliefs shared by a large group of people, it is clear that only the most obvious motives can be identified. Even these are appropriately subject to criticism. Yet it is still important to identify plausible root causes of self-deception as a stimulus for heightened personal reflection.

5. THE UNINTENDED CONSEQUENCE(S). The fifth and final component of Self-Deception Analysis is the unintended consequence. Once we isolate a particular deception, along with the primary defense mechanism and plausible root causes that support it, we are in a position to assess whether participation in self-deception subverts the intended objective. If adherence to a deceptive belief actually foils the objective which that belief is supposed to serve, then it is apparent that self-deception involves us in a vicious circle of self-defeating, unintended consequences.

It is this component of Self-Deception Analysis--the unintended consequence--which supplies the major incentive for exchanging deceptive beliefs about reality for those that illuminate the true nature of the world.

Throughout the book, near the beginning of each chapter, I will identify each of these five elements of Self-Deception Analysis in order to make the presentation as clear as possible.

By illuminating those defensive maneuvers which are incompatible with our true purposes, Self-Deception Analysis helps us clarify our objectives and to find appropriate means to accomplish them. The pain involved in critically examining cherished, sacred beliefs is far surpassed by the joy of a fresh vision, the challenge of unjaded goals and the peace of coming to terms with the reality that is . . . with hope for a reality that is becoming.

CHAPTER 3

THE KINGDOM HAS COME

THE EXPECTATION OF THE KINGDOM OF GOD

The warning reverberated throughout the early
church. Many would arise after Jesus, declaring themselves to be the Christ (Mt. 24:4-5; Mk. 13:5-6).
Given the religious and political milieu of Palestine
at that time, the admonition was not without foundation.

Across the Judean countryside many believed that
the Messiah would appear, endowed with great powers,
to liberate the Jewish people from Roman domination.
It was anticipated that this messianic figure would
be an ideal king who would re-establish the Davidic
Kingdom and usher the nation into a socio-political
Golden Age.

The term 'messiah' itself connotes a political
context. The Hebrew adjective mašiaḥ is derived from
a verb which means "to smear or anoint." With the
definite article, the Hebrew term means "the anointed
one" (equivalent to the Greek ho christos). From
the days of ancient Israel, the ceremony of anointing
by religious officials was an integral part of a leader's claim to legitimate kingship.

When self-styled messianic types attempted to
instigate a popular rebellion against Roman rule,
it was not long before the Roman army intervened.
The same was true for Jesus. He said some rather
pointed things against the local administration and
attracted a remarkable following.

Not only were the Romans suspicious of this young
upstart, but also the Jewish authorities were irritated
by his obnoxious habits. The Galilean regularly had

table-fellowship with tax collectors, publicans and prostitutes (Mt. 11:19; Lk. 15:2). He even had the gall to declare that such social lepers and traitors belonged to the Kingdom of God.[1]

But what sent chills down the spines of Roman and Jewish authorities alike was the strong sentiment that Jesus had stirred among the masses. His 'triumphal entry' into Jerusalem amid the din of "Hosannah's" amounted to a populist coronation of their new king (Mt. 21:8-16; Mk. 11:8-10).

The Gospel accounts depict the crowds hailing Jesus as "the Son of David"--a royal title that was a veiled way of addressing him as king. Needless to say, it did not help quell the fears of the local authorities when Jesus took it upon himself to purge the Temple of corrupting influences by removing, by force, its profit-making enterprises (Mt. 21:10-7; Mk. 11:11; Lk. 19:45-46). The action was a dramatic display of authority . . . Jesus' first act of 'kingship'. It seems likely that this event precipitated Jesus' arrest and ensuing crucifixion.[2]

A GLORIOUS VISION

Beyond the immediate frustrations that accompanied the Roman occupation of Judea, the Jewish hope for the Messiah was fueled by a glorious vision of the anticipated New Age. For example, the prophetic oracles of the Book of Isaiah are filled with grand depictions of the Messianic Age.

During this Golden Age to be, the Jerusalem Temple will stand at the center of the universe--all the nations of earth will recognize Judah's political,

---

[1]Norman Perrin, Rediscovering the Teachings of Jesus (New York: Harper and Row, 1967), pp. 102-108. Perrin believes that Jesus' practice of eating with "tax collectors and sinners" was so offensive to normal Jewish sensibilities that it was the primary factor that precipitated Jesus' crucifixion.

[2]Joachim Jeremias, New Testament Theology: The Proclamation of Jesus (New York: Charles Schribner's Sons, 1971), p. 145.

moral and religious leadership (Is. 2:2-3; 49:22-23; 60:2-22; 61:5-11). The hoped for global reign of Jerusalem will make war obsolete: "They shall beat their swords into plowshares, and their spears into pruning hooks." (Is. 2:4).

Natural enemies will be reconciled once and for all in this utopian era: "The wolf shall dwell with the lamb, and the leopard shall lie down with the kid" (Is. 11:6). Disease will be supplanted by health and wholeness (Is. 35: 5-6); political oppression will be eradicated by the effective administration of justice (Is. 11:4); and even hardened criminals will be set free (Is. 49:9). Hereafter there will be no unsatisfied human needs (Is. 49:10), and the experience of evil will be a thing of the past (Is. 11:9; 65:25).

Sound nice? It's no wonder why people were enthralled with the prospect that Jesus would immediately usher in this utopian era of peace and tranquility.

THE DISAPPOINTMENT

When Jesus was hoisted onto a cross, the hopes of many were dashed. Despair and disillusionment sapped all the dreams and enthusiasm that Jesus had fostered in his disciples.

But, when reports of the resurrection filtered back to Jesus' followers, their despair melted into joy. The excitement of the moment renewed their hope that Jesus would establish the Kingdom of God within a matter of months . . . if not days or hours (Acts 1:6).

The expectation of Jesus' imminent return pervaded the primitive Christian community. For example, Paul's reflections on celibacy are strongly influenced by the belief that Jesus' coming was right around the corner (I Cor. 7:25-31). Similarly the Gospel of Mark conveys something of this belief in Christ's impending return through its portrayal of Jesus' life and teachings.

As time when on, though, the early church gradually had to adjust their informal timetable for Jesus' return. They had to shape the Christian proclamation to account for "the delay of the parousia" (meaning 'coming' in Greek).

This process of adjustment and reorientation had a dramatic impact on early Christianity, which is reflected in the formulation of the Gospel accounts of Jesus' life and in the institutionalization of the primitive Christian community (what is called 'Early Catholicism'). Both Matthew and Luke-Acts still anticipate the coming Kingdom; yet, both Gospels relegate the return of Christ to a more distant point in time.[3] Hence the notion of an interim period of Christian mission began to form. The followers of Jesus were to preach the "Good News" of the risen Lord and teach his commandments (Mt. 28:18-20) in "Jerusalem, in all Judea and Samaria and to the end of the earth" (Acts 1:8).

As we know, the anticipated, imminent return of Christ did not take place; the glorious Messianic Kingdom was not established; and evil continued to ravage the earth. Periodically, though, throughout the course of Christian history, self-appointed prophets have announced the end of the world, labeling their enemies as 'the Antichrist' and gathering their remnant of true believers. Yet human existence survived their predictions of apocalyptic disaster. Life in all its joy and misery persisted.

But the vision of a better world--a Kingdom whose foundation is not laid by men--was still alive in the tears, the martyrdoms and the works of love by those who named themselves among the disciples of Jesus.

A WARNING UNHEEDED

The warning that many would arise after Jesus proclaiming themselves as the Messiah--promising to usher in an age of peace and wholeness--has not been well-heeded by Popular Christianity.

Of course, no self-respecting participant in

---

[3]Norman Perrin, The New Testament: An Introduction (New York: Harcourt Brace Jovanovich, 1974), pp. 163-166, 172, 197-198.

mainstream Christianity is going to run off into the wilderness after a self-proclaimed messiah to await the end of the world. But, in a much more subtle way, many Christians unwittingly convey the belief that the Kingdom of God has arrived.

In particular, two ideas need to be addressed in this regard. Both imply, to some extent, that the Kingdom of God is in place, and both omit important considerations which definitively indicate that the Kingdom is not yet a present reality. These beliefs are: (1) the belief that whatever we 'give' to God will be multiplied and returned to us in this life; and (2) the belief that God always grants our requests when they would enhance human well-being.

THE TENSION OF ALREADY/NOT YET

The Kingdom of God is a vision of beauty, wholeness, justice and peace that is founded on the transformation of free, morally responsible human beings through Jesus Christ. Our perception of ourselves and one another will be crystalline clear in that day--no longer clouded by insecurities, fears, greed and hatred. "For now we see in a mirror dimly, but then face to face" (I Cor. 13:12a).

Unfortunately our experience of life is quite unlike the cherished vision of God's new world. We experience glints of the Kingdom from time to time . . . in the smile of a child, in an act of forgiveness, during a gripping spiritual experience, or in the joyous faces of those liberated from political or economic oppression. But these are only a foretaste of things to come. As St. Paul wrote: "We ourselves, who have the first fruits of the Spirit, groan inwardly as we wait for adoption as sons, the redemption of our bodies" (Rom. 8:23). Our experience of the Kingdom is incomplete, provisional and sporadic.

In theological circles it is often said that the Christian's experience of the Kingdom of God must be seen in the tension of 'already/not yet'. That is, in some respects, our experience of God's Reign is a personal, present reality. At the same time, we, along with the rest of creation, await the cosmic redemption that will be effected through Christ. Paul declares: "I consider that the sufferings of

33

this present time are not worth comparing to the glory that is to be revealed to us" (Rom. 8:18).

The arrival of the Kingdom is a hope yet unrealized. To be sure, scattered glimpses of the Kingdom can be discerned right now, but the total picture belongs to the future . . . with the cosmic redemption of the universe.

THE SELF-DECEPTION

Two separate deceptions will be discussed in this chapter. Both deceptions imply that the Kingdom of God is in place. Therefore I have grouped them together in one self-deception. I call it: the Kingdom Has Come Self-Deception. It has the following five components:

1) **The Deceptions:** (a) Whatever you give to God will be multiplied and returned to you in this life; and (b) God always grants our requests when they would enhance human well-being.

2) **The Intended Objective:** To make God's presence immediate in our day-to-day lives.

3) **The Primary Defense Mechanism:** Rationalization

4) **Factors Which Perpetuate Self-Deception:** (a) Human acquisitiveness; and (b) The desire to assume control over our circumstances.

5) **The Unintended Consequences:** (a) Skepticism/disbelief about the Christian faith; and (b) The depersonalization of God.

Now let's examine each of these five components of the Kingdom Has Come Self-Deception.

1.A. THE DECEPTION: Whatever you give to God will be multiplied and returned to you in this life.

Give and it shall be given to you! That is the battlecry of fund raisers, evangelists, successful Christian business people, and upwardly mobile devotees of an acquisitive lifestyle. The principle goes by several names, including: "Seed Faith," the "Law of Giving and Receiving," and the "Principle of Sowing and Reaping."

Taken to its logical conclusion, this Karma-like principle would promise that everyone gets their just deserts in this life. Those who sow good things will reap good things in return; those who practice evil will themselves experience the fruit of their harmful acts. In other words, the just shall be rewarded and the unjust will experience divine judgment.

Attractive? Of course. Unfortunately, though, we cannot discern such an automatic principle of justice that operates throughout the universe.

But those who profess the principle of giving and receiving rarely take it to its logical conclusion. Most often it is assumed that the punishment of the ungodly will be reserved for a final judgment at the end of human history.

However divine rewards are viewed differently. Most true believers in the Gospel of Giving and Receiving expect some reward for their diligence in this life--a reward that will be amplified beyond belief in the life to come. Hence the principle, as it is expressed within Popular Christianity, translates into this: some divine rewards now, more later; divine retribution later. In short, the Kingdom of God has made an agreeable appearance.

1.B. THE DECEPTION: God always grants our requests when they would enhance human well-being.

Prayer, for most Christians, is a baffling aspect of the life of faith. There is often a striking difference between what we request from God and the real world outcome of our supplications.

From a little child kneeling at her bedside to a seasoned theologian, it is sometimes difficult to resist the thought that our prayers never transcend our four walls, that our 'conversations' with God are nothing more than socially acceptable instances of 'talking to ourselves'. In moments such as these, God seems very distant . . . like a figment of our imagination or a crutch to help us overcome our fears of the world.

A key way of combating this sense of distance

is to exercise faith that God does, in fact, hear our prayers. Usually the simple belief that God hears and understands is enough to quell our misgivings. It must be remembered that prayer itself is an act of faith.

Sometimes, though, people are tempted to collect some empirical evidence that God does in fact listen to their prayers. Unfortunately that temptation leads down the primrose path of endless mental gymnastics. Those who succumb to the desire to substantiate that God hears their prayers often base their argument upon God's will. Their reasoning usually corresponds to the following syllogistic argument:

First Premise: All requests consistent with God's will are granted by God.

Second Premise: All requests that enhance human well-being are consistent with God's will.

Conclusion: Therefore all requests that enhance human well-being are granted by God.

The argument is <u>logically</u> valid. The only problem comes when we relate it to the Christian proclamation. In moving from the two premises to the conclusion, one implies that the Kingdom of God is <u>already</u> a present reality . . . something which is not awaited but has in fact come.

As long as God seems to be answering our prayers (at least most of them), the above argument appears quite plausible. But, of course, prayer is rarely this trouble-free. If prayer was simply a matter of submitting our wish lists to the Almighty, with the understanding that our bill of goods would be delivered in the morning, there would be no problem in 'marketing' Christianity.

When our prayers do not obtain the desired results, we can do one of two things. Either we can reassess the validity of the above argument, or we can try to bolster the argument by tacking on one or more of the following conditions: (1) one must pray 'in faith'; (2) one must pray without unconfessed sin; or (3) one must trust that God acts in our best interests (so that what looked 'good' from our perspective may not be God's best plan for us).

36

2. THE INTENDED OBJECTIVE: To make God's presence immediate in our day to day lives.

Certainly no one could be faulted for wanting to discern signs of the Kingdom. Moreover it is important that we are able to see something of the basic outline of the Kingdom of God in the moral precepts and ideals of our present existence. Without these signs, our hope for the Kingdom would be nothing more than a dreamy illusion or a favorite fantasy.

How do we note the presence of God? By what measure can we detect the winds of his Spirit? Which indicators of the Kingdom are regularly seen in everyday life?

The answers to these questions will be strongly influenced by our concept of God and how we view his activity in the world. For the sake of simplicity, I will identify two kinds of signs which point to the Kingdom of God: (1) power-oriented manifestations of the Kingdom; and (2) ethically-oriented manifestations of the Kingdom.

The desire to witness a miracle, to see a vision or to experience some supernatural happening--these are common examples of power-oriented indicators. These signs and wonders remind us of a spiritual realm outside of our ordinary experience which, conceivably, provides the metaphysical framework for the anticipated Kingdom of God. However power-oriented indicators add nothing content-wise to our understanding of the Kingdom.

Ethically-oriented indicators are different. They actually define the shape of the Kingdom of God . . . its composition, its content. Our inchoate notions of justice, our sense of indignation at the sight of needless suffering, the helping hand of a stranger, the peace of a serene mountain walk, the melting of estrangement into tears of joy, a people liberated from oppression, or the warmth of an embrace-- these are signs of a Kingdom which now exists only in our most noble deeds and our aspirations for a better tomorrow. Ethically-oriented manifestations of the Kingdom present an alternate vision . . . the way things ought to be. Apart from the present witnesses of our moral concepts and social ideals, the conceptualization of a Kingdom from above--instantiated by prayers, hopes and deeds from below--would be impossible . . . a symbol utterly void of meaning.

37

I am not suggesting that power-oriented signs of the Kingdom do not exist or are unimportant. Instead my point is that in terms of relative significance, ethically-oriented manifestations of the Kingdom are of much greater consequence.

Unfortunately many Popular Christians conceive of God's presence in power-oriented terms. There is a predisposition to define God's immediacy in terms of his ability <u>to</u> <u>do</u>. This tendency diminishes our awareness of God's image in the regular features of human existence. In short, the Lord of Miracles overshadows the God who approaches us daily in the unpretentious smile of a child or in kind words of appreciation. These too are among life's miracles.

3. THE PRIMARY DEFENSE MECHANISM: Rationalization.

Rationalization is a defense mechanism which helps us avoid discrepant or discomforting information about ourselves or the world around us. It is an extremely common defense maneuver and often operates in conjunction with other defense mechanisms. I define rationalization as <u>the attempt to evade 'unacceptable' motives, needs, feelings, actions or consequences by reinterpreting those disagreeable features within a positive, acceptable framework</u>.

The process of rationalization is often evident in attempts to cope with failure (i.e., an 'unacceptable' consequence). The rationalization of failure usually functions as a face-saving mechanism or as a way of mollifying disappointment. Consider the following example.

A young premedical student failed to secure the admission into medical school which he greatly desired. He was, however, later able to gain entrance into dental school as a substitute. This was for him a major defeat in life, which he had difficulty in accepting. As part of his endeavors to adjust to his new situation, he gradually developed a most critical attitude toward medicine. This included criticisms about individual physicians and the entire medical profession, which a short time past he had sought so hard to join.

> . . . He remarked one day, 'I wouldn't
> be a doctor for anything. . . . They are
> on call 24 hours a day, and have no life
> of their own. . . . Even if they make any
> kind of living, they will never find time
> to benefit much from it with the schedules
> they have to keep. . . . It's a terrible
> way to live! . . .'[4]

In the case of the Kingdom Has Come Self-Deception, rationalization functions as a means of reinterpreting failures of the principle of giving and receiving or the belief that God will grant our requests
when they are consistent with human well-being. In
spite of strong evidence challenging the validity
of these "spiritual principles," the defense of rationalization effectively insulates these beliefs from
criticism and endows them with an air of authenticity.
I will illustrate this as the chapter develops.

4. FACTORS WHICH PERPETUATE SELF-DECEPTION:
(a) Human acquisitiveness; and (b) The desire to mani-
pulate our environment.

The two deceptions of the Kingdom Has Come Self-
Deception ultimately relate to the desire to acquire
and to control.

ACQUISITIVENESS. The first deception--whatever
you give to God will be multiplied and returned to
you in this life--appeals to our basic acquisitive
instincts. The desire to accumulate and possess seems
to be among the defining characteristics of human
behavior. Short of endorsing Thomas Hobbes' famous
assertion that there is "a general inclination of
all mankind, a perpetual and restless desire of power
after power, that ceaseth only in death,"[5] it seems
fair to say that the desire to amass wealth is a powerful urge which has found varied expression through

---

[4]Henry P. Laughlin, The Ego and Its Defenses (New York:
Appleton-Century-Crofts, 1970), pp. 259-260.

[5]Thomas Hobbes, Leviathan, ed. by M. Oakeshott (New
York: Macmillan, 1962, first published in 1651),
p. 80.

the ages of man.

CONTROL. The second deception--God always grants our requests when they would enhance human well-being--relates to the universal desire to manage one's environment. The impulse to control is, no doubt, born from the feelings of insecurity that confront us from Day One. Thrust into a cold, stark environment from the moment we left the warmth of the womb, our cries of infancy are manifest in an endless variety of permutations as we walk through life.

For the most part, we have been able to quell our fears and insecurities through technological development and political organization. But, of course, there are several key areas of human concern over which we do not have control.

Among those unmanageable facets of life, incurable disease, physical imperfection and the aging process rank near the top of the list. We can build houses to protect us from the elements, and we can create judicial systems and law enforcement agencies to protect us from one another; but, at some time, all must partake of death's bitterness . . . none can escape. Our mortal bodies always remind us of the precarious nature of our existence, no matter how skillfully we may construct our pretenses of security.

5. THE UNINTENDED CONSEQUENCES: (a) Skepticism/disbelief about the Christian faith; and (b) The depersonalization of God.

Self-deception has a way of foiling our best intentions. Instead of reinforcing our belief in God's promise of a better world, the assertion that the Kingdom has come leads to skepticism, disbelief and disillusionment. This exercise in self-deception destroys the necessarily vague tension between the Kingdom as a present actuality and a future expectation. We have no more need of ambiguous 'signs' of a potentiality yet unrealized.

Ironically, Popular Christianity's enthusiasm for demonstrating the Kingdom as a present reality actually subverts a powerful theological concept. We are left with a dissected, vitiated, narrow concept of the Kingdom. As a consequence, the powerful image of the Kingdom of God becomes a mere tool to accomplish human purposes, instead of being a standard for

40

critiquing those purposes. Moreover the Kingdom Has Come Self-Deception can even depersonalize God in certain instances, by unwittingly reducing God to a few objective 'spiritual' principles.

Now that the basic components of this self-deception have been outlined, we are ready to examine the first deception in greater detail.

THE GOSPEL OF GIVING AND RECEIVING

Those convinced of the principle—give and it shall be given to you—are usually armed with a long list of experiences which seem to confirm the principle. Testimonials in support of the principle imply that God returns 'gifts' to him either by (1) an increased quantity of what was given or (2) in the form of another kind of 'good'.

The first sort of 'return' on one's investment in God's work might be typically expressed like this:

I decided to put God first in spite of our bills, and started seeding [i.e., presumably making a donation to a religious organization] for a miracle in our finances. Within four weeks . . . my sales tripled until I was receiving $800 and $900 a week in commissions. In addition to paying my bills the Lord helped me make a large downpayment on a six-room brick home—the first home we'd ever owned. Also, I was able to get a luxury model car.[6]

An example of the second type of 'return' is found in the story of a young couple who were separated and planning to be divorced. In hopes of improving the dismal situation, the woman decided to donate $25 to a religious organization from her meager financial resources. About three days later—after her husband learned that she had made this faith commitment—the thought struck her husband: "You love her. You love the baby. You should call her and work things out." He phoned his wife and they were eventually

---

[6] From Oral Roberts, The Miracle Book (Tulsa, Okla.: Pinoak Publications, 1972), p. 257.

able to reconcile their differences.[7]

It is important to emphasize that proponents of the principle of giving and receiving do not insist that 'gifts' to God have to be in the form of a monetary donation to a religious organization. Non-pecuniary gifts also qualify. One might donate time to some service project or perhaps share personal resources (e.g., home, car) with others in need. Moreover, as the principle gets worked in practice, it begins to look like a religious version of pop psychology: if you need love, give love; if you're lonely, reach out to others; if you want personal affirmation, affirm others. Nonetheless there is some room for cynicism in the recurrent suggestion that gifts to God and donations to religious organizations are synonymous.

TRIAL BY PROOF TEXT

Heralds of the Gospel of Giving and Receiving frequently cite two passages of scripture in support of the idea. One of these texts is Luke 6:38a:

> Give, and it will be given to you; good measure, pressed down, shaken together, running over, will be put into your lap.

The other passage is Mark 10:29-30:

> Jesus said, 'Truly, I say to you there is no one who has left house or brothers or sisters or mother or father or children or lands, for my sake and for the gospel, who will not receive a hundredfold now in this time, houses and brothers and sisters and mothers and children and lands, with persecutions, and in the age to come eternal life'.

Taken in isolation from their context, both passages appear to provide impressive scriptural support for the Gospel of Giving and Receiving. However the

---

[7]From Oral Roberts, _Miracle of Seed-Faith_ (Tulsa, Okla.: Oral Roberts Association, 1970), pp. 45-51.

context of these scriptures points in a different
direction.

A MISQUOTED SERMON

The first text--Luke 6:38a--is part of a famous
discourse by Jesus commonly known as "The Sermon on
the Mount." The immediate context of the verse concerns Jesus' warning that we should not judge or con-
demn others (Lk 6:37-42).

> Judge not, and you will not be judged;
> condemn not, and you will not be condemned;
> forgive, and you will be forgiven; give,
> and it will be given to you; good measure,
> pressed down, shaken together, running over,
> will be put into your lap. For the measure
> you give will be the measure you get back.
> (6:37-38)

This section on judgment continues with a statement
that the blind cannot lead the blind and that no pupil
is greater than his teacher. The paragraph concludes
with an admonition that one should not look at "the
speck that is in your brother's eye" while paying
no attention to "the log that is in your own eye"
(6:41-42).

Clearly this discussion on judgment must be placed
in the eschatological setting of the anticipated Kingdom of God. The passage warns of the type of justice
that will be administered at the end of the age.
"Give to others, and God will give to you" is simply
another way of saying that everyone will get their
just deserts in the final analysis. If you judge
others harshly, God will judge you with sternness;
if you demonstrate kindness and consideration toward
others, God will reciprocate with respect and forgiveness.

To extract verse 38 out of this context of eschatological justice is surely inappropriate. We cannot
use this text to buttress the Gospel of Giving and
Receiving. Otherwise one would be constrained to
say that Jesus also claimed that his followers would
never be condemned, ostracized and persecuted (because,
if one follows the same line of argument, God will
not heap condemnation upon you in this life, if you
refrain from condemning others).

43

Furthermore the whole atmosphere of Luke's "Sermon on the Plain" is permeated with the expectation of the Kingdom along with the accompanying reversal of present miseries.

> Blessed are you poor, for yours is the kingdom of God.

> Blessed are you that hunger now, for you shall be satisfied.

> Blessed are you that weep now, for you shall laugh.

> But woe to you that are rich, for you have received your consolation.

> Woe to you that are full now, for you shall hunger.

> Woe to you that laugh now, for you shall mourn and weep. (Lk. 6:20-21, 24-25)

IN PRAISE OF THE ITINERANT

The second text invoked by advocates of the principle of giving and receiving is Mark 10:29-30:

> Jesus said, 'Truly, I say to you, there is no one who has left house or brothers or sisters or mother or father or children or lands, for my sake and for the gospel, who will not receive a hundredfold now in this time, houses and brothers and sisters and mothers and children and lands, with persecutions, and in the age to come eternal life'.

It is interesting that those who treat this passage as a mandate for the Gospel of Success ("God wants us to have the very best") are oblivious to the fact that the text comes on the heels of Jesus' radical condemnation of the rich: "It is easier for a camel to go through the eye of a needle than for a rich man to enter the kingdom of God" (10:25).

Moreover it seems odd that proponents of the Gospel of Giving and Receiving are not troubled by

44

the fact that their interpretation of Jesus' promise never came true! Jesus' disciples did not pass their time on expansive estates, living as Medieval feudal lords. Instead their lot was one of hardship and persecution; they died in obscurity with limited material possessions.

The passage in question is set in the context of Jesus' encounter with the rich young man. As the story goes, a young man approached Jesus and asked him what was necessary in order for him to receive eternal life. Jesus told him that he needed to obey the ethical directives of the Ten Commandments. The young man responded that he had already followed these since he was a boy.

Perceiving a special quality in the lad, Jesus invited him to join his itinerant band of disciples, admonishing him: "Go, sell what you have, and give to the poor, and you will have treasure in heaven; and come, follow me" (Mk 10:21). Sadly, the young man's countenance fell. He walked away distressed, "for he had great possessions" (vs. 22).

The poignant scene aroused the disciples' emotions. How could Jesus have been so demanding? If it is so difficult for the wealthy to enter the Kingdom of God, "then who can be saved?" (vs. 26). Peter hastily interjected a reminder that he, along with the other disciples, had relinquished much in following Jesus' call. It was as if Peter was fishing for a reassuring pat on the back to allay his feelings of insecurity. The Gospel writers depict Jesus in an affirming stance. He promised his disciples that their sacrifices would be worthwhile in the final analysis.

But how are we to interpret the promise of a hundred-fold more houses, fields, brothers, sisters, etc. to Jesus' disciples in <u>this present age</u>? Could Jesus have so grossly misread the sort of life that his followers would lead? How could he warn about the dangers of wealth and then immediately contradict himself by promising magnificent worldly wealth to his inner group of disciples?

I believe that we should interpret the passage as a commendation for the itinerant life . . . as an apology for voluntary poverty. One may give up a home, leave family and friends, abandon property and forego economic security; yet, in the midst of

45

material want, there is plenty. Messengers of the
Gospel, poor as they may be, are enriched by the ex-
tended family of the people of God. The itinerant
has hundreds more brothers, sisters, mothers and children than he would have otherwise (Mk. 3:31-35).
In a sense, every home of Jesus' followers is his
abode, every field his field.

Essentially Jesus is simply recommending to his
disciples that any sacrifice--no matter how great--is
an acceptable price to pay for heeding his call.
The disciples' decision to leave their secure circumstances to announce the coming Kingdom brought great
intensity to their otherwise mundane vocations. They
could expect both deep satisfaction and keen excitement, as well as profound despair and distressing
persecutions.

WHY THE PRINCIPLE SEEMS TO WORK

As we have seen, the Gospel of Giving and Receiving lacks support in two key New Testament passages
which are claimed by its proponents. Nonetheless
many would assert that the principle of giving and
receiving is confirmed by their own life experiences.

No doubt, on many occasions, the principle does
seem to work. I suggest that there are two reasons
for this: (1) reciprocity is a fundamental building
block of human societies; and (2) when the principle
fails, the failure can be easily reinterpreted (ration-
alized) into a success.

As to the first reason for the principle's apparent validity, it is true that most people in 'nearly
just' societies lead fairly successful lives when
they are 'other-oriented'. People generally respond
favorably to those who are sensitive to the needs
of others or are generous with their personal
resources. It is not surprising that this 'favorable'
response gets translated into successful business
enterprises, enriched personal relationships and a
confident attitude toward life.

But it is one thing to claim that the principle
of giving and receiving is a generally valid pragmatic
principle, quite another to declare that the principle
is a religious truth. To assert that the principle
of giving and receiving is a religious truth means

that the principle comes with a divine guarantee and implies that it can be applied in divergent cultural contexts.

In suburban, middle-class American society, it often seems that people who give to others are rewarded for their beneficence. Unfortunately the same is not true in societies where severe injustices are the norm . . . where rigid inequalities diminish most semblances of reciprocity within the social order. Predictably the Gospel of Giving and Receiving loses its relevance the further it strays from its socially-advantaged constituency. It could never survive in the teeming slums of Calcutta or on the parched earth of Somalia.

A second factor that gives the principle an air of credibility concerns the many ways that one can claim to have received something from God. For instance, if I send $50.00 to my favorite evangelistic organization with the expectation that God will multiply that gift and return it to me, I could readily interpret many commonplace events as fulfilling that expectation. Perhaps I got a raise or an overdue personal loan was finally paid back. Even if God did not 'return' my gift in the form of money, practically any positive feature of my life could be viewed as the result of God upholding his side of the bargain. Perhaps I recently made a good friend, felt a renewed love for a family member, or sensed a closer relationship with God. Even if something terrible happened, the event could be interpreted as something which will ultimately be good (e.g., losing a loved-one who is now in heaven). Needless to say, the potential for rationalization is considerable.

And, of course, there is always the dynamic that people naturally advertise their success stories and are reticent to cast doubt on a 'scriptural' principle when it fails.

THE ACQUISITIVE STYLE

Perhaps the greatest pitfall of the Gospel of Giving and Receiving is neither related to its lack of biblical support nor its inability to be applied in cross-cultural settings. The most weighty liability of this religious idea is that it encourages Christians to adopt giving lifestyles by appealing to their acquisitive instincts. People are motivated to give for reasons that often fall far short of Jesus' example of sacrificial giving. It will not do to dismiss this as a minor flaw of the Gospel of Giving and Receiving with the excuse that the end justifies the means.

There is a world of difference between an act of giving that is motivated by the desire to get (a gift with strings attached) and an act of giving that is inspired by love (a gift freely given). The Gospel of Giving and Receiving not only treats one's motivation for giving as irrelevant, but also legitimates every acquisitive tendency in our moral fiber. It prompts us to forget the "widow's mite" (Mk. 12:41-44; Lk. 21:1-4) by focusing our attention on ostentatious displays of material wealth that "God wants to give you, if you just release your faith and let him."

Christian giving must rise above the calculus of a pedestrian cost-benefit analysis. Our gift-giving must be motivated by a simple desire to render good to others, instead of issuing from a fancy to get more for ourselves. When our personal resources are stretched to meet the needs of others, the only thing we can be certain of knowing is that we have obeyed God's will, the only thing we can be assured of expecting is that we may be a little poorer, and the only thing that we can be confident of hoping is that giving to others may be contagious, beginning a cycle of human concern for the need of others.

Some may counter that many people will not give of their resources if they cannot expect something in return. But surely the Christian ideal of sacrificial giving should not be corrupted in order to fill evangelical coffers. After all, is God's work in the world ever accomplished at the expense of his message?

PRAYER AND THE AMBIGUITY OF THE KINGDOM

The second deception of the Kingdom Has Come Self-Deception relates to the meaning of prayer. This deception asserts that God always grants our requests when they would enhance human well-being.

The concept of prayer properly encompasses a wide spectrum of interaction between the human and the divine, ranging from specific supplications to meditations on the nature of God and his creation to inexpressible responses to the divine that are mediated by ecstatic experience, religious symbolism or concrete works of love. The common denominator of these varied expressions of prayer is <u>communion</u> with God.

The particular deception under consideration understands prayer in terms of petition. This form of prayer consists of articulating specific sorts of human needs, wants, goals, and the like to God. Prayer as petition seeks to influence God in some way, whether by calling a certain problem to his attention or by asking for his assistance in some matter.

Although supplicatory prayer has some specific, desired outcome as its primary goal, often the experience fulfills several other functions as well. In the process of articulating his problems and aspirations to God, a supplicant simultaneously reminds himself of his fondest hopes and most profound desires, as well as attains perspective on the life struggles that monopolize his attention and energies. Moreover the prayer of petition is primarily a prayer for others. The act of prayer prompts us to break out of our limited circle of narcissistic concerns to touch the lives of others.

In sum, prayer as petition--like all forms of prayer--has a dual aspect: man approaching God and man approaching himself.

A PROBLEM WITH PRAYER

An important theological quandary of supplicatory prayer concerns how human beings can be said to 'influence' or 'sway' God.

Several interpretations of man's influence upon God can be ruled out at the outset. Clearly it is ridiculous to think that people can coerce or blackmail the Supreme Deity in order to get their own way. Similarly it is unacceptable to conceive of man's influence upon God in terms of begging. The image of a lowly subject, with a plea in hand, who fearfully approaches his king, amid an intimidating courtly entourage, does not dignify the biblical revelation of a God who created humanity in his own image (Gen.

1:26). Furthermore one cannot say that prayer influences God because it apprises God of human needs. Since God is omniscient, the Scriptures teach that he is aware of our every need and deepest aspiration, "before you ask him" (Mt.6:8).

It appears that the most plausible sense in which we can say that man 'sways' God is through the friendship that exists between God and humanity through Christ. As stewards of God's creation, in partnership with the Creator, we must exercise supplicatory prayer responsibly. A responsible use of prayer will not require God to contradict his creation--a creation in which both joy and sadness, fortune and tragedy, health and illness, kindness and brutality, coexist.

Prayer is powerful enough, metaphorically, to command mountains to be thrown into the sea (Mt. 17:20, 21:21: Mk. 11:23); prayer is realistic enough to help us gracefully accept the mountains that silhouette human existence (Mt. 26:39; Mk. 14:36; Lk. 22:42; II Cor. 12:7-9).

Of course, there may be a miraculous healing here, a supernatural intervention there; but, these intermittent, fleeting appearances of God's grace are no more than signs of the Kingdom . . . a Kingdom that we pray for . . . a Kingdom that we act toward . . . but nonetheless a Kingdom not yet come.

THE GOSPEL ACCORDING TO ST. NICK

The holiday sight is familiar. Children lined up in shopping malls waiting anxiously to see Santa. Armed with lengthy wish lists or, perhaps, just a clear idea of that one special item that will modernize their toy collections, the supplicants of the man from the North Pole approach the bearded figure with feelings that range from awe to disbelief.

Often, in a child's eyes, the jolly man in the red suit possesses semi-divine attributes. He is able to be at many places at the same time. Santa is kind, wise and his white hair befits him. He will give you whatever you want, that is, if you satisfy certain moral criteria (Have you been a good boy or girl this year?) Furthermore, despite the deluge of Christmas lists, Santa is somehow able to fill the orders and coordinate their delivery at just the right time. But as every schoolboy knows, Santa's elaborate organization is useless if you fail to make your Christmas list a matter of public domain . . . Santa and his agents cannot read your mind!

I imagine that childhood fantasies about Santa Claus stay with us long after that brief moment of confusion and disillusionment when we discovered that this wonderful personage did not exist. Sometimes people's concept of God is strikingly similar to a child's image of the man who flies in the company of reindeer. I will refer to this tendency as "the Gospel according to St. Nick."

STORING EARTHLY TREASURE IN GOOD CONSCIENCE

The fundamental tenet of the Gospel According to St. Nick is that "God wants to give you his very best." The basis of this claim is that (1) God is good and (2) every material resource in the universe is at his disposal. What gets defined as "God's best" might range from a healthy life to a $200,000 lakeside condominium. As the reasoning goes, why wouldn't God want to give us things that enrich human life?

When it seems that God is not upholding his side of the bargain by giving us what we ask, two types of explanations are commonly employed to account for God's inaction. The first explanation emphasizes special considerations relating to God's sovereignty; the second class of explanations focus on some deficiency in the supplicant himself.

The first, most common reason for God's inaction is that a particular request was not in his will. For instance, it may be that something seemed good from our perspective when, from God's standpoint, it would have been detrimental to our welfare. Those who justify God's inaction on the basis of his sovereignty have ultimate recourse to the argument that we cannot understand the mysterious workings of God . . . we can only trust in his goodness.

The second class of reasons for God's inaction pins the blame--in one way or another--upon the supplicant. Often it is said that the person did not pray with enough faith or, perhaps, there was some 'unconfessed' sin that stood in the way of God granting the request. This class of explanations

51

views unanswered prayer as the result of overlooked technicalities. The implication is that if one just exercised a little more faith or confessed his sin, God would grant the request.

Both types of explanations can be interpreted as rationalizations for God's failure to act when some response was expected. Both explanations imply that the Kingdom has come.

THE EQUALITY OF PREFERENCES

The Gospel According to St. Nick assumes that all human preferences are equal in God's sight. If one simply masters the correct prayer format, the riches of the Kingdom will be opened to him. This theology portrays a God who busies himself by delivering new cars, arranging promotions and healing the common cold for an elite group of believers. By implication the plight of starving infants and children on the other side of the globe is outside the purview of God's interests.

The God proclaimed in the Gospel According to St. Nick sees only wants, wishes and desires. He is oblivious to global need. Like a shopping mall Santa Claus who refrains from telling a child that he does not <u>really</u> need an expensive toy, we see a God who lacks the moral fiber to cry out against the injustices that engulf our world. Instead of challenging us to search out the needs of others, the Gospel According to St. Nick only promises that our stockings will be filled with goodies.

SELF-DECEPTION TO THE MAX

In some religious groups on the fringe of Popular Christianity, the Gospel According to St. Nick is taken to its extreme. These groups believe that God will answer any prayer if it is "confessed" enough by the believer. Confessing one's faith, according to this viewpoint, means that you should act <u>as if</u> you are healed once you have prayed for healing, or you should act <u>as if</u> you have received some material good once it has been requested from God.

For example, with respect to divine healing,

a distinction is often made within these groups between an illness and its symptoms. It is believed that once one prays for physical healing, one must announce to others that the healing has taken place for the prayer to be effectual. Therefore a person might be deathly sick and sincerely claim to family and friends that the illness has been healed, even though the symptoms persist (perhaps one of Satan's tricks). The rationalizations needed to sustain this peculiar type of religious belief are legion.

Most of the time this extreme form of the Gospel According to St. Nick does not have detrimental real world consequences beyond creating unnecessary guilt or embarrassment. Sadly, though, there are some horror stories where unnecessary deaths were caused by delayed medical care (especially in the early detection of cancer) and due to the withdrawal of medication (eg., the discontinuation of insulin).

GOD IN THE FORMULA

Extreme manifestations of the Gospel According to St. Nick border on magic. The outcome is a depersonalized view of God who resides in a tidy formula for success.

The God of the Formula can be easily manipulated. As long as you pay attention to all of the technicalities, you can get God to work for you. Like instructions for a do-it-yourself kit, the implication is: Follow the steps carefully and you will get the desired outcome. This understanding of prayer makes true communion with God an impossibility because it reduces prayer to an incantation.

THE KINGDOM AS AN ALTERNATE VISION

Religion . . . wears many hats. Down through the ages, it has performed many roles within human societies. Some good; other bad.

Any student of history is painfully aware of the blatant misuses of religion--religiously inspired crusades, inquisitions, and intolerance toward religious minorities to name a few. Religion has legitimated unjust social structures; it has sacralized longstanding prejudices which pit one social class, race or nation against another; and it has spiritualized the political frustrations of the poor and oppressed, functioning as "the opiate of the masses."

On the other hand, religion has many positive accomplishments to its credit. In every epoch of human existence, religious symbols have helped man interpret his environment--the nature of the physical world, the meaning of human life and the shape of his moral obligations to others. Religiously inspired reformers have been prominent at nearly every step of moral and social progress ventured by humankind. Moreover under normal social conditions, but especially in moments of crisis and social dislocation, religious practices have been powerful cohesive forces that bind human beings together in families, tribes, migrant communities and incipient nations.

In the contemporary situation religion has another important social role. It has a responsibility to present humanity with an alternate vision of life on earth, the prospect of birthing a better world through the transformation of self and society.

The alternate vision presented by Christianity is epitomized in the idea of the Kingdom of God. The Christian's hope for the Kingdom warns him that man cannot technically create his own utopia--a heaven on earth--apart from God's intervention. Yet the Kingdom as a future event, beyond human control, in no way diminishes its relevance to the present. As an alternate vision, the Kingdom of God is the Christian's resource or guide for action in the time being. The vision of the Kingdom inspires personal transformation, prompts us to rectify social injustices, and reinvigorates Christian communities with a fresh love for God and one another.

The 'already' aspect of the Kingdom of God provides us with an optimistic vision of what can be accomplished now in partnership with God; the 'not yet' aspect of the Kingdom endows us with a realistic vision of the human condition that does not preclude a genuinely positive stance toward the world.

Unfortunately the Kingdom Has Come Self-Deception destroys the potency of this Christian idea. It trades the vision of a new world for an unimaginative, privatized concept of the Kingdom. Instead of critiquing human motivations and social injustices, Popular

54

Christianity's Kingdom of God is reduced to a tool that does whatever we want it to do. The concept extends no further than our native perspectives on life permit. By contrast, the genuine inbreaking of the Kingdom is accompanied by the flight from narcissism and a desire to engage the world around us.

No . . . the Kingdom has not come. Like Jesus' first disciples, we must stand ready to adjust our expectations of the Kingdom in the face of necessity. Until the end of the age, the words of the Lord's prayer--"Thy kingdom come"--will be on the lips of those who carry Jesus' cross into uncharted realms.

CHAPTER 4

CHRISTIANITY WITHOUT TRAGEDY

EVIL AS A PERCEPTUAL PROBLEM

A family is killed by a drunken driver; a famine in East Africa takes the lives of countless children; a young man in Latin America is tortured and killed by a "moderately repressive" military dictatorship; the hopes of an Eastern European nation for political freedom are crushed by a swift, brutal military machine; a gas station attendant is mercilessly shot by robbers without provocation; an earthquake in Asia takes the lives of thousands; a conflict in the Middle East leaves orphaned children and grief-stricken parents; a teenager is trapped in the self-destructive snare of drugs and prostitution; an elderly person sits alone, waiting, watching, abandoned; a human fetus too small to think, yet developing in anticipation of its first breath, is conveniently disposed of; a tornado wipes out in seconds what took years to build; a terrorist's bomb takes the lives of innocent bystanders; and 800 million people on planet earth are trapped in a form of poverty so severe and devastating that North Americans and Europeans who have not travelled in the poor regions of the less developed world have no first-hand knowledge of it.

By whatever name you choose to call it, evil keeps a constant, unceasing vigil over humanity. Its ugliness can be avoided and its effects may be postponed; but, in every person's life, at some time, the fact of evil must be reckoned with.

Evil is a part of everyone's reality. It thwarts the best intention and can strain the human spirit far beyond its breaking point.

The alternative to facing the horror and reality of evil is to deny its existence in some way. It is not difficult to understand why we would rather avoid evil than peer into its cavernous face. It disrupts our lives and leads us into paths of fear and insecurity.

Freud described this basic human tendency to avoid unpleasant aspects of life as "the Pleasure Principle."[1] In view of the adeptness of humans to avoid distressing features of their existence (whether by geographic or emotional distancing), one would imagine that evil is a perceptual problem, in addition to the more obvious problems it poses for our existence.

THE SELF-DECEPTION

The self-deception presently under consideration concerns the perception of tragic events. While the perception of evil is a problem for anyone, the issue deserves special attention on the part of Christians.

I call this self-deception the Denied Tragedy Self-Deception. By 'tragedy' I mean to denote a class of events which are destructive, purposeless and undeserved. As I define the term, all of these conditions must be present before an event can be genuinely labeled 'tragic'.

The Denied Tragedy Self-Deception has the following five components:

1. **The Deception:** For any 'child of God', the outcome of a bad event will be an identifiable, proportionate good.

2. **The Intended Objective:** To create hope by affirming God's control over grievous events.

3. **The Primary Defense Mechanism:** Denial

---

[1] Sigmund Freud, "Formulations Regarding the Two Principles in Mental Functioning," in Collected Papers, Vol. IV, trans. by J. Rivere (New York: Basic Books, 1959), p. 14.

4.   A Factor Which Perpetuates Self-Deception:
reduction of cognitive dissonance.

5.   The Unintended Consequence: (a) An unreal
portrayal of the human condition; and (b)
Skepticism about God's sense of 'fair play'.

Now that these five elements have been presented,
let's take a closer look at them.

1.   THE DECEPTION: For any 'child of God', the
outcome of a bad event will be identifiable, proportionate good.

"In everything there is a purpose"--this message
reverberates throughout sanctuaries from coast to
coast. Indeed it is encouraging to hear that we can
endure trials with the assurance that sometime, somewhere, somehow, we will discover the purpose of our
present sufferings.

A sense of purpose sustains us through the most
difficult times. People regularly submit themselves
to excruciating pain or voluntarily deprive themselves
of material comforts if they believe that some worthwhile purpose is served by their sufferings. Patients
undergo complicated surgical procedures to prolong
their lives. Parents often scrimp and save so that
their children can have an opportunity to get an education and a decent career. Throughout history people
have risked their lives for the sake of freedom from
political oppression.

In a Christian context, to say that every event
has a purpose translates into the religious conviction
that God 'uses' events to obtain aims which are consistent with his plan for us and in our best interests.
Often when it is asserted that God is using a particular situation--however horrible--to accomplish his
will, it is tantamount to affirming simply that "God
is good and he deserves our trust."

According to this view, we might not understand
the why and wherefore of our afflictions; but, in
the final analysis, we can take heart that God is
fitting these circumstances into some redemptive design. A scripture often invoked to buttress this
view is Romans 8:28. The paraphrase in the Living
Bible most explicitly conveys the idea: "And we know
that all that happens to us is working for our good
if we love God and are fitting into his plans."

The idea that some redemptive design stands behind the most chaotic, horrible events is sometimes illustrated by two sides of a finely woven rug. On the back side of the rug, no pattern is evident and the threads appear in disarray. As the analogy goes, we see the events of life as disordered and confused from a human perspective. Yet, from God's vantage point, those disjointed events fit into a grand design --a design that only becomes apparent when we take the perspective of the rug-maker who sees the intricate pattern on the front side of the rug.

Of course, the religious claim that God 'uses' events to obtain aims consistent with his plan for us and in our best interests is an <u>unfalsifiable</u> claim. We cannot prove or disprove it by reading the empirical facts of the world around us.

Most of the time, though, when Christians assert that God had some purpose in this event or that situation, they have in mind some sort of tangible, redeeming consequence that one day will be manifest. For example, the loss of a job might renew a person's appreciation of family and friends; a close brush with death might strengthen one's faith in God; or a painful divorce might release two discontented people from a vicious circle of self-destructive behavior to rediscover the fulfillment and joy that life can bring.

To say that an event has some 'purpose' is to imply that the event was a <u>proportionate</u> means to a desired end. The word 'proportionate' is important. The means must fit the end. A homeowner who chooses to rid his house of termites by dynamiting the house would, by all conventional standards, be someone "not playing with a full deck." Although his action eliminated the termites (a 'good' end), the means selected to achieve that end were so malfitted that it would be correct to say the action was purposeless. Nothing proportionately beneficial resulted from the action.

A <u>falsifiable</u> version of the unfalsifiable claim that "God uses events to obtain aims which are consistent with his plan for us and in our best interests" might go something like this: For any 'child of God', the outcome of a bad event will be an identifiable, proportionate good. The term 'child of God' denotes a class of people and can be interpreted in a variety of ways. Most Popular Christians hold views which fall somewhere between using the term to refer to all of humanity and the extreme belief that only a few select believers are chosen to be God's children. Certainly all spokespersons of Popular Christianity would class all 'born-again' Christians among the company of God's children. Moreover, nearly all would be constrained, on theological grounds, to regard every infant and child throughout the world as a 'child of God', irrespective of the religious beliefs of his or her parents.

In this chapter it is argued that many events that regularly befall humanity are utterly pointless and destructive, without rhyme or reason. In itself, this is a very uncontroversial claim; but, when taken in relation to the way we view God's participation in moments of crises, it can have a profound effect on how we articulate the Gospel to a world traumatized by tragedy.

2. THE INTENDED OBJECTIVE: To create hope by affirming God's control over grievous events.

Most who proclaim the Gospel According to St. Purpose offer the good news--in everything there is a purpose--as a soothing balm, words of consolement, to those gripped by pain, frustration and remorse. The assertion that every bad event is purposeful is not the result of a carefully designed survey or the outcome of a series of detached observations about the world. Instead the claim is guided by a pragmatic concern--to create hope in the midst of despair.

Hope is a precious quality. It is the sustenance of every worthy goal and the thread that retains important human values in times of severe crisis. At least two basic types of hope can be identified: (1) the hope of an ordered past; and (2) the hope of an open future.

Those who posit that every event is permeated with purpose hold out the hope of an ordered past. This type of hope is backward looking. Its retrospective vision strains to find some orderly pattern woven into the fabric of human history. The hope of an ordered past offers the promise that soon that which appears senseless and destructive will be recognized later as one piece in the puzzle of God's beneficent masterplan, coalescing into a history of meaning.

Another source of hope could be called 'the hope

of an open future'. In contrast to the hope of an ordered past, this type of hope is forward-looking, drawing its sustenance from possibilities that lie just beyond our reach--in the real of promise, redemption, creativity and partnership with God. The simple, comforting words--"this too shall pass"--reflect this perspective, in that beyond our present, transitory sufferings there lies the prospect of a better future.

The so-called "theologies of hope" emphasize Christianity's essential openness to the future, which is the ground of its "openness to the world." Jürgen Moltmann, the central figure of this recent movement in Christian theology, locates the ground of our hope for a future of possibility in the death and resurrection of Christ. A future brimming with possibility, created by Jesus' sacrificial love, in turn inspires the Christian to assume a stance of being authentically open to the world.[2]

Of these two sources of hope, the hope of an open future provides the only plausible framework for the Christian hope. Unlike the hope of an ordered past, the hope of an open future can be integrated with our experience of the tragic in a way that nourishes freedom and creativity in the light of a renewed future.

3. THE PRIMARY DEFENSE MECHANISM: Denial.

One of the most basic mechanisms of defense is denial. Denial can be defined as the attempt to evade threatening aspects of one's environment by simply rejecting their very existence. It is avoidance by disbelief.

Denial is manifest in many different contexts, to varying degrees. In extreme cases, denial is psychopathic, causing a person to lose touch with their ordinary reality. In more subtle forms, denial is manifest in our 'looking behavior', what we selectively omit from our socially-constructed notions of reality. This is the type of denial to which I refer. It places limitations on the way we process information about the world, leading us to adopt a kind of 'ostrich

---

[2]Jürgen Moltmann, "Theology as Eschatology," in The Future of Hope, ed. by F. Herzog (New York: Herder and Herder, 1970), pp. 23, 45-46.

mentality' in coping with unpleasant features of reality.

4. A FACTOR WHICH PERPETUATES SELF-DECEPTION: The reduction of cognitive dissonance.

Like any mechanism of defense, denial implies some type of motivating force which helps us to understand why self-deception is perpetuated. I suggest that one of these motivations is the desire to reconcile two contradictory ideas: (1) the belief that God is perfectly good and all powerful; and (2) our knowledge of the tragic dimension of human life. These opposing thoughts or 'cognitions' generate dissonance or 'noise' in our minds which, naturally, we try to reduce.

The theory of cognitive dissonance attempts to explain aspects of human behavior in terms of the mental conflict or discomfort that is induced by simultaneously entertaining two inconsistent thoughts. Leon Festinger, the originator of the theory, sets forth its basic hypotheses as follows:

> 1. The existence of dissonance, being psychologically uncomfortable, will motivate the person to try to reduce the dissonance and achieve consonance.

> 2. When dissonance is present, in addition to trying to reduce it, the person will actively avoid situations and information which would likely increase the dissonance.[3]

The avoidance of dissonance-producing situations can take a variety of forms. For example, we may effectively suppress a discomforting thought which we acknowledge as being perfectly valid. This type of dissonance reducing maneuver could be illustrated by people with chronic problems of smoking or overeating. On the one hand, they like to smoke or consume large quantities of food. On the other hand, they are well aware that this sort of habit endangers their health and threatens their future happiness. They are caught in a dilemma. Admonitions by physicians, family and friends are mentally noted, but the urge

---

[3] Leon Festinger, A Theory of Cognitive Dissonance (Stanford, Cal.: Stanford University Press, 1957), p. 3.

to smoke or overeat persists. The dissonance that this produces within a person's mind is usually reduced either by suppressing the knowledge that his habits are adverse to good health or by employing some type of rationalization (e.g., "I'd rather live a shorter, happy life than a longer, boring one").

Another means of reducing cognitive dissonance is to become very selective about the kinds of information we decide to look at. Several studies suggest that persons who experience moderate levels of cognitive dissonance tend to seek information sources which agree with their own preconceived opinion on a matter.[4] Hence dissonance is reduced by finding material that seems to buttress a particular belief which has been challenged by some experience or 'discrepant information'.

Apparently cognitive dissonance also has an effect on a person's memory. One study found that information which generates dissonance tends to be forgotten much more quickly (a week after the initial exposure) than information which agrees with one's own opinion.[5] Hence dissonance was reduced by the subtle process of selectively forgetting discrepant information.

The reduction of cognitive dissonance is a significant factor which perpetuates the Denied Tragedy Self-Deception because of an especially thorny philosophical issue known as "the problem of evil," which will be introduced momentarily. Many Popular Christians have resolved the psychological dissonance created by the problem of evil in the mistaken direction of redefining evil in a positive light. I will say more about this later.

5. THE UNINTENDED CONSEQUENCES: (a) An unreal portrayal of the human condition; and (b) Skepticism

---

[4] D. Ehrlich, et al., "Postdecision Exposure to Relevant Information" (Journal of Abnormal Social Psychology 54:98-102, 1957); Festinger, A Theory of Cognitive Dissonance, pp. 162-176; and Judson Mills, et al., "Selectivity in Exposure to Information" (Journal of Abnormal Social Psychology 59:250-253, 1959).

[5] See J. W. Brehm, and A. R. Cohen, Explorations in Cognitive Dissonance (New York: John Wiley, 1962), pp. 93-97.

about God's sense of 'fair play'.

Self-deception takes its toll on our sensibilities. It blinds us to obvious facts of reality and generates a less than accurate portrait of the world.

The Denied Tragedy Self-Deception attempts to seek out some semblance of purpose in situations which can only be described as destructive expenditures of hatred, intolerance and insensitivity. The Gospel According to St. Purpose articulates an emaciated version of the Christian hope which has nothing to say to the true sufferers of this world. Its message can only reach the 'marginally distraught'--those who suffer from 'developmental' pains which are the inevitable concomitants of human existence (e.g., the death of a loved one, illness, a 'broken heart').

Those who are trapped in the vortex of human barbarity and brutality do not have recourse to the comforting thought that their misfortune falls into some beneficient master plan penned by God Almighty. Their 'clouds' have no silver-linings. Their experience of evil does not permit them the luxury of seeing the worksmanship of a divine hand where the savagery of the human hand is so conspicuous. Consequently, the Gospel According to St. Purpose offers no hope to those in desperate need of hope. Instead it can only undermine our noblest beliefs about God's sense of fairness, his commitment to justice, by attributing to God that which the human heart alone must claim full responsibility.

THE PROBLEM OF EVIL

Evil is a perceptual problem for any human being, but it is a problem which deserves special attention from Christians. This is because of a difficult philosophical issue known as "the problem of evil."

The problem of evil is not a bone of contention for every religion. Only those religions which claim that God is both a good being and omnipotent or all-powerful are confronted with this issue.

The classical formulation of the problem of evil is this: How can evil exist in a world that was created by a God who is all-powerful and perfectly good? The problem is sometimes referred to as the issue of 'theodicy'. The term comes from two Greek words that mean 'god' and 'justice'. Hence a theodicy refers to a particular attempt to defend the justice or fairness of God in relation to our experience of evil.

Most theodicies or attempts to resolve the problem of evil imply one of three things: (1) that God's power is limited in some respect; (2) that there is some deficiency in God's goodness; or (3) that our experience of evil must be reinterpreted in a positive light. Of course, one obvious, and inappropriate, solution to the problem of evil is to deny the very existence of evil itself. This proposal is advocated by a religious group known as Christian Science. According to their theological perspective, evil is an illusion and has no actual basis in reality.

SHORT-CIRCUITING THE PROBLEM

Two commonly used avenues of side-stepping the problem of evil assert either that: (1) the problem of evil is irrelevant to the real world concerns of humanity; or (2) the questions raised by the problem of evil reflect an impious attitude toward God.

The first approach avoids the issue by making the pragmatic assertion that evil is to be resisted and not philosophized about. According to this view, the theoretical issues surrounding evil pale into insignificance when compared to the devastating experience of evil itself. One should wage war on evil, instead of standing on a distant hill to observe the course of a battle and speculate on its outcome.

Actually such pragmatic criticisms of the problem of evil neither address the matter as a theological issue nor make it an irrelevant concern. The criticism simply reminds us that the alleviation of evil takes precedence over our attempts to philosophize about it. But such philosophizing is hardly peripheral to the Christian task. In fact, it is of crucial importance, especially in view of the influence of the problem of evil in generating skepticism about Christianity.

The second means of avoiding the problem of evil is to argue that any attempt to defend God's justice or sense of fairness is doomed from the very start. According to this view, such a project is an exercise in futility, misfounded on the assumption that we, as human beings, have a right to make any judgment about God's intentions or to offer a defense on his behalf. God's will is so mysterious and inscrutible that his ways are beyond human comprehension. This sort of approach was taken by the author of the Book of Job.

THE STORY OF JOB

The author of the Book of Job attempted to discredit the belief that God uses suffering as a means to punish sin.

Job--a faithful servant of God--is tested by "the adversary" (ha satan)[6] with God's permission. The trial is severe. His children are killed and all of his worldly possessions are taken away. As if this was not enough, Job himself is afflicted with a painful disease.

Despite all of his sufferings, Job remains firm in his faith and refuses to curse God for his predicament (2:10). Job's 'friends' try to help him by exploring the cause of his demise. They consistently reiterate the belief that human suffering must be the result of some sin or affront committed against God.

Job rejects the charge that his suffering was born from an act of sin. Instead he takes the offensive and impugns God's alleged 'good' intentions.

When I say, 'My bed will comfort me,
    my couch will ease my complaint,
thou does scare me with dreams
    and terrify me with visions,
so that I would choose strangling
    and death rather than my bones.
    (7:13-15)

Job manifests little reticence in pinning the blame for his condition upon God.

---

[6]It is improper to translate this Hebrew word as a proper noun (i.e., Satan), as it is grammatically incorrect to use the article ha before proper names in Hebrew.

> He has stripped from me my glory,
> and has taken the crown from my head.
> He breaks me down on every side, and I am gone,
> and my hope he has pulled up like a tree.
> He has kindled his wrath against me,
> and counts me as his adversary.
> (19:9-11)

Job is cast as a man obsessed with the truth. He longs to penetrate the nature of his miserable existence. Job's friends brand his searching questions as exercises in futility, reflecting an impious, self-righteous posture toward God.

One is struck by the honest and insightful depiction of the human condition that one finds in Job's dialogues. In contrast to Job's friends (who argue that divine justice is regularly enacted here on earth), Job observes that evil men often seem strangely exempt from suffering and misery.

> Their houses are safe from fear,
> and no rod of God is upon them. . . .
> They spend their days in prosperity,
> and in peace they go down to Sheol.
> They say to God, 'Depart from us!
> We do not desire the knowledge of thy ways.
> What is the Almighty, that we should serve him?
> And what profit do we get if we pray to him?' (21:9, 13-15)

Job notices that even in death the wicked are honored (21:32-33).

Job's distaste for simple answers in explanation of his own sufferings prompts him to portray realistically the social injustices that surround him. Evil men steal, enslave orphans, oppress widows, deny the poor of adequate shelter and exploit their laborers (24:2-11). Yet, in all this, God is silent.

> From out of the city the dying groan,
> and the soul of the wounded cries for help;
> yet God pays no attention to their prayer. (24:12)

Considering all of the depth of insight and poetic finesse displayed by the author of Job, it is unfortunate that the drama closes on a weak note. God's response to Job's probing questions is essentially a flowery rendition of: "It's really none of your business."

The author of the Book of Job portrays God as a deity who behaves like an insecure professor, suddenly exasperated at the incessant questions of an inquisitive student.

Who are you to question my wisdom
     with your ignorant, empty words? . . .
Were you there when I made the world?
     If you know so much, tell me about
     it.
Who decided how large it would be?
     Who stretched the measuring line over
     it?
Do you know all the answers? (38:2,4-5,TEV)

Having been spoken to by the Almighty, Job understandably feels intimidated by this line of questioning. God continues his reproof by saying:

Are you trying to prove that I am unjust--
     to put me in the wrong and yourself
     in the right?
Are you as strong as I am?
     Can your voice thunder as loud as mine?
     (40:8-9, TEV)

Job wisely repents of all his questions and concedes his case.

I know, Lord, that you are all-powerful;
     you can do everything you want.
You ask how I dare question your wisdom
     when I am so ignorant.
I talked about things I did not understand,
     about marvels too great for me to know.
     (42:2-3, TEV)

The drama concludes with the reinstatement of all of Job's wealth, and his family is miraculously brought back to life. Job is healed of his debilitating ailment and, proverbially, everyone lives happily after. Of course, the reinstatement of Job's personal fortune in no way addresses the pointed questions Job posed about the suffering of others.

The moral of the story is this: Don't assume that the experience of suffering is a form of divine judgment, but don't ask too many questions either. In fairness, though, we cannot be too hard on the author's attempted resolution of the drama. In a brilliant style, the author has raised many salient questions about our experience of evil.

The approach taken in the Book of Job exalts God's power to the point that we lose sight of God's goodness. Certainly we can conceive of an all-powerful deity who can do anything exactly as he pleases--manipulating people as puppets and overriding human freedom. But a deity such as this would not evoke our admiration and inspire us to love him voluntarily. Instead our worship of such an unprincipled deity would be motivated by fear and dread.

AN ANALOGY WITH CLAY FEET

The Apostle Paul, in discussing a dilemma concerning God's justice, takes an approach similar to the one in Job. He models our relationship to God with the analogy of a clay pot and its potter.

> But who are you, a man, to answer back to God? Will what is molded say to its molder, 'Why have you made me thus?' Has the potter no right over the clay, to make out of the same lump one vessel for beauty and another for menial use? (Rom. 9:20-21; cp. Is. 45:9ff.)

Paul's analogy of a clay pot and its potter provides a picturesque depiction of the power inequality between God and man; but, it in no way solves the dilemma of God's justice. First, it is incorrect to model human beings--endowed with spiritual potentialities, a conscience, rationality and a free will--in terms of an inert clay pot. The clay pot never questions its maker because it is a clay pot. Second, Paul's line of argument is a variant of the age-old theme: "might makes right." Hence he attributes to a loving, compassionate God a moral attitude that we commonly consider unsound and despicable among human beings!

Is God somehow exempt from compelling moral

considerations by virtue of the fact that he is God and may do as he pleases? Of course not. Such a view may dignify God's sovereignty, but it ultimately places him on one side of an impassible power gap with humanity on the other side--a chasm that cannot be bridged by moral concepts common to both God and man. In sharp contrast to the redeeming, reconciling God of the Hebrew-Christian tradition, such a deity would establish a cosmic double-standard by exempting himself from the very moral principles that he enacted for man. Therefore it is not possible to side-step the problem of evil by arguing that God's sense of right and wrong is none of our business.

GOD AS CREATOR AND GOD AS PARTICIPANT

The problem of evil is concerned about God's relation to his creation. This relation can be explored from two vantage points: (1) God as the creator who stands before his creation; and (2) God as a participant who stands alongside his creation.

The image of God as creator depicts God as an all-powerful and all-knowing being who calls the universe into existence according to one particular 'blueprint', chosen from a set of possible designs. Of course, God's loving and compassionate character--as reflected in the life and teachings of Jesus--would naturally limit the possible options before him. For example, God could have created a certain class of human beings who were physically and intellectually inferior in order to serve as slaves for the rest of humanity. To have created the world in this way would have been within God's power but would surely contradict his character.

The image of God as participant portrays God in his ongoing creative activity. Creation did not stop with several distinct acts which brought the universe into being. The Scriptures teach that God is involved with his creation as a continuing event, largely through his covenant relationship with humanity.

Of course, the extent of God's participation in the affairs of the universe can be conceived in a variety of ways. A minimalist view of God's participation might attribute only the regular operation of natural laws (e.g., gravity) ultimately to God's sustaining participation in the universe. At the other end of the continuum, a maximalist view would assert that God actually _causes_ every event in the universe according to some foreordained, detailed plan.

Most of us initially confront the problem of evil when we reflect on God's role as participant in creation. When evil befalls us, often questions arise in the back of our minds like: "How could God have allowed this to happen?"; "Am I being punished for something?"; "Is God trying to teach me some lesson through this misfortune?"

Often, once having come face-to-face with the problem of evil from the standpoint of God as participant, our questions and doubts focus on God's responsibility as creator. We might ask, for example, why God chose one mode of his participation over another when he initially set up the universe? Perhaps some minor engineering improvements could have significantly reduced the amount of pain and suffering we now experience. Why couldn't God have excluded M.S., malaria, leprosy, cancer or leukemia from his blueprint of creation without interfering with human autonomy or the fundamental shape of the world?

Traditionally reflections on the problem of evil by philosophers and theologians have focused on God's responsibility as creator. In keeping with the aims of the book, though, I will discuss the issue only from the standpoint of God as participant. This point of entry will help us focus the discussion on evil as a _perceptual_ problem. Admittedly, in following this course, I am begging some important questions which relate to God as creator. Yet, to take up even a few of those questions would be prohibitive. Besides, others have analyzed these issues at length with far more skill and nuance than I could provide.

---

[7] For thorough and accessible discussions on this matter, see David Griffin, _God, Power and Evil: A Process Theodicy_ (Philadelphia: Westminster, 1976); John Hick, _Evil and the God of Love_ (New York: Harper and Row, 1966); and especially S. Paul Schilling, _God and Human Anguish_ (Nashville: Abingdon, 1977).

TURNING DOWN THE NOISE

I suggest that the philosophical problem of evil, viewed in conjunction with the psychological theory of cognitive dissonance, explains why many Christians seem to understate the full destructive significance and magnitude of evil. In the context of Popular Christianity, the pervasiveness of human tragedy is denied by the insistence that every event which befalls a child of God--no matter how terrible--has some purpose.

Most, if not all, Popular Christians firmly believe that God is both good and all-powerful. Generally God's omnipotence is viewed in quite literal terms: "God can do anything"; "There is no obstacle too great for him"; "God can handle any and every problem in your life"; "He can protect us from any evil." The only limitation generally placed on God's power within Popular Christianity is that God may not choose to exercise his power because it is outside of his 'will'. Since this limitation is self-imposed (and presumably benefits us because his will is perfect), it does not alter the claim that God is all-powerful. Because Popular Christians heartily endorse the theological affirmations that God is good and all-powerful, the perception of radical evil or tragedy naturally creates cognitive dissonance.

One way of reducing the dissonance generated by the perception of tragedy is to re-evaluate evil in some positive light, in a way that attenuates its destructive and aimless nature. This redefinition of evil can be accomplished by asserting that bad events always have some redemptive purpose (e.g., to draw us closer to God, to teach us some lesson, the conversion of a loved one, or some positive outcome that cannot be identified until some time has elapsed).

Hence the Gospel According to St. Purpose provides a way out of the problem of evil and turns down the 'noise' in our minds. Unfortunately, though, reduced mental distress is purchased at the price of self-deception.

AVOIDING THE FLIP OF THE COIN

Most of us do not want to play the gambler when

it comes to interpreting the major events that shape our lives. We do not like to think of our lives in terms of chance, probability and luck. Those events which we regularly ascribe to 'lady luck' are normally minor happenings that affect us only slightly.

The thought, expressed by Jesus himself, that God "makes his sun rise on the evil and on the good, and sends rain on the just and the unjust" (Mt. 5:45b) injects a discomforting note of the random. Jesus vigorously challenged the popular belief that God orchestrates events for the purpose of punishing the wicked and vindicating the righteous. When his contemporaries sought some lesson from heaven in Pilate's massacre of some Galileans or the eighteen people who were killed when the tower of Siloam fell in Jerusalem (Lk. 13:1-5), Jesus did not satisfy their need to fit these tragic events into neat, little boxes. Instead he emphasized that these unfortunate ones were no worse sinners than anyone else.

Besides satisfying our basic craving for order, the Gospel According to St. Purpose has two subordinate functions: (1) it legitimates our good fortune; and (2) it focuses our thankfulness when we experience a 'close call'.

LUCK AND 'GOD'S BLESSINGS'

Most of us cherish the thought that we somehow deserve our worldly possessions and social status. The Gospel According to St. Purpose conveniently provides a way to place all of our possessions under the umbrella of God's care and bountiful provision. It obscures the incongruity of believing that God 'gave' a new car or a raise to an upwardly-mobile Christian (for the glory of God, of course) but, somehow, cannot find the time to feed a severely malnourished infant on the other side of the globe.

If anyone smugly claims that luck has nothing to do with their 'station in life' or material possessions, he ought to reflect a moment on the nature of his birth. None of us chose the family or country in which we were born. Without a philosophical thought in our heads, we just came into the world.

If you were born in 1980, there would be a one-in-three chance that you would be born into

74

absolute poverty, a devastating form of poverty that currently afflicts approximately 800 million people in less developed countries (excluding China).[8] 'Absolute poverty' is a kind of deprivation so severe that it is virtually nonexistent in North America, Europe, Japan, Australia and the U.S.S.R.

Unfortunately this tragic situation is bound to get worse. By the year 2000, 92% of the world's population growth will take place in less developed countries.[9] An increasing number of these infants will be caught in the debilitating trap of acute poverty.

What if things had been different? What if _you_

---

[8]The probability estimate is based on an estimate by economists at the World Bank that 780 million people suffered from absolute poverty in 1980 (figure excludes China). Assuming that the geographic distribution of the absolute poor is roughly unchanged from World Bank estimates based on 1969 data (Africa, 21%; Latin America, 5%; Asia, 74%) and that births are randomized across geographical regions, 35% of the new population growth would take place in circumstances of absolute poverty. Actually, though, due to the fact that higher fertility rates tend to be concentrated in the poorest regions of less developed countries, the percentage of persons born into absolute poverty would be higher than this figure suggests. The probability estimate assumes that the weighted average annual percentage growth in population is 2.9% for Africa (population 399 million), 2.7% for Latin America (population 325 million), 2.2% for Asia (population 1295 million (excluding China), and 0.5% for the industrialized countries (population 708 million). Sources: U.S. Council on Environmental Quality, and the Department of State, The Global 2000 Report to the President: Entering the Twenty-First Century, Vol. 1 (Washington, D.C.: U.S. Government Printing Office, 1980), p. 9; World Bank, The Assault on World Poverty (reprint) of Rural Development Sector Policy Paper), p. 79; World Bank, World Development Report, 1980 (New York: Oxford University Press, 1980), pp. 33, 142-143.

[9]Council on Environmental Quality, and the Department of State, The Global 2000 Report to the President: Entering the Twenty-First Century, Vol I (Washington, D. C.,: U.S. Government Printing Office, 1980), p. 9.

had been born into absolute poverty? What would your life be like now?

Let us assume, for the sake of speculation, that you were born into a family of ten children. At the time of birth your life expectancy would be 45 years or less (73 years in the U.S.). Before you could be aware of the odds against your own survival, there would be a 30% chance that you would never see your fifth birthday (only 2% in the U.S.). Assuming that you were lucky enough to survive to age five, three of your brothers and sisters would not be so fortunate. Two would have died within a year of their birth and a third before the age of five. Altogether only half of your brothers and sisters would live to age 40.

If you were fortunate enough to escape severe malnutrition during the first five years of life, you would not suffer from any permanent learning disabilities. Perhaps, though, your little brother was not so lucky. If there was a local food shortage when he was four months old, his developing body probably was severely undernourished--causing permanent brain damage.

Having been born into a family suffering from absolute poverty, you may be able to attend some school, but your educational career would be short-lived, probably only through the second grade. Your textbooks, if you were lucky enough to have them, would be of low quality. Perhaps you would be able to achieve some sort of marginal literacy. But if you were born in Mali, West Africa, 90% of your countrymen would be illiterate.

Of course, there would be no proper sewerage facilities where you lived. It is a long way to get water, and the water is foul, infested by parasites. (In Indonesia only 12% of the population have access to a safe water source).

It goes without saying that the nearest medical facility is miles away; medicine is scarce. (If you were born in Ethiopia, there would be an average of one physician per 76,000 people).

There would be a good chance that your father would be landless. What work there is pays little and is seasonal. (A landless family in Malaysia earns a household income on the average of only $73 per

year).   The   possibilities   for   productive employment
are practically nil.[10]

The   intent   of   this   brief exercise in imagining
an 'alternative' birth is to emphasize that the fortui-
tous   circumstances   of   our   birth   was the outcome of
just   plain   luck--the   flip   of   a coin or the draw of
a   card.   It   could have been otherwise.   To think for
a   moment   that   we are special enough, in God's sight,
to   warrant being born in the comfortable circumstances
of   an   advanced,   industrialized   country--instead   of
in   a   poverty   stricken   region of Cambodia, Ethiopia,
Malaysia or Bangladesh--is sheer arrogance.

THE CLOSE CALL

In   addition   to   legitimating   our   good fortune,
the   Gospel   According to St. Purpose finds strong emotional   support   in   the need to express gratitude when
we   experience   a   'close   call'.   All   of us, at some
point   in   our   lives,   have or will experience a close
call.   Perhaps   our   life   was in immediate peril, and
we escaped death's grasp by inches.

Those   who   survive   a   close   call understandably
feel   overwhelmed with gratitude, frequently testifying
to a renewed appreciation for life.   It is only natural
that   we should thank God for seeing us through a close
call.   Who   else   is   there   to receive our gratitude?
We   cannot   thank ourselves and, unless we were rescued
by others, we cannot even be grateful to someone else.

A   problem   exists,   though,   when   we   generalize
upon   the experience of the close call.   There is temptation to reinterpret all of our day-to-day experiences
in   light   of   the   close   call.   Taken to the extreme,
it   can get to the point that every trivial event takes
on   some   divine   significance.   We accept the illusion
that   it   is   an   issue of cosmic importance whether or
not   God 'gives' us a certain job, a new car or a park-
ing spot during rush hour!

In   view   of   the   psychological   'needs' that the
Gospel   According   to   St. Purpose satisfies, it is not

---

[10]World   Bank,   World Development Report, 1980,   pp. 33,
43, 110-111, 152-153.

surprising that Popular Christians have embued it with an aura of sanctity. Sadly, though, the price of our peace of mind is the price of self-deception.

SOURCES OF TRAGEDY

There are two major sources of tragic events: (1) the physical and chemical laws of nature; and (2) human freedom and interdependence. These sources of purposelessness parallel a traditional distinction between two classes of destabilizing events: natural evil and moral evil.

Natural evil ranges from those periodic convulsions of the earth and its atmosphere (earthquakes, tornadoes, volcanic eruptions, hurricanes, tidal waves) to the gamut of diseases that have plagued mankind for millennia.

Moral evil differs from natural evil in that the source of evil can be traced to human actions. Moral evil does not proceed from impersonal forces--the result of inert geological forces or a communicable virus. Murders, rapes, robberies, wars, torture--these cannot be innocuously labeled: 'acts of God'. Moral evil can be traced to the decisions of persons. Granted, in some instances, such as war, the acts of individuals coalesce at such a large scale that they are hardly discernable. Still the ultimate causes are attributable to people.

NATURAL EVIL

Natural evil is a major source of tragedy because 'Mother Nature' is anything but a fine-tuned instrument in the hands of the Almighty. Earthquakes, plagues, hurricanes, tidal waves, floods--they affect everyone in a particular geographic locale with equal devastation. They cannot teach individualized lessons or convey some message from God. Such disasters take both the young and the old; saints and sinners are afflicted irrespective of their virtue or vice. If God used nature to communicate his will, it would be tantamount to releasing a bull in a china closet.

One notable attempt to read the hand of God in the erratic spasms of nature occurred after an earthquake ravaged Lisbon, Portugal, on November 1, 1775. Clergy throughout the British Isles and the Continent pointed to the disaster as a sign of God's judgment. Even John Wesley, in a pamphlet entitled Serious Thoughts Occasioned by the Late Earthquake in Lisbon, argued that the event was a sign of God's disfavor. In general, the literature of that period gave four reasons for God's harsh judgment on Lisbon:

(1) the fabulous wealth of Lisbon . . .; 2) the severity of the Portuguese Inquisition, of which Lisbon was the major center; (3) superstition and the worship of images; and (4) a lax, indulgent, casuistical moral code.[11]

However, some observers of the day, such as Kant and Voltaire, were quick to point out that many cities were just as corrupt as Lisbon, yet they did not taste God's bitter judgment. In a poem written shortly after the earthquake, Voltaire concluded the original version with these words: "We know nothing; nature has no message for us; God does not speak".[12]

Although we can technically restrain the impact of nature upon human communities, it is inconceivable that man will ever be able to 'control' nature in the full sense of the term. We may entertain fantasies of flying through the sky like Superman, but the law of gravity will not be suspended when a deluded LSD victim leaps off a building, attempting to turn his fantasy into reality. We may build massive buildings and large communities around an earthquake fault, but the fact that natural bodies cool more quickly on the outside (thereby creating earthquakes, tidal waves, volcanoes) means that nature will not make exceptions on our behalf.

MORAL EVIL

Moral evil is a source of tragedy because of two invariant features of human existence: freedom and interdependence.

---

[11]S. Paul Schilling, God and Human Anguish, p. 132.

[12]Ibid., p. 57.

The gift of freedom and human autonomy provides many possibilities for creativity or destruction. Freedom is purchased at an incredible price--at the cost of exploitation, savagery, callousness and misery. Nonetheless most would agree that the cost of freedom is not too exhorbitant when compared with the alternatives (e.g., being programmed for 'good' behavior by a divine being, extra-terrestrial creatures or the state).

A favorite theme of many a Hollywood production involves a mad scientist or extra-terrestrial creature who plots to rule the world, holding out the promise that hunger, war and human strife will be rendered technologically obsolete. After the movie's hero or heroine foils the sinister plan for world control, we are left with some variant of the moral platitude: The world would be nice without those evils, but if we have to relinquish our freedom to find utopia, it is not worth it.

We not only value human autonomy above utilitarian considerations, but also it is correct to say that freedom is the prerequisite of those characteristics that define what it is to be human. Love, moral responsibility, rationality, friendship and creativity--these qualities would be impossible without some degree of freedom and autonomy.

The fact of human interdependence means that the price of freedom is not contained to a few 'bad' individuals who have "made their bed and have to sleep in it, too." Because people live in communities (e.g., families, towns, cities and nations), they inevitably partake of both the joys and pitfalls of human community. The victim of a drunk driver shares the burden of human irresponsibility; the passengers killed in a plane crash feel the full weight of human negligence or the finitude of our technologies; the young man who goes to war suffers the brunt of human greed and misunderstanding.

Interdependence deepens both the joy and despair of what it means to be human. Destructive acts born from malice, carelessness or ignorance are not confined to the 'responsible parties'. The fact of interdependence means that the world will always have more than its share of innocent victims.

The presence of natural and moral evil are

incessant sources of purposelessness and waste. They are the inevitable concomitants of human existence. It is difficult to see how Christians could think for a moment that they are somehow exempt from the shadow of tragedy that encroaches upon every contour of human life.

ROMANS 8:28

A verse cited frequently in support of the Gospel According to St. Purpose is Romans 8:28. The translation in the King James Version supports the Popular Christian interpretation: "And we know that all things work together for good to them that love God, to them who are called according to his purpose." Two conditions are implied in this translation: (1) we must love God; and (2) we must be "called according to his purpose." If these conditions are met, the Popular Christian interpretation holds out the promise that every event in a Christian's life "works together for good."

For the sake of argument, let us assume that Popular Christians have grasped the essence of Paul's thought. Is the promise held out in Romans 8:28 valid when applied to the real world? To discover the answer we must first examine the two conditions of the promise.

As to the first condition, let us assume that 'loving God' does not imply any particular gradations of love. In other words, the condition does not imply a cutoff line, below which one's love for God simply isn't up to standards (e.g., unless you have loved God like St. Francis of Assisi, you have not really loved God). Moreover, let's assume that the type of love referred to in this verse includes a child's simple and undefined love for God. Hence it would be correct to say that infants and children satisfy the first condition by virtue of their childlike faith and innocence, irrespective of their cognitive understanding of God or their parent's religious beliefs. This is certainly not a gratuitous assumption. Jesus spoke about children with great tenderness and sensitivity, declaring that the Kingdom of God belonged to them (Mt. 19:13-35; Mk. 10:13-16; Lk. 18:15-17).

The second condition of Romans 8:28--that we must be "called according to his purpose"--is related

81

to Paul's understanding of divine foreknowledge and predestination, alluded to in verses 29-30. Now is certainly not the time to discuss all of the theological problems related to the concept of divine predestination. Moreover the Popular Christian interpretation of this verse does not place any emphasis on the notion of special predestination.

Let us assume that being called according to God's purpose is equivalent to "being in God's will" or "living in accordance with his plan." Given this assumption, the second condition of Romans 8:28 is not a true condition, because it does not supply us with an independent criterion for knowing whether or not we are acting in harmony with God's plans. There is no way for us to know definitively when the second condition is satisfied or unsatisfied, since none of us can legitimately claim to read the mind of God in sufficient detail. Hence I assume that the second condition adds nothing to the first.

The Popular Christian interpretation of Romans 8:28 promises that once the first condition of loving God is satisfied, God will order every event in our lives--no matter how bad--toward some good end. Generally this good end is understood as some positive outcome that emerges from negative circumstances and creates a sense of objective purpose.

Of course, the history of Christian martyrs alone provides plenty of evidence to invalidate the Popular Christian interpretation of Romans 8:28. But, for the sake of argument, let us assume that in the case of a martyr, his or her this-worldly sacrifice will be amply compensated by some special other-worldly reward in the afterlife, specifically reserved for martyrs of the faith. It is important to recognize, though, that this sort of argument cannot be overused. If any other-world reward is the good end of this-worldly suffering, then any and every event that led directly to death could be regarded as 'good' (e.g., murder, illness, natural disaster). This would make our use of the term 'good' absurd and pointless.

SOME CONTRAINDICATIONS

Assuming that the translation of Romans 8:28 in the <u>King James Version</u> conveys the essence of Paul's thought and given the above assumptions, a global application of Romans 8:28 will show that the promise is patently false!

For example, let's take the problem of world hunger. The World Bank has estimated that during the mid-1970's between 400 and 600 million people suffered from severe malnutrition. By the year 2000, the Bank projects a figure as high as 1.3 billion, assuming that __radical__ changes in the distribution of the world's economic resources do not occur.[13]

Most of the victims of international malnutrition are infants and children. One outcome of severe under-nutrition is infant mortality.[14] Another is a high susceptibility to serious diseases throughout child-hood.[15] Furthermore it is widely believed that some extent of mental retardation among children accompanies severe maternal malnutrition at late stages of fetal development or acute undernutrition during infancy and early childhood.[16] If this multitude of children are beneficiaries of God's care, then God is plainly doing a rotten job!

---

[13] Robert McNamara, "Address to the 1978 Annual Meeting of the World Bank - International Monetary Fund Board of Governors," Washington, D.C., Sept. 1978.

[14] Aaron Lechtig, et al., "Maternal Nutrition and Fetal Growth in Developing Countries" (__American Journal of Diseases of Children__ 29:553-561, 1975); Leonard Mata, et al., "Survival and Physical Growth in Infancy and Early Childhood" (__American Journal of Diseases of Children__ 12:561-566, 1975).

[15] John Gordon, Ishwari Chitkara, and John Wyon, "Weanling Diarrhea" (__American Journal of the Medical Sciences__ 245:345-377, 1963); Irwin Rosenberg, Noel Solomons, and Douglas Levin, "Interaction of Infection and Nutrition: Some Practical Concerns" (__Ecology of Food and Nutrition__ 4:203-206, 1976).

[16] Mary Alice Caliendo, __Nutrition and the World Food Crisis__ (New York: Macmillan, 1979), pp. 31-50; Joaquin Cravioto, and Beatriz Robles, "Evolution of Adaptive and Motor Behavior During Rehabilitation from Kwashiorkor" (__American Journal of Orthopsychiatry__ 35:449-464, 1965); Robert Lasky, et al., "Birth Weight and Psychomotor Performance in Rural Guatemala" (__American Journal of Diseases of Children__ 129:566-569, 1975); M. B.

Of course, we cannot begin to sketch the magnitude of suffering throughout history that destroyed lives and created unbearable misery. It is impossible to conceptualize the massive scale of terror and devastation generated by the wars, plagues, famines, natural disasters and genocidal rampages of past generations.

Our own generation alone has witnessed the acts of Adolf Hitler, Pol Pot, Idi Amin; the fates of Hiroshima and Nagasaki; B-52 saturation bombing in Vietnam and Cambodia; the invasions of Hungary, Czechoslovakia and Afghanistan; the gruesome, widespread practice of torture by "moderately repressive" dictatorships throughout the "free world"; and many other dreadful signposts of man's inhumanity to man.

How many dreams have been crushed by senseless barbarity? How many times have tears flooded the eyes of widows and orphans? How many people gasped their last breath with the knowledge that life had ended because of someone else's stupidity? Do we dare utter the trite motto: In everything there is a purpose?

AN ALTERNATE INTERPRETATION

The Popular Christian interpretation of Romans 8:28 cannot stand in the harsh light of reality. It may provide solace for the 'marginally distraught', but it cannot survive the litmus test of a global application.

Does this mean that St. Paul grossly understated the radical dimension of evil? I think not. Instead I suggest that a close reading of Romans 8:28 will show that Popular Christians have taken the verse

Stoch, and P. M. Smythe, "The Effect of Undernutrition During Infancy on Subsequent Brain Growth and Intellectual Development" (S.A. Tydskrif vir Geneeskunde (Oct. 28): 1027-1030, 1967); and Myron Winick, "Fetal Malnutrition and Growth Processes" (Hospital Practice (May):31-41, 1970). For criticism on the relation of severe malnutrition and mental impairment, see Ernesto Pollitt, "Ecology, Malnutrition and Mental Development" (Psychosomatic Medicine 31:193-200, 1969).

out of context. Additionally, there is good reason to believe that an alternate reading of Romans 8:28-- which appears in some ancient manuscripts--reflects the original text.

If you examine Romans 8:28 in its immediate con- text, it becomes apparent that Paul does not view the world as a paragon of order and symmetry. Paul contrasts the pain of the present moment with the glorious Kingdom that will be disclosed at the end of history (8:18). Creation itself "was subjected to futility" (8:20) and is enslaved in corruption and decay (8:21). In this dismal setting of futility and waste, the Christian hope cannot be read from the state of the world. Instead Paul declares that "we hope for what we do not see" (8:25).

In vivid contrast to Paul's vision of a universe distressed and in turmoil, the Gospel According to St. Purpose is predicated upon a well-ordered universe where God oversees and manipulates all the events which befall his 'children'. To ignore the immediate textual context of Romans 8:28, using the verse to support belief in a well-ordered state of affairs, is clearly misguided.

Not only is the Popular Christian interpretation of Romans 8:28 detached from its immediate context, but also there is a strong possibility that another reading should be used for this verse. When the orig- inal biblical texts were handed down from one genera- tion to the next or transmitted from one locality to another, it was necessary to copy the texts by hand. Through this arduous process of textual transmis- sion, some minor variations appeared in the texts. Sometimes these slight deviations were due to common scribal errors. At other times a certain theological bias prompted the scribe to insert a word or to make a deletion.

In the case of Romans 8:28 we have two possible texts to select. The difference between the readings concerns the subject of a Greek verb (sunergei) which means "working together." One reading, employed by the King James Version and some other translations, has the Greek substantive panta ("all things") as the subject. Hence it is translated: "All things work together for good."

By contrast, the Revised Standard Version, Today's English Version and the New International Version opt for the other reading. This reading has God (ho theos) as the subject of the verb sunergei ("working together"). Hence the verse is translated as follows: "We know that in everything God works for good with those who love him, who are called according to his purpose" (RSV).

This textual variation is of some significance in our interpretation of Romans 8:28. Considering the immediate context of the passage, it appears that Paul is simply affirming that God is on the side of the good in all settings of human turmoil. God is striving, aiming and struggling toward the good—in partnership with us. In other words, we can be assured of God's best intentions.

In everything that happens we can take confidence in knowing that God longs for the good to triumph, for the Kingdom to be disclosed in its fullness . . . when darkness is extinguished by the light of his love. Our hope in God is not founded on the perception of the divine hand in human affairs, but upon the confidence that

> neither death, nor life, nor angels, nor principalities, nor things present, nor things to come, nor powers, nor height, nor depth, nor anything else in all creation, will be able to separate us from the love of God in Christ Jesus our Lord (Rom. 8:38-39).

This interpretation of Romans 8:28 stands in sharp contrast to the Popular Christian understanding that all events on planet earth are manipulated by a divine hand for the benefit of God's children, so that "everything that happens fits into a pattern for good" (J. B. Phillips).

Unlike many Popular Christians, Jesus did not treat God as a deux ex machina who pops out of heaven to rescue us from an intractable dilemma. Instead God is our partner in facing life's predicaments, who expresses solidarity with the poor, the helpless and the outcast.

The God revealed through Jesus' life and teachings possesses a love so comprehensive that he is not afraid of dirtying his hands in the process of fully participating in the anguish of each human generation. In short, the deity of the Christian proclamation is a God who suffers.

THE GOD WHO SUFFERS

One survivor of Auschwitz, Elie Wiesel, witnessed
the hanging of three Jews--two men and a child--at
the hands of the Nazi S.S. The gruesome scene was
punctuated by cries of "long live liberty!" from the
adults, but the young boy stood petrified in silence.
One prisoner, standing behind Wiesel, exclaimed in
agony: "Where is God? Where is He?" At that moment
the executioner overturned the chairs positioned on
the gallows and the nooses snapped tight. The two
adults died instantly. But the child, because of
his small frame, dangled helplessly--thrashing the
air--for about a half hour. He gasped for breath
and struggled in futility, in full sight of thousands
of prisoners. Again Wiesel heard the distraught voice
from behind him: "Where is God now?" Then, within
himself, an inaudible voice responded: "Where is
He? Here He is--He is hanging here on this gallows."[17]

Not far from the horrors of Auschwitz, Poland,
a young German pastor sat in a prison cell in Berlin.
Until the time of his imprisonment, he had all the
makings of a brilliant theological career. In 1937
he wrote The Cost of Discipleship, a book whose influence endures to this day. Following a lecture tour
in America, in 1939, he returned to his troubled homeland, against the insistence of friends who pressed
him to stay in America to protect his life. Although
he formerly held strong pacifist convictions, he began
to see pacifism as an escape from Christian responsibility and joined the Resistance upon returning to
Germany. His activities with the Underground led
to a two year period of imprisonment, beginning on
April 5, 1943. Later he was implicated in the unsuccessful assassination attempt on Hitler's life ("the
officer's plot") which took place on July 20, 1944.
After being relocated in several prisons, he was executed by the Gestapo in the concentration camp at
Flossenbürg, on April 9, 1945, just a few days before

---

[17]Elie Wiesel, Night, trans. by S. Rodway (New York:
Hill and Wang, 1960), pp. 70-71.

the Allies liberated the camp. His name? Dietrich Bonhoeffer.

From his prison cell in Berlin, in a letter dated July 16, 1944, Bonhoeffer penned these words:

> Before God and with God we live without God. God lets himself be pushed out of the world on to the cross. He is weak and powerless in the world, and that is precisely the way, the only way, in which he is with us and helps us. Matt. 8:17 makes it quite clear that Christ helps us, not by virtue of his omnipotence, but by virtue of his weakness and suffering.
>
> Here is the decisive difference between Christianity and all religions. Man's religiosity makes him look in distress to the power of God in the world: God is the _deux ex machina_. The Bible directs man to God's powerlessness and suffering; only the suffering God can help.[18]

For Bonhoeffer, the God who suffers is the God who demonstrates his solidarity with mankind. He is neither a deistic deity who stoicly observes the progression of human history from a distant abode, nor is he an interventionist deity who paternalistically manipulates human affairs like some cosmic puppet show. Instead he is a God who is _loving_ enough to become woefully aware of the plethora of pain suffered by all his creatures--from the least to the most complex; a God who is _powerful_ enough to become vulnerable, touchable and susceptible to sorrow; and a God who is _good_ enough to allow humanity to fail, witnessing the disruption of his best intentions without thought of reprisal . . . only redemption.

The primitive Christian community captured a glimpse of the God who suffers in its understanding of the events on Good Friday.

The nature of Jesus' crucifixion, apart from the resurrection, reveals something of the character

---

[18]Dietrich Bonhoeffer, _Letters and Papers From Prison_, ed. by E. Bethge, trans. by R. H. Fuller (New York: Macmillan, 1972), pp. 360-361.

of God. We tend to view the cross solely in light of the resurrection. Our detached, retrospective vision helps us understand the significance of the cross, but it clouds our perception of the horror at the cross.

Generally speaking, we have overdosed on romanticized portraits of an unperturbed Christ who witnesses his final moments with the demeanor of an English gentleman. As a consequence, we rarely peer into Jesus' anguish-filled eyes as he hung on the cross. Unlike the death of Socrates and other martyrs of history, Jesus' death was not a 'fine death', as Jürgen Moltmann reminds us.

> The synoptic gospels agree that he was 'greatly distressed and troubled' (Mark 14:33 par.) and that his soul was sorrowful even to death. He died 'with loud cries and tears', according to the Epistle to the Hebrews (5:7). According to Mark 15:37 he died with every expression of the most profound horror . . . Mark 15:34 reproduces the cry of the dying Jesus in the words of Psalms 22:2: 'My God, why hast thou forsaken me?'[19]

The dimension of suffering experienced by Jesus at the cross clearly transcended simple physical pain, transporting him to the depths of human despair and spiritual darkness. We find it impossible to fully comprehend Jesus' overwhelming feeling of abandonment by his Father in heaven. One wonders whether Popular Christianity's "praise the Lord" theologians would have censured Jesus' cry at Calvary . . . a cry of profound despair: "My God, my God, why hast thou forsaken me?" (Mk. 15:34).

The vision of the suffering God not only finds expression in the details of Jesus' passion but also surfaces in a perspective on Good Friday that gained a lot of currency in the early church. That perspective interpreted Jesus' life and crucifixion by the portrait of Isaiah's "suffering servant of God."

The so-called Servant Songs of Deutero-Isaiah

---

[19]Jürgen Moltmann, The Crucified God (New York: Harper and Row, 1974), p. 146.

(Is. 42:1-4, 49:1-6, 50:4-9, 52:13-53:12) refer to the nation of Israel as the servant of Yahweh who is destined to effect salvation among the Gentiles worldwide, a salvation purchased by Israel's sufferings.[20] It is a moot question whether Jesus himself perceived his passion in light of the suffering servant imagery.[21] Nevertheless there is widespread evidence that the Christian community soon appropriated Isaiah's suffering servant motif in its understanding of the events of Good Friday and the nature of Jesus' messianic calling.[22] The most prominent identification between Jesus and Deutero-Isaiah's suffering servant appears in I Peter 2:21-25:

> . . . Christ also suffered for you [cp. Is. 53:4], leaving you an example, that you should follow in his steps. He committed no sin; no guile was found on his lips [cp. 53:9]. When he was reviled, he did not revile in return; when he suffered, he did not threaten [cp. 53:7]; but he trusted to him who judges justly. He himself bore our sins [cp. 53:11] in his body on the tree, that we may die to sin and live to righteousness. By his wounds you have been healed [cp. 53:5]. For you were straying like sheep [cp. 53:6], but have now returned to the Shepherd and Guardian of your souls.

This image of the suffering God stands in sharp contrast to the traditional Hellenistic concept of a deity who is immutable, omnipotent, self-sufficient, aloof and untouchable. Traditionally we have tended to think of God as a being who stands in need of nothing and is influenced by no one. God is the all-powerful but solitary figure of the universe.

By contrast, a recent school of theology, known

---

[20]J. Lindbloom, Prophecy in Ancient Israel (Philadelphia: Fortress Press, 1962), pp. 400-402.

[21]Werner Kümmel, The Theology of the New Testament (Nashville: Abingdon, 1973), pp. 88-90.

[22]For an extensive listing of allusions to Isaiah 53 in the Gospels, see Joachim Jeremias, New Testament Theology, trans. by J. Bowden (New York: Charles Scribner's Sons, 1971), pp. 286-287.

as "Process Theology," offers an alternate portrait of God. God, according to Process theologians, is not an amalgam of absolute divine qualities which isolate God from his creation. Instead God participates in a dynamic interaction with the entirety of creation, a process which involves change and creativity. Unlike the traditional understanding of God, the Process theologian argues that God is influenced by his creation, that God's 'eternalness' does not imply that he is changeless, and most of all, that God cannot be 'omnipotent' in the sense of possessing the totality of power in the universe. Schubert Ogden expresses the significance of the Process perspective in this way:

> . . . it follows that nothing whatever, not even God, can wholly determine the being of something else. Taken in a completely generalized, analogical sense, 'freedom' means self-creation and, therefore, determination by self in contrast to determination by others. . . .

> This implies, then, that even the greatest conceivable power over others--the 'omnipotent' power than which none greater can be conceived--could not be all the power there is. . . .[23]

The image of the God who suffers--who is touched by a world of pain and whose best laid plans are vulnerable to human irrationality--opens the way for an articulation of the Christian faith that is able to integrate the experience of the tragic within an overall context of meaning and hope. A Christianity with tragedy is a form of faith and practice that unmasks the pretenses of an age characterized by a narcissistic flight from suffering, staring straight into the faceless abyss of evil . . . partaking of the tragic vision of life.

THE GOSPEL AND TRAGEDY

From Sophocles' Oedipus Rex to Shakespeare's

---

[23]Schubert Ogden, Faith and Freedom (Nashville: Abingdon, 1979), p. 76.

King Lear to Hawthorne's The Scarlet Letter, tragic knowledge is well-attested throughout the history of literature. But how can we reconcile the proclamation of the Gospel ("good news") with the fact of human tragedy? Tragic events are destructive and aimless; the Gospel generates life and meaning.

One approach is to say that the two are irreconcilable, beyond any conceivable harmonization. This approach views religious belief as inherently inimical to tragic knowledge. As I. A. Richards put it,

> Tragedy is only possible to a mind which is for the moment agnostic or Manichean. The least touch of any theology which has a compensating[24] Heaven to offer the tragic hero is fatal.

But must we define tragedy in terms of ultimate despair, hopelessness or folly? Are there not intermediate categories which do not preclude the possibility of meaning and hope? Even those who speak of tragedy in the sense of ultimate folly celebrate the nobility of the human spirit, as it is crushed by the cold, determined machinery of fate.

If we interpret the vision of the tragic as something less than ultimate despair, it is clear that the Gospel can be articulated in a way that makes tragic knowledge an integral part of the Christian proclamation.

Obviously such an integration between the Gospel and tragedy is impossible if we insist on interpreting the "Good News" through rose-colored glasses. It will not do to sell Christianity as the surest way to "life, liberty and pursuit of happiness." If we treat the Gospel as an additive to the 'good life', something which augments our personal well-being or enhances our relationships, then we will never see the cross, as it stands uninvitingly at the center of Christian discipleship.

The offense of the cross stands at the heart of the Good News. At the cross we remember that tragedy is an inescapable fact of human existence; at

---

[24] I. A. Richards, Principles of Literary Criticism (New York: Harcourt, Brace & Co., 1959), p. 246.

the cross we remember that a glimmer of hope can penetrate even the darkest moment. But the cross is in no way a 'paradigm' of the way God regularly transforms bad events into meaningful, purposeful ones. Instead the cross (as seen from the resurrection) is the one great <u>exception</u> to the rule, an exception which generates the first rays of the authentic human hope.

D. D. Raphael has suggested that tragedy always has <u>conflict</u> as a necessary ingredient. Not any sort of conflict will do. It must be of a special type. The conflict inherent in tragic dramas is between an "inevitable power," which Raphael labels "necessity," and the response to this "inevitable power" by the tragic hero.

> Tragic conflict differs from the conflicts presented by other forms of drama in that the victory always goes to necessity. The hero is crushed.[25]

Raphael distinguishes classical Tragedy from modern Tragedy in this way. The 'inevitable power' in classical Tragedy is labeled 'fate'; whereas, in modern Tragedy, the 'necessity' against which the tragic hero struggles--which eventually crushes him--is related to human character.

Raphael's concept of tragic conflict offers us a clue as to how the experience of the tragic can be an integral part of the Christian proclamation. In our previous discussion of natural and moral evil, it was emphasized that these factors, inherent in human experience, are major sources of purposelessness. They are 'inevitable powers' which sap the most noble aspiration, which disrupt our best laid plans, and which crush the brightest prospects for change.

If hope can possibly exist in a world racked by tragic conflict, it is the hope of an open future--the hope of possibilities yet unforeseen or unrealized, the promise of an outcome whose testimony resides in the hearts of the faithful.

If the God revealed in Jesus the Christ is

---

[25] D. D. Raphael, <u>The Paradox of Tragedy</u> (Bloomington, Ind.: Indiana University Press, 1960), p. 25.

believable in a world overwhelmed by tragedy writ
large, then he is a God who suffers, who weeps, who
cares more deeply than any being in the universe.

The Gospel According to St. Purpose cannot appreciate the theological significance of tragic conflict
because it denies the reality of tragedy itself.
We must take stock of the tragic proportions of human
existence and seek solace only in the "sure and stead-
fast anchor of the soul" (Heb. 6:19)--the one named
Jesus, from Nazareth.

CHAPTER 5

APOCALYPSE NOW?

STARGAZING--CHRISTIAN STYLE

Is the Rapture going to come before or after
the Tribulation? What is the Millennium? Who will
be the Antichrist? What does the number 666 mean?
Is it necessary for the Temple to be rebuilt in Jerusalem before the end comes? Will there be a worldwide
Christian revival before the return of Christ?

Questions like these and many others are often
heard on the lips of well-meaning Christians. One
need not look far to find books, songs and movies
that depict the horrors of the end time. The theme
is always the same. Christians are admonished to
get serious with their faith before they are drawn
into Satan's web. The signs of the times are clear;
the end is near.

Some brace themselves for the final conflict
while others anticipate a mid-flight rendezvous with
Christ in the clouds . . . something called 'the Rapture'. A few overly zealous types talk of stockpiling
food or heading for the hills to avoid Armageddon.
Some warn of computers and innovative credit systems
that will one day be used to implement the Antichrist's
program of global religious persecution; others
interpret any movements of international cooperation
as the harbinger of the Antichrist's one-world government.

There seems to be no end to this kind of armchair
speculation within Popular Christianity. Ministers
instruct their congregations to use the Bible as a
kind of <u>Poor Richard's Almanac of the End</u>. Everyone

has their own theories, their divinely inspired interpretations of Revelation, Ezekiel, Joel, Daniel and Matthew 24. No one wants to miss an opportunity to witness the fulfillment of biblical prophecy; everyone wants to augur the future.

Stargazing--from the beginnings of astronomy to the horoscopes of contemporary astrology--holds a certain fascination. The idea that individual fates can be discerned in the heavens appeals to our desire to know the unknowable. But like their ancient predecessors, contemporary stargazers face the predicament of not knowing for sure whether they discern in the heavens the mysterious ways of God or simply gaze at a reflection of themselves.

SIGNS OF THE END OR SIGNS OF THE TIME?

From banal predictions headlined in Hollywood tabloids to computer generated scenarios of life on earth at 2025, our preoccupation with the future is a defining characteristic of our culture. Our sometimes inordinate fascination with the future stems from both our boredom with the present and our anxiety toward the future . . . but probably anxiety prevails as the primary cause.

The grounds for future-oriented anxiety are manifest. Technological and social change have proceeded at breakneck speed. We are all victims of the malaise that Alvin Toffler diagnosed as "future shock." We wonder what life will be like just over the horizon. Is there any hope for the great experiment we call 'the human experience'? Will we all be vaporized in a moment of madness or by a slight miscalculation?

It should not surprise us that Popular Christianity is similarly preoccupied with the future. Visions of an appointed Armageddon transmute our general societal anxiety into a call to obedience and faithfulness. Middle Eastern conflicts cease to be simple political struggles over scarce resources and claims to national autonomy. Instead they take on a religious aura.

Many Popular Christians believe that world events are taking place according to a prearranged timetable, wrought in heaven, which will converge in a final conflict between the forces of good and evil:

Armageddon. Famines, earthquakes, wars and rumors of wars--these are the things that must precede the end. They are the birthpangs of the coming new world. It is believed that the appointed time has arrived. Like a well-oiled machine, humanity is on a collision course with unprecedented horrors and God Almighty is in the driver's seat.

THE 'CHRISTIAN' RESPONSE?

In the face of the impending panorama of destruction, Popular Christianity proffers two 'Christian' responses.

The first response is to acquiesce to this ghoulish scenario, sitting back to reflect on God's hand in world events, taking comfort in the belief that God is completely in control. After all, it is assumed that these horrible events must precede the end. Biblical prophecy is irrevocable. According to this view, we might lose a hundred million people here and a few million people there, but these are 'acceptable losses' for the Son of Man's 'red carpet'.

A second 'Christian' response offered by Popular Christianity is--believe it or not--to speed up the whole process! Matthew 24:14 has inspired a new breed of efficiency engineers of the end. They stress that a world-wide evangelization campaign must precede Christ's return. Once this aggressive program capitalizes on the world's communications networks, so that everyone 'hears' the Gospel, then the end will come. The doctrine provides a handy rationale for world missions with the gruesome justification that Christians are morally obligated to rush humanity headlong into Armageddon. After all, if it has to happen, you might as well get it over with . . . or so the reasoning goes.

Stargazing. What a pleasant way to observe our destinies . . . fixed in the heavens . . . inalterable, controlled and secure. Who needs horoscopes when you have Bible prophecy? There is no need to fret; nothing can really be done to avert the appointed destruction. The Gospel According to Armageddon translates the Aramaic invocation on the lips of the first Christians--Maranatha (O Lord, come)--into a stark hymn of desolation: Apocalypse, now.

THE SELF-DECEPTION

I will call the particular self-deception under consideration the Apocalypse Now Self-Deception. It has the following five components:

1. **The Deception:** Social conditions today are so bad they cannot be changed.

2. **The Intended Objective:** To foster allegiance to the Christian faith by affirming God's control over the end of history.

3. **The Primary Defense Mechanisms:** (a) Overcompensation; and (b) Isolation.

4. **Factors Which Perpetuate Self-Deception:** (a) Diminishing personal influence over complex social issues; and (b) The tendency to distance ourselves from suffering.

5. **The Unintended Consequences:** (a) The evasion of personal moral responsibility; and (b) The loss of compassion.

Let's examine each of these elements of the Apocalypse Now Self-Deception.

1. **THE DECEPTION:** Social conditions today are so bad they cannot be changed.

Nowadays one often gets the feeling that people have lost confidence in their ability to shape their own destinies. The social order seems too complex, too massive to be malleable to the human will. Every step in social progress seems to be enshrouded in futility . . . like rearranging the deck chairs on the Titanic.

But is it really true that these are the darkest of days? An inhabitant of Europe in the 14th century who beheld the fury of the Black Death would surely disagree. Those who were unfortunate enough to witness the earthquake of 1556 at Shen-shu, China or the Indian famine of 1770 would have rightly felt that the end of the world was upon them.

By any measure, there are no historical grounds for claiming that our lifetimes have seen unprecedented tribulation. Contrary to the pessimistic view, an excellent case could be made for the claim that our epoch has unparalleled opportunities to make remarkable strides in moral and social progress. Of course, the obverse is also true. We are in a position to set back human progress millenia, or perhaps annihilate it altogether, if our generation persists in its short-sightedness.

We stand at a unique juncture of human history. The possibilities for good seem almost limitless; the potential for self-destruction is awesome.

Technology has perched man on a frightful precipice where perspective and balance are the only threads which steady his quivering stance. There . . . at the precipice . . . man is victimized by his own genius. His technological capabilities have far outdistanced his meager achievements in moral and social progress. Morally speaking, humanity is not too far ahead of the discovery of fire.

Split-second communications, global intercourse, universal public education, economic interdependence and open, democratic societies--these are a few of the reasons why our generation is able to exercise more influence over the events of history than generations of times past.

Especially in the past two hundred years, the signs of humanity's moral progress have been extraordinary. During this brief segment of human history, we have witnessed the worldwide abolition of slavery, the near universal rejection of overt colonialism and racism, a developing concept of individual human rights, remarkable accomplishments in international organization, and the spread of constitutional democracies. These are no mean achievements! Our ancestors would have viewed such social developments as practical impossibilities from their vantage points.

Of course, there have been many tragic developments also. Two World Wars, the nuclear arms race, the rise of totalitarian regimes, acute global economic inequalities, the Holocaust--we could go on for pages to describe the manifestations of greed, malice and mistrust in recent history.

Yet, as terrible as these events are, the small accomplishments in our ongoing moral advancement are enough to convince us that the aspiration for peace and justice has never fared stronger within the human breast.

2. THE INTENDED OBJECTIVE: To foster allegiance to the Christian faith by affirming God's control over the end of history.

Keep the faith . . . for the end is near! This message is a central feature of what is called 'apocalyptic literature'. The term 'apocalyptic' is derived from a Greek word which means 'revelation' or 'disclosure'. In a religious context the term refers to auditory or visionary communications from a deity who discloses some hidden truth, perhaps a spiritual insight into political conditions or detailed 'predictions' of certain events couched in symbolic, enigmatic language.

The diverse kinds of literature which have been labeled 'apocalyptic' all have at least one thing in common: the apocalypticist 'disinterestedly' interprets historical events in terms of a comprehensive pattern or plan which[1] moves history toward a certain, determined conclusion. The apocalypticist lays claim to special knowledge unavailable to the uninitiated. He is a 'determinist' in the sense that he is convinced that he is privy to an unalterable design that impels history to a specified end. That end--whether it is a messianic kingdom or a Marxist utopia--is all that matters. Historical events themselves are irrelevant features of the grand design. Obviously apocalypticists usually make much better social critics than social reformers.

It should not surprise us that the apocalyptic, as a literary genre, flourishes during periods of severe social turmoil or persecution. When historical events become meaningless, if not inherently evil, there is an acute need to detach oneself from tragic circumstances in order to seek meaning from sources beyond history.

The major representatives of apocalyptic literature within the Bible--Daniel and Revelation--were written during periods of intense religious

---

[1] Walter Schmithals, The Apocalyptic Movement, trans. by John E. Steely (New York: Abingdon Press, 1975), pp. 17ff.

persecution. Apostasy was rife, and graphic depictions of God's judgment were used to summon the faithful to obedience. The Book of Daniel closes with these words:

> And you, Daniel, be faithful to the end. Then you will die, but you will rise to receive your reward at the end of time (12:13, TEV).

Similarly John's Revelation is full of admonitions enjoining believers to stay true to the faith until the end.

> Be faithful unto death, and I will give you the crown of life (2:10b).

The Book of Daniel emerged from the severe persecution of the Jews by Antiochus IV (Epiphanes) between 168-163 BCE, and Revelation was penned during a period of persecution under the Roman Emperor Domitian (81-96 CE). At these historical junctures things looked very dismal for Jewish/Christian communities. Many turned away from the faith of their fathers. Circumstances were so bad that good could conceivably come only by totally annihilating the evil of the present age, starting over again with a clean slate.

Those who remained true to their confession of faith were promised a new world order that would reward them dearly:

> To those who win the victory, who continue to the end . . . I will give them authority over the nations, to rule them with an iron rod and to break them to pieces like clay pots (Rev 2:26-28a, TEV).

The apostate's fate would be much different. His end would be as gory as the faithful's reward was glorious. Faith was fostered by an incentive system of heavenly design. The threat of punishment scared would-be apostates and the promise of incalculable reward encouraged the faithful to continue their fidelity.

Of course, it goes without saying that a divine incentive system such as this is nourished on sentiments which are less than noble. The prospect of heavenly crowns decorating our heads or hellish flames lapping at our feet appeals to our child-like craving for approval and our fears of pain and rejection. From the standpoint of apocalyptic literature, allegiance to the faith is sustained by a careful calculation of the costs and benefits that lie ahead. Fidelity is cast as the prudent course to follow.

It is understandable that apocalyptic writers, living in periods of severe turmoil, were anxious to portray religious commitment as a rational choice. Many of their countrymen were disillusioned with the faith of their fathers or despaired of the ostracism and persecution which their religious commitment had brought upon them. It was necessary to show why religious fidelity was sensible.

However, the social setting of Popular Christianity does not even remotely resemble the turbulent eras during which the apocalyptic literature of the Bible was written. Popular Christianity basks in religious freedom, not persecution, and its base of political power is anything but ineffectual. Its apocalyptic spirit is born from comfort, not turmoil: 'cheap apocalypticism'.

It is a truism that people motivated by love, instead of fear, will more consistently uphold their cherished values. Moral and religious ideals move us by drawing us to new heights of insight and vision. By contrast, threats of impending doom or promises of heavenly reward only compel people in one direction or another . . . no substantial inner transformation is required. Jesus' transforming gospel is 'good news' because it leads us to a higher plane of insight, love and life. Our obedience does not have to be guaranteed by external compulsion.

3. THE PRIMARY DEFENSE MECHANISMS: (a) Overcompensation; and (b) Isolation.

OVERCOMPENSATION. The ego defense of compensation is probably the most visible of the mechanisms of psychological defense. All of us feel certain deficiencies relating to our physical appearance, personality or social position which we try to compensate for by emphasizing strengths in other areas. Compensation is usually a helpful defense mechanism because it develops strong aspects of our personality, nurturing our self-concept, while displacing the self-consciousness we feel toward our perceived weaknesses and deficiencies.

Sometimes, though, the healthy operation of compensation gets out of balance. In such cases the urge to compensate for one's felt deficiencies creates many blind spots and a myopic concern to be successful in one's areas of compensation. This is called overcompensation.

I will define overcompensation as <u>the exaggerated attempt to evade felt deficiencies by developing qualities or perspectives that appear to counteract or mollify those deficiencies</u>. For example, overcompensation is evidenced in the behavior of the graduate student described in the following case study:

> A 24-year-old graduate student was the smallest member of his class. Among his associates however he was considered 'a real scrapper'. His general attitude and demeanor left no doubts about his outer feelings of self-confidence. . . .

> On occasion he might lightly (or sometimes less than lightly!) punch, push, or jostle his fellow students about. While usually done in a friendly enough manner, this was still as though to lay claim to some kind of physical dominance of the relationship. He was quick to respond to an intellectual challenge, which from his history, proved to be a similar kind of automatic response to earlier boyhood physical challenges. At times, a comment or statement would be taken by him as a challenge, where none had been intended. . . .

> Under therapeutic study his relative aggressiveness, defensiveness, and cockiness proved to be an attempted compensation for inner and more hidden doubts and fears of inadequacy. These stemmed in particular from his limited physical endowment and his pervasive inner feelings about his lacks in this area. As the needs became clarified in therapy they lessened. His demeanor became gradually less aggressive.[2]

---

[2] Henry P. Laughlin, <u>The Ego and Its Defenses</u> (New York: Appleton-Century-Crofts, 1970), p. 19.

I suggest that the defense mechanism of overcompensation can be discerned in Popular Christianity's appropriation of apocalyptic literature. By marshalling apocalyptic themes within the Christian tradition, Popular Christians overcompensate for their felt inabilities to influence the course of human events. In so doing, Popular Christians have tended to adopt a pessimistic outlook on their own abilities to exercise effective social responsibility. Structural evil is viewed as beyond transformation. Only the complete annihilation of the present age will allow the good to shine forth. The apocalyptic perspective, adopted by many Popular Christians, substitutes divinely ordained timetables for movements of social change; it sees the future as closed and predetermined, instead of being open and responsive to man's partnership with God.

ISOLATION. A second defense mechanism that seems to be operative in Popular Christianity's use of apocalyptic themes is the mechanism of isolation. Every normal human being--who possesses minimal powers of imagination and an ordinary capacity to empathize--finds the sight of another's suffering to be a distressing experience. It should not surprise us, then, that the mind constructs various ways to insulate us from the painful perception of suffering. One defense mechanism that aids our avoidance of suffering is isolation.

Isolation can be defined as the attempt to evade threatening situations by divorcing one's emotions from objects or ideas which generally evoke an emotional response. The divorce of affect from object can be accomplished in innumerable ways. For example, an emotionally charged situation can be redescribed in cool, detached, intellectual terms, where the emotional force of the situation is defanged. This sort of isolation (sometimes called 'intellectualization') is evident when people recount especially painful events--a divorce, being raped, the death of a loved one--in dispassionate, detached, matter-of-fact tones.

The defense mechanism of isolation is also manifest in attempts to substitute non-emotive terminology for emotive words; the impact being that the unpleasant impressions created by the emotive words are avoided. Everyday examples of this type of isolation range from common euphemisms (e.g., 'passed away', 'affair' or 'restroom') to distancing, technical jargon (e.g., referring to an abortion as a 'termination of pregnancy' or a fetus as 'the products of conception').

Isolation is profuse in military lingo. Strategic planners speak of "neutralizing" the enemy; a soldier "mows down" combatants with his machine gun during "an engagement." Some of the more disturbing examples of isolation appear in the pages of international weapons catalogues, where the British BAC 167 Strikemaster jet "offers a uniquely cost-effective solution for counter-insurgency" and a French 30-mm aircraft round is described as being "very effective against persons."[3]

In sum, the defense mechanism of isolation functions to insulate us from emotional pain. Isolation allows us to contemplate suffering in mass proportions with little concurrent emotional turmoil . . . from a cool, detached perspective.

I suggest that Popular Christianity's appropriation of apocalyptic motifs has the effect of distancing sensitive Christian people from the preventable pain and suffering which currently ravage the earth. In short, I interpret apocalypticism as a form of isolation. I will elaborate on this suggestion momentarily.

4. FACTORS WHICH PERPETUATE SELF-DECEPTION: (a) Diminishing personal influence over complex social issues; and (b) The tendency to distance ourselves from suffering.

DIMINISHING PERSONAL INFLUENCE. Massive bureaucracies, endless red tape, special interests groups, political haggling--trying to get anything done these days seems doomed to failure from the very start. Social institutions seem too complex and impersonal. Referendums and cumbersome legislative procedures have supplanted the town meeting; gargantuan corporations have replaced the family business; and we need "Good Samaritan" laws to shield us from lawsuits when we extend a helping hand to another. No doubt, this real sense of diminishing personal control over social institutions contributes to the fatalistic conviction that our only hope lies in starting over from scratch.

Our frustration with the complexity of modern life is understandable, but it must not lead us to

---

[3] Kurt Andersen, "What Money Can Buy" (Time, Oct 26, 1981).

to "call fire down from heaven" (Lk. 9:54) while possibilities for transformation still exist.

Christian communities have no business leading the parade of defeatists and prophets of doom, as a means of overcompensating for our feelings of powerlessness. To do so betrays the Christian task of being "like salt for all mankind" (Mt 5:13). The pessimist should not feel at home with true Christianity. Pessimism is a kind of balm for disappointment. Like the disillusioned lover who exclaims that she will never love again, the pessimist averts disappointment by disengagement. The pessimist's hope that "does not disappoint" (Rom 5:5) is a hope void of expectation . . . actually not a hope at all.

The first Christians were optimistic enough to affirm the transformative potential of the Gospel; they were realistic enough to recognize that insofar as the Christian mission is concerned, the cross goes with the territory; but, they did not partake of pessimism's chalice by interpreting their failures as mandates for inaction.

INSULATION FROM SUFFERING. A second factor that supports that Apocalypse Now Self-Deception concerns the long recognized human tendency to remove ourselves from the proximity of suffering. The perception of another's distress sometimes creates so much emotional turmoil that the instinct to withdraw overcomes our learned abilities to empathize and respond with compassion.

Signs of emotional or geographic distancing can be discerned throughout our culture. Nursing homes shield us from the inevitability of old age and help sustain 'the cult of youth'; superhighways skirt blighted slum areas which cordon off the 'undesirable'; and reports of famine in Chad or Ethiopia, when they make the evening news, can be turned off with a flick of the switch.

The Gospel According to Armageddon emotionally isolates us from millions who suffer. It preaches that humanity's final hour is ticking away according to a prearranged plan that cannot be reversed. Because the fuse is set, we need not feel pain on behalf of those who are victims of the ordeal . . . we can relax with a mind game that comforts us at the cost of extinguishing the fires of compassion with apathy and acquiescence.

5. THE UNINTENDED CONSEQUENCES: (a) The evasion of personal moral responsibility; and (b) The loss of compassion.

EVADED MORAL RESPONSIBILITY. A recurring theme of this book is that self-deception ultimately subverts a person's true intentions. In the case of the Apocalypse Now Self-Deception, the subversive consequences of self-deception are especially pronounced. In their attempt to foster loyalty to the Christian faith, Popular Christians unwittingly undermine the Christian mission.

By overcompensating for a felt sense of powerlessness, Popular Christianity embraces a world view which sees meaningful social reform as a forlorn cause. As the reasoning goes, because we are in the last days, terrible events must take place before Christ's return. Those events cannot be changed; they are predetermined and executed by God himself. Hence the Christian's only moral responsibility is to remain true to her religious convictions (especially under severe persecution) and to uphold her personal moral code.

Ought implies can. That is, we are not morally responsible in situations where we cannot exercise any influence or control. Because the Gospel According to Armageddon esteems the world as beyond the point of no return, there is nothing we can do to avert the coming disaster . . . nothing we should do.

The clock is ticking; events are moving rapidly toward their own conclusion. The apocalypticist can point to a famine as 'a sign of the end' while failing to recognize his own moral obligations to aid those who starve needlessly. He need not feel any moral compunction at the sight of a malnourished infant. By implication, the 'end time' renders the Golden Rule obsolete.

DIMINISHED COMPASSION. Besides leading us down the path of evaded moral responsibility, the Apocalypse Now Self-Deception has the unintended consequence of reducing our capacity to feel compassion. I have often been struck by the glib, matter-of-fact way that many Popular Christians speak of the horrible events that will signal Christ's return. Famines, wars, earthquakes, convulsions in the heavens—the prospect of such terrors do not even evince a tear on behalf of one's fellow man. Instead Christians are instructed that they themselves should not dread these impending disasters--either they will be 'raptured' away or God will grant them supernatural strength to undergo 'the Tribulation'.

The Gospel According to Armageddon looks upon the world's inequalities, injustices and conflicts with a glint in its eye. Its adherents have insider information. They know that diplomats expend their energies in futility and that peace treaties are only cosmetic measures to dress up a world without a 'last request'. This gospel does not elevate peacemakers (Mt. 5:9), but instead displays a morbid fascination with warmongers.

How is it that otherwise sensitive Christian people can catalogue these global horrors with a disposition not unlike that of an accountant's listing of debits and credits? The only answer that seems reasonable to me is that Popular Christianity's appropriation of apocalyptic themes within the Bible has created a sense of emotional isolation, insulating Christians from compassion they would normally feel otherwise. They feel little to no pain because their normal emotional responses have been short-circuited. Because this suggestion may seem confusing or untenable, I will elaborate upon it further.

DOOMSDAY AND PERSONAL DISTANCE

One especially unfortunate effect of isolation is that it increases what Lawrence Becker has called "personal distance." This term refers to the degree of emotional/cognitive separation between one person and another. Becker notes that "for most people, an increase in the amount of personal distance involved correlates directly with an increase in the injuries they are capable of doing to their fellows."[4] Of course, this principle could be expanded to include the 'sins of omission' (actions which would greatly benefit others that we fail to do) which we commit routinely in the course of our social relations. That is, the greater the personal distance, the less apt we are to be aware of another's need.

---

[4]Lawrence C. Becker, "The Neglect of Virtue" (Ethics 85/2:110-122, 1975), p. 121.

The unfortunate consequences of high degrees of personal distance have been documented in laboratory experiments. Stanley Milgram conducted a fascinating set of experiments at Stanford which demonstrated that people more readily inflict pain on others when audio or visual contact with the victim is obstructed in some way.[5]

The same dynamic is attested in the testimonies of bombadiers. One American pilot who flew in Vietnam explained it like this:

> For the pilot it's a set of coordinates. It's an altitude, it's a distance, it's flipping a switch, it's all these things that are so abstract. . . . You depersonalize the enemy and you depersonalize the civilians. . . . You don't see the effect of what you do. Except the closer you get to the ground, the more that changes.[6]

One young Air Force captain, Donald Dawson, who flew in B-52 Arclight strikes (sixty 750 lb. bombs dropped simultaneously on a 'box' one-half mile wide and two miles long) in Nixon's secret airwar over Cambodia, became obsessed with the death and destruction he had inflicted. One day he learned that a Cambodian wedding party had been 'boxed' by a B-52 Arclight strike.

> This made him think constantly of the 'reverence' in which he held his own wedding--he considered it the most important event in his life, and 'having the actual ceremony devastated by a B-52 attack is beyond comprehension'.[7]

In June of 1973 he refused to fly.

---

[5] Stanley Milgram, Obedience to Authority (New York: Harper and Row, 1974), p. 34.

[6] Kit Lavell, "The Flying Black Ponies," in Everything We Had: An Oral History of the Vietnam War. . .," pp. 133-140 (New York: Random House, 1981, p. 140.

[7] William Shawcross, Sideshow: Kissinger, Nixon and the Destruction of Cambodia (New York: Simon & Schuster, 1979), p. 291.

Perhaps there is no more poignant instance of personal distance and emotional isolation than the case of Otto Adolf Eichmann. He was the low-level, Nazi bureaucrat who was responsible for assembling and transporting millions of Jews to their deaths. Despite his gruesome charge, there is no record that he himself actually killed anyone.

Eichmann was obsessed with doing his duty and being a 'good' citizen in Hitler's Third Reich. He partook of the view--prevalent in the S.S.--that they were privileged to be a part of a unique and glorious segment of world history. Eichmann frequently quoted a maxim of one of his superiors: "These are the battles which future generations will not have to fight again."[8] Of course, such noble "battles" were fought against women, children, the elderly, the infirm and the mentally retarded.

Eichmann successfully intellectualized his task of conducting the most terrible, systematic exercise in genocide that history has ever known. He convinced himself that he was only doing his duty, being a good citizen. In spite of his many visits to Auschwitz, Eichmann managed to avoid witnessing an execution. Once, though, when visiting a death camp in Poland, he saw a group of Jews who were going to be gassed in a mobile van. Eichmann recounted the distressing experience like this:

> I cannot tell [how many Jews entered], I hardly looked. I could not; I could not; I had had enough. . . . I then drove along after the van, and then I saw the most horrible sight I had thus far seen in my life. The truck was making for an open ditch, the doors were opened, and the corpses were thrown out, as though they were still alive, so smooth were their limbs. . . . There I got enough. I was finished. I only remember that a physician in white overalls told me to look through a hole into the truck while they were still in it. I refused

---

[8]Hannah Arendt, <u>Eichmann in Jerusalem</u>, 2nd ed. (New York: Viking Press, 1964), p. 105.

to do that. I could not. I had to disappear.[9]

Ironically, Eichmann slaughtered millions of innocent people as an efficiency expert of genocide but did not have stomach to witness the gassing of a few people.

It is noteworthy that the official correspondence within Nazi Germany shows much evidence of emotional isolation when the extermination of the Jews was discussed. Since cooperation at various levels of the German bureaucracy was essential, strict "language rules" were followed. Words such as "extermination," "liquidation" or "killing" were inadmissible in official documents. Instead, officials had to use the terms: "final solution," "evacuation" and "special treatment." When reference to the deportation of the Jews was necessary, the 'language rules' dictated that writers should use "change of residence" or "resettlement." The logistics of gassing, forced sterilizations and the disposal of bodies were described later as "medical matters." As Hannah Arendt notes,

> the net effect of this language system was not to keep these people ignorant of what they were doing, but to prevent them from equating it with their old, 'normal' knowledge of murder and lies.[10]

Of course, these examples of personal distance are extreme. But, at a much more subtle level, I believe the same dynamic operates in the Gospel According to Armageddon. For example, there is a tendency among Popular Christians to view a famine as a sign of the end, instead of as an occasion to express love to our neighbors in faraway lands. Most Popular Christians have enough material resources to significantly improve the lives of large numbers of acutely poor, undernourished people. Unfortunately, the Gospel According to Armageddon is preoccupied with auguring the next move on the divine chessboard--a game of wits that makes famine relief look uninteresting by

---

[9] Arendt, p. 88.

[10] Arendt, p. 86

111

comparison.[11]

Jesus was not aloof to human suffering. He was neither a dreamy-eyed mystic seeking union with the

---

[11]It is important not to overstate my case. Some who believe that Christ's second coming is imminent are actively engaged in famine relief and other important social concerns. Two possible explanations could account for this.

First, it could be that those who have mixed their belief in the imminence of the end of history with social activism are motivated by strong (admirable) moral convictions which sustain their activism, in spite of the credo that there are no prospects for meaningful social change.

A second explanation is more plausible. It could be that for such persons, their eschatological convictions are a more-or-less 'formal' element of their overall belief system. For example, Gary Schwartz, in his study of Seventh-Day Adventism, found that the group's belief in the imminence of the end of the world did not inhibit its members from demonstrating great concern for their own upward social mobility and their children's future economic prospects [Sect Ideologies and Social Status (Chicago: University of Chicago, 1970), pp. 220ff.]. Schwartz explains this phenomenon by making a distinction between a religious movement's "formal theology" and its "ideology." Similar distinctions have been made by anthropologists who have studied the social impact of religious belief systems. David Aberle [The Peyote Religion Among the Navaho (Chicago: Aldine Publishing Co., 1966), p. 317] draws the distinction between a group's "official ideology" and its "directing ideology," and Clifford Geertz ["Religion as a Cultural System," in Anthropological Approaches to the Study of Religion, pp. 1-46, ed. by Michael Banton (New York: Praeger, 1966), pp. 26ff.] distinguishes between "religious" and "commonsense" perspectives or symbol systems.

Often Popular Christians who hold a dire outlook on the course of world affairs are anything but apolitical. Many display an adamant concern for political issues (e.g., school prayer, anti-pornography legislation, etc.) The somewhat 'reactionary' cast of their political involvements is probably due to the highly selective way in which certain social issues are deemed as 'religiously significant', and the notable lack of a comprehensive, integrated approach to Christian mission.

divine and disdaining contact with the world, nor was he an apocalyptic fanatic who clustered his disciples in an isolated commune to await the death throes of the earth. Why should his followers obscure the transformative light of his message under a bushel of pessimism, passivity and portentous scenarios of the future?

THE ARGUMENT FROM PROPHECY

Some may counter that I am missing the whole point. Just because the Gospel According to Armageddon diminishes Christian social awareness is no reason to dismiss it. If the end of the world really <u>is</u> upon us, the truth should prevail irrespective of the consequences for Christian mission.

This is certainly a legitimate point if one can justify the claim that these, in fact, are the last days. Yet those who glibly set forth this claim must be cognizant of the many times that Christians in past generations believed that they were witnesses of the end of human history. As I mentioned in Chapter 3, the early followers of Jesus anticipated the coming of Christ within their lifetimes. Of course, the early Christians had to readjust their timetables as the years passed.

Throughout the history of Christianity, prophets of doom have warned believers that they had better prepare themselves for the final conflict between the forces of good and evil. Like a broken record, all of their predictions of evil's cosmic demise never came about . . . and man continued to live in moral ambiguity.

Contemporary prophets of Armageddon emphasize that our historical epoch is unique in that we are witnessing the convergence of conditions which are supposed to attend the end. Actually, though, nearly every one of these 'signs' could be more readily applied to past historical periods. Consider the following.

Famines? What our generation has witnessed is small-scale compared with famines that ravaged the earth in times past. In 436 BCE thousands of starving Romans ended their tribulation by drowning themselves in the Tiber River; in 1333-7 four million people died from starvation in only a <u>single</u> region in China; in 1770 about ten million died during a famine in India; the potato famine in Ireland killed about one-fifth of the population between 1845 and 1851.[12]

Wars and rumors of wars? The hegemony of the nuclear powers threaten mankind with unparalleled destruction, but it has also brought about an era of relative international stability. Of course, no apology for nuclear weapons intended. My point is simply that warfare was a more frequent, endemic fact of life in earlier periods of world history.

Earthquakes? Compared to the earthquake that struck Shen-shu, China in 1556 CE (approximately 830,000 perished), the 20th century has seen no earthquake disaster comparable in scope. Moreover the idea that earthquakes seem to be more frequent in recent times is easily explained by the dramatic technological advances which allow us to detect and record tremors worldwide.

Pestilence? Our century has not witnessed anything even remotely similar to the plagues that plundered the earth in the past eras. The Black Death (bubonic plague) of 14th century Europe decimated one-fourth of its population . . . approximately 25 million persons!

False prophets? Contemporary religious 'cults' pose no real threat to mainstream Christianity. Their influence has been wildly overrated. By comparison, Gnosticism and Manicheanism posed <u>real</u> challenges to the integrity of the Christian faith in its early development.

Ominous signs in the heavens? We now view comets, meteor showers, and solar and lunar eclipses as natural occurrences. To the ancients, though, these heavenly phenomena were forboding omens that struck great fear in people's hearts:

> . . . the sun will be darkened, and the moon will not give its light, and the stars will fall from heaven, and the powers of the heavens will be shaken" (Mt. 24:29).

---

[12]Amartya Sen, <u>Poverty and Famines</u> (New York: Oxford University Press, 1981), p. 39.

Latter day revivals? The Pentecostal, Evangelical and Charismatic movements in this century have had nowhere near the influence of past religious revivals. Insofar as the American scene is concerned, the 'Great Awakening' of the 18th century and the 'Second Great Awakening' of the 19th century were far more influential. Moreover the monastic movements of the Middle Ages make contemporary attempts at church renewal look anemic.

In spite of the ambiguities of these familiar 'signs of the end', many Popular Christians would argue that they have irrefutable evidence that we witness the final days of life on earth. That 'evidence' consists of the formation of the Jewish state of Israel in 1948. According to this view, it was prophesied in the Bible that Israel must be reunited as a nation before the second coming of Christ. Now that the Jewish people have a national identity, watchmen of the end clamor that the appointed time is at hand. This is the crux of Popular Christianity's claim that we live in the final hour.

THE STATE OF ISRAEL AND THE STATE OF PROPHECY

Proponents of the Gospel According to Armageddon assert that the formation of the Israeli state in 1948 was predicted by some Old Testament prophets. To buttress this assertion, they point to a few prophetic oracles which allude to a great war that will bring about the demise of all nations hostile to Israel (Ezek. 38-39; Is. 66; Zech. 14; Mic. 4:11-13; Joel 3; Dan. 11:40-45).

The Hebrew prophets who referred to this great war believed that it would be the harbinger of a glorious New Age. The prophets envisioned that Israel would enjoy worldwide political, moral and religious supremacy, and that the earth would be cast under the spell of universal peace, wholeness and tranquility.[13]

The biblical passages which speak of this great

---

[13]Peter Ackroyd, Exile and Restoration (Philadelphia: Westminster, 1968), pp. 115-117; Walter Eichrodt, Ezekiel, trans. by Cosslett Quin (Philadelphia:

war were written after a grave national crisis which threatened the religious and cultural identity of the Jewish people: the Babylonian Exile. In 597 and 587 BCE the Neo-Babylonian Empire deported several thousand of Judah's inhabitants--landed citizens, national officials, priests--in order to pacify Palestinian resistance to Babylonian hegemony. With the destruction of the Temple, the deportation of the priestly class, and foreign occupation, these were dark days for the citizens of Judah. The poignant poems of the Book of Lamentations testify to the prevailing mood of national despair.

The social turmoil of the Exile set the stage for an intensely fertile period of religious development: Judaism was born. Ancient Israelite traditions about Abraham, the Exodus from Egypt and the Davidic Kingdom were reinterpreted in light of Judah's contemporary plight. Much of the Hebrew scriptures received their final form during this period. The Deuteronomic History (Deuteronomy through II Kings), the Priestly Work (roughly Genesis through Numbers), and the towering figures of Jeremiah, Deutero-Isaiah and Ezekiel were products of this age.

The prophets of the Exile emphasized God's righteousness and interpreted Judah's demise as a divine judgment, which God's sense of justice required. Yet Judah's sufferings were viewed in a redemptive context. The Babylonian Exile became a symbol of both punishment and promise.[14] The tribulation of the Exile would ultimately lead the people to repent of their wickedness and return to God. It was believed that God would remain faithful to Judah, in spite of the nation's disobedience, and would establish a new covenant with the people (Jer. 31:33-34).

The new covenant anticipated by the prophets of the Exile not only involved the return of the exiles to Palestine, but also God also promised to restore the Davidic Kingdom and to anoint an ideal king to lead the people into prosperity (Ezek. 37). Despondency melted in the face of glorious visions of a New Age where Jerusalem would be supreme, where sickness, suspicion and strife would reign no more (Is. 65-66). It was to be a veritable religious, social

---

[14]See Peter Ackroyd, Exile and Restoration, pp. 237ff.

and political Golden Age.

The Babylonian Exile ended in 539 BCE with the defeat of Nabonidus, King of Babylon, by Cyrus, founder of the Persian Empire. Cyrus instituted a policy of religious toleration throughout the empire. He was viewed by the exiles as a kind of messianic figure (Is. 45:1). This policy of toleration--attested in the Cyrus Cylinder--eventually led to the return of many of Judah's exiles to Palestine and to the restoration of the Jerusalem Temple, a building program that was helped by the patronage of the Persian government.

DISAPPOINTMENT AND REINTERPRETATION

Unexpectedly the return of the exiles from Babylon and the reconstruction of the Temple did not usher in a Golden Age for Israel. Judah became a province of the Persian Empire and the people still struggled for their cultural and religious survival. The writer of Malachi lamented that the newly constructed Temple was not even being supported by the people's tithes and offerings (3:8-23). Moreover the tragic Samaritan 'schism' crushed hopes for an immediate reunification of Israel. Judah was far from reaching the pinnacle of international prestige. Contrary to the exilic prophecies, the country was obscure, unimportant and dominated by those who did not believe in Yahweh, the God of Israel.

The intense despair of the Exile had generated unbounded religious creativity and the hope for a bright new world. But the mood of the post-exilic period was much more subdued: disappointment mixed with occasional moments of anticipation. The prophecies which had promised a quick end to Israel's sufferings and a rosy future about to unfold remained unfulfilled. The moment called for some sort of creative reinterpretation. How would the New Age come about? What events would precede Israel's accession to world leadership?

In seeking to explain why the New Age had not come about, the post-exilic prophets emphasized certain themes which were present in Israel's prophetic traditions. From these themes, two different scenarios evolved as alternate explanations of how God was going to place Israel in the international limelight: (1)

the Missionary Option; and (2) the Holy War Option.

THE MISSIONARY OPTION

The Missionary Option interpreted Israel's claim to world leadership in terms of the moral and spiritual excellence of Judaism. It was thought that the nations would flock to Zion, submitting themselves voluntarily to Judah's rule, when they beheld the marvelous works of Yahweh (Jer. 3:17, 16:19-21; Is. 2:2-3, 19:23-25, 45:22-24, 56:7; Zech. 8:20-23; Mic. 4:1-5). The theme of Israel's salvific role to the rest of the world became especially prominent between 170 BCE and 70 CE, when Jewish missionaries zealously sought converts among the Gentiles (cp. Mt. 23:15).[15]

The story of Jonah is a fanciful testimony to the conversionist mood among many Jews in the period following the Exile. The reluctant prophet was instructed by God to journey to the capital city of Assyria (Nineveh) to deliver a stinging message of death and destruction to Israel's dreaded enemy. After three days in the belly of a whale, Jonah was ready to deliver his ominous dispatch to the Assyrians. Unpredictably, the people of Ninevah repented of their sin and begged Yahweh for mercy. The display of penitence impressed Yahweh and he decided to spare the city from destruction.

Jonah was not thrilled with God's change of heart and sulked because Israel's enemies were not obliterated. Implicit in the story is a criticism of those who anticipated Israel's expanding influence in terms of waging destruction upon her enemies.

THE HOLY WAR OPTION

The Holy War Option interpreted Israel's rise to international prominence as the outcome of a great war against the nations. The Gentiles were depicted as objects of Yahweh's wrath (Is. 13:1ff, 34:1ff,

---

[15]For evidence of the conversionist attitude in 'intertestamental literature', see D. S. Russell, The Method and Message of Jewish Apocalyptic, pp. 299-300.

35:4, 41:11-23, 47:1ff, 51:22-23, 60:12; Ezek. 28:26, 36:5-7; Mic. 5:8-9, 7:13; Zep. 3:19). Yahweh was portrayed as a blood-thirsty warrior who breathes havoc and longs for revenge (Jer. 25:29-38, 46:10; Is. 42:13, 63:3-6). Israel would make slaves of their enemies . . . the once enslaved would exploit their opportunity to enslave (Is. 14:2, 45:14).

In stark contrast to the vision of the nations flocking to Jerusalem voluntarily, the holy war scenario envisioned coerced participation in Israel's religious holidays, on pain of drought or disease if they chose not to comply (Zech. 14:16-19). In short, the Holy War Option echoed the familiar theme of zealous nationalism: convert or die. This generalized hostility toward the Gentiles was strongly evidenced in many later religious writings that were produced in the interval between the Old and New Testament.[16]

The holy war interpretation of Israel's glorification foresaw a great war which would be waged against Israel by the nations of the earth (Is. 66; Ezek. 38-39; Joel 3; Zech. 14; Mic. 4:11-13; Dan. 11:40-45). This final conflict was to be the mechanism that Yahweh used to subjugate all of the world's peoples to Israel's rule. Israel's road to religious and moral leadership was to be paved with hatred, blood and destruction.

THE BOOK OF DANIEL

An interesting appropriation of the Holy War Option appears in the Book of Daniel. The visions in Daniel (chapters 7-12) are attributed to a Jewish hero who lived during the Babylonian Exile. In actual fact, though, the visions were written at a much later date, ca. 166 BCE. At that time it was not considered dishonest for an author to claim that his writings were produced by a great prophetic figure of the past. The practice of writing under a pseudonym was considered to be a perfectly acceptable way of lending authority to one's message, due to the late post-exilic belief that prophecy had ceased.

---

[16]Russell, pp. 300-303.

Daniel's visions open with a description of four beasts which symbolically represent the historical succession of four kingdoms: the Babylonian, the Median, the Persian and the Hellenistic empires (7:3-7). It was the fourth beast (the Greek kingdom of Alexander) that attracted the author's interest.

The fourth beast had ten horns (7:7) which probably represent a succession of rulers from the Ptolemaic dynasty in Egypt and the Seleucid dynasty in Syria. As the vision progressed, Daniel saw a little horn emerging from the other ten on the fourth beast (7:8). This little horn represented a king who would make arrogant claims against God and persecute God's people for 3 1/2 years (7:8, 25; 8:24). This king undoubtedly refers to the Seleucid ruler named Antiochus IV (Epiphanes) who believed that he was the incarnation of Zeus. Antiochus Epiphanes vigorously persecuted the Jewish people, beginning in the autumn of 169 BCE and ignobly found his place in world history as the engineer of history's first case of genuine religious persecution.

As Daniel's visions unfold, the figure of Antiochus Epiphanes grows in prominence. A goat with four horns inhabits Daniel's second vision. The author of Daniel leaves no doubt that the goat represents the Hellenistic Empire of Alexander the Great, and that each of the four horns refer to the four monarchies which Alexander's generals formed after his untimely death in 323 BCE (8:21-22). From one of these four horns (the Seleucid kingdom), a "little horn" emerges who would stop the daily sacrifices and desecrate the Temple (8:11). Again the reference unmistakably is to Antiochus Epiphanes who set up a pagan altar on the great altar of sacrifice ("the abomination of desolation") and dedicated the Jerusalem Temple to Zeus on December 6, 167 BCE. In Daniel's last vision there is a rather detailed account of the historical conflicts between the Seleucid and Ptolemaic kingdoms (11:5-20), but the infamous career of Antiochus Epiphanes is given the center stage (11:21-39).

For the writer of Daniel, the figure of Antiochus Epiphanes was evil personified . . . the incarnation of everything exalted against God. At the time of his writing (ca. 166 BCE), it seemed as if Antiochus' power would go unchecked.

When it came time for the author to augur the

fate of his arch villain, he naturally appropriated the holy war scenario. In comparison to the writer's masterful presentation of past historical events in apocalyptic imagery, he was much less successful in his only attempt at making a genuine prediction of the future.

The author of Daniel predicted that Antiochus Epiphanes would launch a massive, blitzkrieg attack on the Ptolemaic kingdom in Egypt which would end in complete success (11:40-44). Part of the campaign against Egypt would spill over into Palestine and "tens of thousands" would be killed. But Antiochus' military success would be short-lived. The author cryptically predicted that Antiochus Epiphanes would perish somewhere between Jerusalem and the Mediterranean Sea (11:45). Apparently he believed that Antiochus' death would trigger an intense period of tribulation which would end in the resurrection of the dead and the onset of Israel's Golden Age (12:1-3).[17]

Contrary to the writer's premonitions, Antiochus Epiphanes never launched this whirlwind campaign against Egypt. Also he did not die in Palestine but perished in 163 BCE while fighting a war against the Parthians. Obviously the New Age anticipated by Daniel failed to materialize. The author's reliance on the holy war scenario led to an ambitious interpretation of current events that proved incorrect.

In later Jewish writings the antipathy toward Antiochus Epiphanes was transferred to Herod the Great and the Roman general Pompey. Moreover the idea of 'the Antichrist' in the Christian tradition (I Jn. 2:18; Rev. 13) drew inspiration from the vilified figure of Antiochus Epiphanes.[18]

---

[17] For further reading, see E. W. Heaton, The Book of Daniel (London: SCM Press, 1956); André Lacocque, The Book of Daniel, trans. by David Pellauer (London: SPCK, 1979); W. Stewart McCullough, The History and Literature of the Palestinian Jews from Cyrus to Herod (Toronto: University of Toronto Press, 1975), pp. 196-199; Norman W. Porteous, Daniel: A Commentary (Philadelphia: Westminster Press, 1965).

[18] See D. S. Russell, The Method and Message of Jewish Apocalyptic, pp. 276-280.

THE CANAANITE CONNECTION

The holy war scenarios of Trito-Isaiah, Ezekiel,
Micah, Zechariah, Joel and Daniel depicted a great
war which Yahweh would incite against Israel. In
the midst of what looked to be a hopeless conflict,
Yahweh would personally enter the fray on Israel's
behalf in order to humiliate her enemies. Yahweh's
hand in the outcome would be unmistakably evident
(Is. 42:10, 63:3-6). The nations would stand in awe
of Israel's god, loyally submitting to the authority
of Jerusalem, whether by fear or admiration. From
the devastation and confusion created by this cosmic
conflict between the forces of good and evil, a new
world order would appear. Israel's New Age of unparallelled glory would be born from unprecedented tribulation . . . order would emerge from chaos.

The holy war motif ultimately finds its source[19]
of inspiration in Canaanite mythology. Since the
incredible discovery in 1928 of ancient Ugarit (modern
Ras Shamra, Syria), with its extensive library, biblical scholars have recognized the widespread influence
of indigenous Canaanite religious ideas upon the development of Israelite religion.

The mythological texts at Ugarit reveal a 'pan-
theon' of gods headed by a deity named El. El's position in the universe is pre-eminent. He is called
"the creator of created things," "the Kindly One,
El, the Merciful," and "the father of men."[20] Other
gods mentioned in the Ugaritic texts include the
storm-god Baal, the fertility goddess Anat, the mother-
goddess Asherah, the sea-god Yamm, the god of the
evening-star Šlm, and Mot, the god of sterility and
death. It was thought that these gods assembled on
a mountain which lies twenty miles north of ancient
Ugarit, named Mt. Saphōn (modern Jebel Aqra). This
mountain exercised so much religious influence over
the region that Psalm 48:2 identified Mt. Zion, the

---

[19]See Frank M. Cross, Canaanite Myth and Hebrew Epic
(Cambridge, Mass: Harvard University Press, 1973),
pp. 105-111, 135-144, 343-346.

[20]John Gray, The Legacy of Canaan, 2nd ed. (Leiden:
Brill, 1965), pp. 159-160.

throne of Yahweh, with "the heights of S̲ā̲p̲h̲ō̲n̲" (cp. Is. 14:13).[21]

The earlier traditions within the Old Testament bear witness to the formative influence of the religious culture of Canaan upon Israelite religion. For example, the Canaanite sky-god El was adopted by the early Israelites as their central deity. The Bible refers to El by names which were commonly attributed to him throughout the ancient Near East: ꜣĒl ꜥelyōn [El, the Highest One (Gen. 14:18; Ps. 78:35)]; ꜣĒl ꜥôlām [El, the Ancient One (Gen. 21:33)]; and ꜣĒl šadday [El, the One of the Mountain (Gen. 17:1, 28:3, 35:11, 43:14, 48:3)].

The deity who revealed himself to Jacob was "El, god of your father [Isaac]" (Gen. 46:3, cp. 33:20). When Yahwehism was introduced to Israelite religion, the god Yahweh was associated with El.[22] The identification of Yahweh with El is described explicitly in Exodus 6:2-3:

> God spoke to Moses, saying: 'I am Yahweh; and I appeared to Abraham, Isaac and Jacob, as El, the One of the Mountain, but I did not disclose my name to them: Yahweh'. (my translation)

Often the Old Testament juxtaposes the name Yahweh with El, a form which usually is misleadingly translated as "Lord God." As Yahwehism became predominant in Israelite religion, Yahweh's strong association with El diminished. Jeremiah and Hosea, two of the prophets most hostile to Canaanite culture, assiduously avoided the use of ꜣēl in their references to the

---

[21]Helmer Ringgren, Religions of the Ancient Near East (Philadelphia: Westminster, 1973), p. 133. The Hebrew word ṣāphôn is usually translated 'north'. However even if the term is not translated as a proper noun, the reference alludes to Mt. Saphon, as Mt. Zion is located geographically in the south.

[22]Gösta W. Ahlström, Aspects of Syncretism in Israelite Religion (Lund: C. W. Gleerup, 1963), pp. 12-13; Cross, Canaanite Myth and Hebrew Epic, pp. 60ff.

God of Israel.[23]

El was not the only Canaanite god who helped shape the religion of Israel in its earlier phase. The Canaanite storm-god, Baal, was considered Yahweh's archfiend by many of the later prophets. However early descriptions of Yahweh portrayed Israel's god as a storm-god (Dt. 33:26-29; II Sam. 22:8-16; Ps. 29, 68:8-9; 77:15-20; Hab. 3:3-15) and bear remarkable resemblance to Baal's attributes in the Ugaritic texts.[24] Also Saul, Jonathan and David each named one of their sons after Baal: Ishbaal (man of Baal), Meribaal (great is Baal), and Beeliada (Baal knows). The editor of I and II Samuel did not look favorably on this fact and either deleted the Baal component of their names or replaced it with bŏšeth, the Hebrew word for 'shame' (II Sam. 2:10, 5:16, 21:7). The Chronicler, writing after the Exile, had enough distance from Israel's Canaanite heritage to report the true names without embarrassment (I Chr. 9:39-40, 14:7).

Anat, Šlm and, especially, Asherah are also mentioned in the Old Testament. One of Israel's 'judges'--Shamgar--was called "son of Anat" (Jg. 5:6). David named two of his sons--Absolam and Solomon--after Salem, the most prominent deity of the city of Jerusalem during its Jebusite period. The name 'Jerusalem' itself means "foundations of Salem." This god (Šlm) is also mentioned in the Ugaritic texts and elsewhere.[25] Also, we have every reason to believe that El's consort, Asherah, was consistently worshiped in the Jerusalem Temple and throughout Israel until the Babylonian Exile, excepting the short-lived religious innovations of Hezekiah and Josiah (II Kg. 18, 23). Both textual evidence from the Bible and archeological evidence throughout Palestine attest to

---

[23]Arvid S. Kapelrud, The Ras Shamra Discoveries and the Old Testament, trans. by G. W. Anderson (Norman, Okla.: University of Oklahoma Press, 1963), p. 57.

[24]For a full discussion, see Cross, Canaanite Myth and Hebrew Epic, pp. 147ff.

[25]Gray, The Legacy of Canaan, p. 185.

Israel's strong cult of Asherah.[26] Even some of Jeremiah's contemporaries blamed their nation's misfortunes on the fact that sacrifices were no longer being offered to "the queen of heaven" (Jer. 44:18-19).

In view of the generous attitude assumed by most Israelites toward the religious ideas of Canaan, it is not surprising that the holy war motif found its origins in this fertile mythological climate.

DRAGON-SLAYING--CANAANITE STYLE

The fragmented mythological texts from ancient Ugarit are centered on the turbulent careers of Baal and Anat. As the storm-god, Baal had the important role of insuring that enough rain fell for the crops to grow. When Baal reigned as king, the citizens of Ugarit were assured that their fields would be fertile and that the destructive forces in the universe would be subdued. Otherwise the demise of Baal meant that the powers of chaos, sterility and death would be unleashed upon the earth.

Baal and his consort Anat, a fierce fertility goddess, wage their war for order, life and fecundity by battling their traditional adversaries: Prince Yamm (the sea), Judge Nahor (the river), Mot (the underworld god of disease and death), and Lotan (a dragon-like monster). These representatives of chaos, death, sterility and destruction threaten to usurp Baal's throne, an outcome that would envelop the world in darkness.

In one cuneiform text the fearsome messengers of Prince Yamm (the sea) and Judge Nahor (the river) approach El's divine council and arrogantly demand

---

[26] See Ahlström, Aspects of Syncretism in Israelite Religion, pp. 51ff. Ahlström notes that more "Astarte plaques" (terra cotta depictions of a naked goddess) have been found at Jerusalem than any other site in Israel and Judea. Moreover, at Kuntillet ᶜAjrud, a Judean fortress in the 9th-8th centuries BCE, an inscription was found that reads: "may you be blessed to Yahweh . . . and to his Asherah." (See Royal Administration and National Religion in Ancient Palestine (Leiden: E. J. Brill, 1982), pp. 43, 82.)

them to deliver Baal into their hands as their slave. The gods were intimidated by awesome powers of Prince Sea and Judge River and decided to comply with the request. Of course, the hero, Baal, was not going to give up without a fight. Even though Baal's prospects for success looked dim, he went into battle and defeated his adversaries, thanks to a couple magical clubs that Kothar, the craftsman of the gods, gave to him. The heavens rejoiced that Baal had restrained the forces of destruction once again.[27] A palace was completed for Baal on Mt. Saphōn.

The mythological texts from ancient Ugarit convey the belief that order is born from a cosmic conflict with the unruly forces of chaos and destruction. Baal's claim to kingship (and the human prospect for life and fertility) is threatened on all sides by belligerent combatants. But even though Baal, and the hope for life, may be challenged periodically by Prince Sea, Judge River, Death (Mōt) and the dreaded monster, Lotan, the citizens of Ugarit believed that Baal, and the forces of good, would ultimately prevail.

We have every reason to believe that the myths about Baal and Anat were not localized at Ugarit, but were familiar tales throughout the religious culture of Canaan. The Bible even alludes to these prevalent mythological motifs. Baal's dreaded enemy, Lotan, the dragon-like monster, is called Leviathan in the Old Testament (Is. 27:1; Ps. 74:14, 104:26; Job 3:8, 41:1). Yahweh not only displays his power over the sea monster Leviathan, but also subdues the destructive force of the Sea and the River (Ps. 93:3-4; Hab. 3:8; Job 38:7-11; Nah. 1:4). The Bible also refers to a primeval monster named Rahab who battled against Yahweh and was overcome (Is. 51:9; Ps. 89:10; Job 26:12). In Psalm 74 and Isaiah 51 the imprint of Canaanite mythology is especially pronounced.

> Yet God, my king, is from ancient times,
> working salvation in the midst of the earth.
> You shattered Yam (Sea) with your might,
> and smashed the heads of the sea monsters;
> You crushed the heads of Leviathan,

---

[27]For this story, as well as others from Ugarit, see James Pritchard, The Ancient Near East, Vol. I (Princeton: Princeton University Press, 1958), pp. 92ff.

and gave him as food for the desert-dwellers.
(Ps. 74:12-14, my translation)

Awake, awake, put on strength,
    O arm of the Lord;
Awake, as in days of old,
    the generations of long ago.
Was it not thou that didst cut Rehab in pieces,
    that didst pierce the dragon? (Is. 51:9)

The seasonal battles of Baal of Canaan were histor-
ified in the primeval acts of Yahweh of Israel, who
demonstrated his power over mankind's foes by annihilating the beasts who threatened to subvert his creation. In ancient times Yahweh's rule was challenged,
the fierce moment of battle arrived, Yahweh was victor-
ious and creation was born . . . a creation which
proclaims Yahweh's undisputed rule. It should not
surprise us that this cosmic drama, involving Yahweh's
battles with his primeval foes, was appropriated by
those prophets who foresaw a new creation . . .
Israel's glorious New Age . . . which would not only
testify to Yahweh's sovereignty over nature, but also
his supremacy over Israel's enemies.

The Holy War Option--born from the religious
milieu which produced Baal's fateful confrontations
with Prince Yamm, Mot and Lotan--promises a New Age
of peace and prosperity when Israel's historical enemies 'bite the dust'. It preaches transformation
by annihilation . . . the birth of a New Age from
the total destruction of the present world order.
It is a not so subtle irony that some within the Christian community confidently interpret their futures
by a theme that ultimately hearkens back to the soil
of Canaan.

Unfortunately the seers of holy war are always
on the lookout for the beasts from without but rarely
contemplate the beasts from within. Greed, mistrust,
apathy and arrogance--the dragons that devour human
communities--roam undeterred in the hearts of those
who echo the cry: Convert or die!

ARMAGEDDON: HOLY WAR PAR EXCELLENCE

Popular Christians who believe that the end of
the world is upon us must show why the formation of
the State of Israel in 1948 was significant in terms

of biblical eschatology. Unless advocates of the Gospel According to Armageddon can substantiate that claim, their dire predictions of doom and destruction lack foundation.

The argument used by contemporary proponents of the Gospel According to Armageddon goes something like this. The first step of the argument is to admit that some events predicted by Israel's exilic and post-exilic prophets did not take place after the Babylonian Exile. Although the prophets' predictions concerning the return of the exiles from Babylon and the reconstruction of the Jerusalem Temple were fulfilled, the great war and subsequent New Age about which they spoke never took place.

The second step of the argument assumes that none of Israel's prophets could have predicted the future incorrectly. Hence these unfulfilled prophecies must refer to events that lie beyond the reconstruction of Jewish society in the post-exilic period. Because the Jews were no longer a national, political unit after 70 CE, it would be logically impossible for these prophecies concerning a great war against Israel to be fulfilled. However with the formation of the State of Israel in 1948, the stage was set for this cataclysmic event. Obviously the frequent conflicts in the Mideast and the strategic importance of the region for the superpowers have helped to galvanize the conviction that the final war between the forces of good and evil is about to erupt: Armageddon.

The first point of the argument offered by defenders of the Gospel According to Armageddon is patently true. The great war prophesied by some Old Testament prophets did not take place. However the second stage of the argument is fraught with difficulties.

First, the claim that prophecies written after the Babylonian Exile refer to a precise sequence of events nearly 2500 years later should be considered suspect at first blush. There is no question that the prophets themselves believed that the great war against Israel was imminent; otherwise, one would be hard pressed to explain their obvious sense of urgency.

Second, the only reason that can be given to support a modern application of these prophecies is that they have not been fulfilled. This assumes gratuitously that biblical prophets infallibly foresaw the future. As we saw in our discussion of Daniel's visions, the holy war scenario led the author to make an extravagant prediction about Antiochus Epiphanes that never came true. The popular belief that biblical prophets never made a 'bad call' (and, hence, are unerring guides to the future) is very incorrect.[28]

It is neither intellectually honest nor a sign of 'true faith' to reinterpret failed prophecies as instances of deferred prophecy. Obviously it is possible to avoid passing judgment on any and every prediction of the future by relegating its fulfillment to an undetermined tomorrow.

It should be emphasized, though, that while proponents of the Gospel According to Armageddon assert that God has given them a rough agenda of what happens next, few get bogged down in the details. Most are consumed by the excitement of seeing God's hand at work in world events, readily perceiving some hidden, cosmic significance in a Middle Eastern conflict or some new technological development. They share the rapture of every apocalypticist down through the ages: now . . . at last . . . God will reveal himself without ambiguity, evil will bare its ugly head only once more, to be silenced forever.

Yet, unfortunately, the modern Christian stargazer shares more than enthusiasm with the apocalypticist; he embraces the world view of the latter . . . a perspective on life that is deterministic, tends toward fatalism and is at odds with Jesus' redemptive message of love and liberation.

THE PROPHET VS. THE APOCALYPTICIST

A helpful way of describing the world view reflected in apocalyptic literature is to contrast the religious ideas of the apocalypticist with the message of his predecessor: the Hebrew prophet.

Any comparison between the prophet and the apocalypticist must proceed in the knowledge that the latter

---

[28]On the subject of unfulfilled prophecies in the Old Testament, see Robert P. Carroll, When Prophecy Failed (New York: Seabury Press, 1979).

selected and exaggerated certain themes which can be found in the oracles of Israel's prophets. Hence their differences must not overshadow important points of similarity. Yet the peculiar emphases of the apocalypticist--along with his tendency to borrow liberally from the religious ideas of Canaan, Persia and Greece --meant that apocalyptic literature developed distinctive qualities which contrast sharply with the Hebraic, prophetic outlook.

Our stereotypical apocalypticist views history from a deterministic perspective. For him world events are manipulated to fit into some sort of grand design. The apocalypticist views God's judgment as fixed and irrevocable. Those who practice evil cannot escape impending doom. The only recourse for true believers is to 'hang tough' and to avoid being swept up into the vortex of apostasy and rebellion.

The final act of human history for the apocalypticist will feature the separation of good from evil with the final destruction of the latter. Because he remains convinced that the sequence of events revealed to him must precede the end, the apocalypticist is fundamentally unconcerned with the historical events themselves. History is only significant in that it reflects the conflict between the forces of light and darkness. Although the message of the apocalypticist brims with hope for the redeemed, the chosen remnant of true believers, his attitude toward the social order is undeniably pessimistic . . . everything will perish in a brief, cataclysmic moment.

By contrast, the Hebrew prophets viewed history in terms of a dynamic interaction between God and man. Unlike the deterministic view of the apocalypticist, the prophet assumed that history was in a state of flux. Covenants, unfaithfulness, fidelity, rebellion and repentance all played a role in shaping history. Our stereotypical Hebrew prophet viewed God's judgment as mutable--a fate that could be avoided by a sincere act of repentance.

When judgment came upon Israel, the prophets generally took an optimistic perspective on the outcome: Israel would eventually repent of her sin. This prophetic optimism was founded on the hope that the end of history will witness the complete redemption of all God's creation . . . redeemed from pain, alienation, grief and sickness. The hope of a better tomorrow propelled the prophet into the arena of history;

130

he was involved, active and engaged.

A salient theme common to both the apocalypticist and the prophet is that of transformation. Both were unsatisfied with the religious, moral and social conditions which surrounded them. Both longed for change. Yet their respective approaches to transformation were radically different.

The apocalypticist views transformation in cosmic terms: the old age is passing away; the new age is about to appear. The transfiguration of our present existence will be cataclysmic, unambiguous and 'extraterrestrial'. The conflict between the forces of good and evil will result in the glorification of the faithful and the annihilation of the wicked. The apocalypticist's salvation is decidedly individualistic. Only those who continue in obedience will survive the coming onslaught—whether by divine protection or resurrection. The rest of God's creation will lie in ruins.

One sees a very different concept of transformation among the Hebrew prophets. Transformation was a process built upon repentance and fidelity to God's commands. For the prophet, transformation was wrought in the context of community, not catastrophe; it was inspired by God's covenantal relationship with man, not by unyielding threats of destruction. More than a few select disciples would partake of God's glorious salvation. All of creation would be reconciled to the Creator.

Although apocalyptic literature found its way into the New Testament (i.e., Revelation and the apocalyptic discourses in the Gospels), it is not difficult to see why a strict apocalyptic perspective is at variance with Jesus' transforming message of forgiveness and love. Jesus' hope for the Kingdom propelled him into the world, not away from it; his proclamation was not a mediation on impending disaster, but a declaration of forgiveness; and his disciples caught a vision of the Christian task in this world which went far beyond resisting apostasy.

Jesus spoke as a prophet.[29] Like his Old Testament forebears, he was intensely interested in the day to day affairs of life. All human relationships were religiously significant (Mt. 5:23-24). Neither the tax collector nor the prostitute were excluded from the Kingdom of God. Jesus proclaimed in word and deed that neighbor-love, justice and compassion are the defining features of friendship with God. He resisted attempts to compartmentalize man's relationship with God. For Jesus, a glimpse of the sacred was readily apparent in the mundane. The detached religious piety of many of his countrymen struck him as distasteful and irrelevant.

Jesus' life was a celebration of transformation. No aspect of creation was beyond God's healing touch. The keynote of his public ministry was a text from Isaiah 61.

> The Spirit of the Lord is upon me,
>> because he has anointed me to preach
>> good news to the poor.
> He has sent me to proclaim release to the
>> captives and recovering of sight to the
>> blind,
> To set at liberty those who are oppressed,
>> to proclaim the acceptable year of the
>> Lord. (Lk. 4:18-19)

As Joachim Jeremias has observed, it is significant that Jesus broke off his quotation of Isaiah in the middle of a sentence: "to proclaim the acceptable year of the Lord. . . ." The text in Isaiah concludes the sentence with these words: " . . . and the day of vengeance of our God."[30] Jesus' task was about the redemption of creation, not its obliteration.

Ardent believers in the Gospel According to Armageddon should give pause to inquire whether they have

---

[29]Joachim Jeremias, New Testament Theology (New York: Charles Scribner's Sons, 1971), pp. 76ff.; Norman Perrin, Rediscovering the Teachings of Jesus (New York: Harper and Row, 1967), pp. 72ff.

[30]Jeremias, New Testament Theology, p. 206.

underestimated the power of Jesus' transforming gospel. The quest for a new heaven and a new earth can take many forms; there is no reason why it should be sought in the aftermath of a nuclear fireball or horrid orgies of destruction.

Those who squint heavenward, seeking visions of the final hour, await an unmistakable revelation of God that will literally shake heaven and earth. Unfortunately, though, their narrow focus blinds them from frequent moments of God's self-disclosure in less earthshaking contexts.

In his concern to see the Lord of Armageddon, the apocalypticist forgets that Jesus' face can be discerned daily in the dazed look of a marasmic infant, in the suspicious glance of a stranger, in the complaints of a sick person, and in the heart of the most callous criminal.

> . . . for I was hungry and you gave me food, thirsty and you gave me drink, I was a stranger and you welcomed me, I was naked and you clothed me, I was sick and you visited me, I was in prison and you came to me. (Mt. 25:35-36)

If Christians availed themselves of all the opportunities to witness God's presence in the face of human need, perhaps the spectacle of holy war would hold less fascination.

Contrary to the prophets of doom, the path ahead winds through unbounded regions of possibility. God's moments of creativity are as near as we choose to look. But like the irresponsible servant who buried his one talent in preparation for his master's return (Mt. 25:14-30; Lk. 19:12-27), we can choose to limit the reach of Jesus' transforming touch by reclining on Armageddon's bleachers, passing up opportunities to flesh out God's love to a suffering humanity.

No injustice can dim the Gospel's light; no political power can silence its piercing truth; no good task lies beyond its vision. We must shed our self-deception and face the future responsibly, lest we be accused of "holding the form of religion but denying the power of it" (II Tim. 3:5).

CHAPTER 6

NARCISSISM AND THE PURSUIT OF VIRTUE

SELF-UNDERSTANDING OR SELF-ABSORPTION?

"Know thyself." Down through the centuries Socrates' dictum has inspired many to risk the pain of introspection and self-discovery in order to attain a 'true' estimate of themselves. All who seek genuine self-understanding know that their unceasing journey is paved with moments of disillusionment and authenticity, joy and despair.

The quest for self-knowledge is a moral endeavor. It transcends the banality of mere "self-awareness." Authentic self-understanding is more than "getting in touch with yourself." Seminars on assertiveness, goal-setting, the life cycle, or values clarification may superficially raise our awareness of what we want and how we can get it . . . but true self-understanding is something different.

Who am I? What is the purpose of my existence? Who is my neighbor, and what does he mean to me? These are questions of self-understanding. They contrast sharply with the pedestrian inquiries of self-awareness: What do I want? How can I get it? How can I use others to accomplish my goals? Unfortunately, many today confuse self-awareness with self-understanding. The former leads to narcissism and self-absorption, the latter liberates us to love our neighbor.

Our generation has been unaffectionately dubbed the "Me Generation." Christopher Lasch, in his incisive critique of American culture, The Culture of Narcissism, attributes our self-centeredness to the pessimism and lack of vision that permeate our

135

society. He writes:

> After the political turmoil of the sixties,
> Americans have retreated to purely personal
> preoccupations. Having no hope of improving
> their lives in any of the ways that matter,
> people have convinced themselves that what
> matters is psychic self-improvement: getting
> in touch with their feelings, eating health
> food, taking lessons in ballet or belly-
> dancing, immersing themselves in the wisdom
> of the East, jogging, learning how to 're-
> late', overcoming the 'fear of pleas-
> ure'. . . .   Since 'the society' has no
> future, it makes sense to live only for
> the moment, to fix our eyes on our own 'pri-
> vate performance', to become connoisseurs
> of our own decadence. . . .[1]

The predominant instinct of "the culture of narcissism"
is simply "to survive"--nothing more, nothing less.

Lasch's criticism of the general culture is apro-
pos to our discussion of Popular Christianity. As
we saw in the last chapter, the Gospel According to
Armageddon proffers a basically survivalist view of
Christian life. The apocalyptic vision sees only
death and destruction in the near term; true possibilities for transformation lie outside human history.

Because Popular Christianity lacks a positive
this-worldly vision, a sense of Christian mission
beyond evangelizing the 'unsaved' (so they can be
rescued from God's wrath), its focus turns inward.
Christian moral obligation becomes introverted, privatized and individualistic. In Lasch's metaphor, we
have nothing to do except to become "connoisseurs"
of our own virtue. The noble quest for self-understanding deteriorates into a mere exercise in self-absorption.

PRIVATIZED RELIGION

The narcissistic tenor of our times is indicative

---

[1]Christopher Lasch, The Culture of Narcissism (New
York: Warner Books, 1979), pp. 29,31.

of more profound, structural changes that have shaped Western culture over the past few centuries. Thomas Luckmann, in his revealing essay on religion and modern society, The Invisible Religion,[2] describes the impact of institutional specialization in modern, industrial societies upon traditional religious institutions.

Luckmann argues that religious institutions have become increasingly specialized and relegated to the "private sphere" of life. One consequence of the church's involuntary withdrawal to the "private sphere" is that religious institutions are forced to compete on the open market for prospective consumers, who shop for "models of 'ultimate' significance" in order to satisfy their private needs. Obviously the desire to get an edge on the competition has a profound impact on the way traditional religious values are articulated or 'revised'.

Luckmann identifies several themes which character-ize the disconnected "assortments of 'ultimate' mean-ings" from which the consumer selects in assembling his own private 'religion'. The dominant themes of the "invisible religion"--what Luckmann calls "the modern sacred cosmos"--include individual autonomy, self-expression, self-realization, sexuality and fa-milism. These themes are evidenced throughout 'secu-lar' culture and generate a sense of personal content-ment by supporting the illusion of subjective freedom and autonomy without posing any fundamental challenge to the social order. In other words, all that really matters has to do with the "inner man." Social, eco-nomic and political structures are 'good' or 'bad' only to the degree that they facilitate or obstruct personal fulfillment in the "private sphere."

Generally speaking, Popular Christianity has entered the market of assorted religious ideas with the enthusiasm of a 19th century entrepreneur. A quick browse through most Christian bookstores will confirm the impression that Popular Christianity has let the "modern sacred cosmos" dictate its own relig-ious agenda. Consumers are wooed with titles like: Handbook to Happiness; Richer Relationships; Overcoming Stress; How to Win in a Crisis; The Christian's Secret

---

[2]Thomas Luckmann, The Invisible Religion (New York: Macmillan, 1969), see especially chapters 6 and 7.

of a Happy Life; Quality Friendship; Sex Begins in the Kitchen; Maximum Living in a Pressure-Cooker World; Stress in the Family; Getting Control of Your Life; Power in Praise; Discover Your Possibilities; The Christian Family; Slim for Him; You Can be the Wife of a Happy Husband; How to be a Winner; The Christian Couple; How to Live Like a King's Kid; You Can Become the Person You Want to Be; The Total Woman and The Total Man.

The themes of the "modern sacred cosmos" are expecially prominent in the lyrics of contemporary Christian music. Like their secular counterparts, Popular Christian songwriters tend to make personal contentment the summum bonum of human existence. Both contemporary Christian songs and secular music evidence a myopic concern for private gratification. The differences between a "me and Jesus" spirituality and the secular theme of "me and my lover, girlfriend, husband, etc." are not worth mentioning. Popular Christianity's love-affair with privatized religion is evidenced in song titles like "The Lord and I Together," "Clean Before My Lord," "Filled to Overflowing," "I am Safe," "Happiness is Following Jesus," "Only Jesus Can Satisfy Your Soul," "He'll Take Care of You," "Set My Spirit Free," "I am so Happy," "Give Your Heart a Home," "I'm Gonna Live Forever," "Sheltered in the Arms of God," "Rescue Me," and "Feel the Love."

It is difficult to know how or whether the trend of religious privatization can be stemmed or reversed. One thing is certain, though, the process can be retarded.

Christians have no business celebrating the entrenchment of Christianity in the "private sphere." Hopefully we can address the human condition with something other than trite mottos like "Let Jesus fill your every need" . . . better to let Jesus show us our neighbor.

The overstatement of individual need usually coexists with an understated version of public moral responsibility. The priest-image of privatized Christianity is the therapist (the 'Christian counselor'), and the Christian faith is presented as good therapy. There is little need for the prophetic core of the Christian faith when psychic contentment is the primary goal of religious commitment.

The self-deception under consideration concerns the way that people view their moral (or religious) obligations. I will call it the Compartmentalized Morality Self-Deception. It has the following five components:

1. **The Deception:** Virtue is the mark of Christian living.

2. **The Intended Objective:** To change certain kinds of behavior which are viewed as negative or unhealthy.

3. **The Primary Defense Mechanism:** Compartmentalization.

4. **Factors Which Perpetuate Self-Deception:** (a) The therapy orientation of contemporary American culture; and (b) The felt need to assume 'control'.

5. **The Unintended Consequences:** A privatized form of Christian commitment that is blind to areas of public moral responsibility.

Let's take a closer look at each of these elements.

1. THE DECEPTION: Virtue is the mark of Christian living.

Virtue. The term has taken on a restricted connotation in popular literature, often being associated with sexual continence. Actually, though, the proper meaning of the term is quite broad.

Virtue refers to positive 'character traits' or 'dispositions' which are acquired in some way. Virtues may be instilled by one's upbringing; they may be acquired through practice; or they may be the gift of some divine grace ("infused virtue"). Honesty, courage, faith, gratitude, trustworthiness, prudence, temperance, fortitude, wisdom, love, generosity—these qualities are often considered to be virtues. They motivate 'good acts'; and, in a limited sense, they help define the scope of our moral obligations toward others.

My point in this chapter is not that virtue is

unimportant to the Christian life. On the contrary, the presence of virtuous qualities (often called "fruits of the Spirit") has always been a reliable indicator of mature Christian living. Instead of disparaging the importance of virtue, I am suggesting that a Christian's religious obligation to be virtuous must be balanced by his moral obligations to others. Ethicists often refer to this 'golden mean' between the cultivation of internal virtue and the fulfillment of one's external moral obligations toward others in terms of the balance between an "ethics of virtue" and an "ethics of duty."

Some may charge that I am building a 'straw man' type of argument by suggesting that Popular Christians adhere strictly to an 'ethics of virtue' interpretation of their religious moral obligations. I concede that the issue is more a matter of emphasis than an either/or proposition. Nonetheless the 'ethics of virtue' position is so dominant in Popular Christianity that I believe the characterization is warranted. I will have more to say about an 'ethics of virtue' and an 'ethics of duty' later in the chapter.

2. THE INTENDED OBJECTIVE: To change certain kinds of behavior which are viewed as negative or unhealthy.

It goes without saying that each of us would like to change certain aspects of our disposition. Perhaps it is a fiery temper, inordinate jealousy, an incapacitating fear or some bad habit. It can be safely assumed that we will never be completely satisfied with ourselves. As soon as one 'dragon' is conquered, another arises to take its place. In short, we must learn to accept our imperfections without being complacent about self-improvement.

In general, two approaches can be taken in the development of our characters: (1) the 'hard focus' approach; and (2) the 'soft focus' approach.

The hard focus approach views personality change in terms of concentrated effort. If enough attention were given to this or that matter, the problem could be solved. Even those who are convinced that only God can effect a real change in one's character may be just as committed to the hard focus approach as the "carnal Christian" who is "walking in the flesh." I am impressed, for example, by the way the prayers are often preoccupied with a whole regimen of personal change: "Lord please help me do better in this; Lord, give me victory over that, etc."

The biggest drawback of the hard focus approach is that, invariably, whatever we are working for or against is exaggerated way out of proportion. Our achievements are overvalued, and our failures consume us. The hard focus approach sees personal development in terms of an endless set of hurdles to jump. It feeds on one's compulsive, perfectionistic tendencies.

A second approach to character development is the 'soft focus' approach. Instead of concentrating on details, this approach takes an integrated view of personality development by focusing on an exemplary personage or ideal. Perhaps we long to emulate a religious leader, a hero, a saint or some admired 'significant other'. The soft focus approach defines character development in terms of a well-integrated vision. The specifics are important only in the sense that they contribute to the whole.

I believe that many Popular Christians tend to mix a 'hard focus' approach to personality development with a one-sided 'ethics of virtue' understanding of Christian moral obligation. The outcome of this 'mix' is a narcissistic articulation of Christianity which is preoccupied with piddling priorities that sap our moral vision. I recommend that the 'soft focus' approach is much more consistent with Christian personal development and that the ethics of virtue approach must be tempered by an ethic of duty.

3.   THE DEFENSE MECHANISM: Compartmentalization.

Compartmentalization can be defined as <u>the attempt</u> <u>to evade a threatening aspect of one's internal or</u> <u>external reality by segmenting and labeling it to</u> <u>fit into 'acceptable' categories</u>. What is too painful to see in its entirety, compartmentalization attempts to make palatable by means of dissection and classification.

A familiar example is the so-called 'Sunday Christian'. This person lives a dual existence. His religious and ethical values are at full strength on Sunday but diluted beyond recognition during the rest of the week. The contradiction and guilt which would normally arise from this dual behavior is evaded by compartmentalization. One type of conduct is appropriate during one day of the week; another sort of

141

behavior is permissible for the rest of the week.

Similarly the classical portrait of the Mafia Don epitomizes the defense of compartmentalization. He considers himself a true American patriot while continuously breaking the law, or he strongly upholds 'conservative' family values while being about the business of selling drugs and promoting prostitution in the workaday world.

In the case of the Compartmentalized Morality Self-Deception, this defense mechanism functions to support a constricted circle of moral obligation which, when viewed from a larger perspective, would be readily seen as woefully inadequate. The process of compartmentalization effectively limits the Christian's perception of his moral obligations. The 'proper' sphere of moral action is seen in terms of 'having' more 'fruits of the Spirit', being a 'good' spouse or parent, being an 'obedient' citizen or a faithful church member. Any suggestion that Christian moral obligation is global--extending beyond the confines of one's immediate family, friends or church--is abruptly labeled as "political", "liberal" or "that's your special calling."

I make the assumption that we can 'read' the general outlines of human moral obligations from reality, which, of course, includes our capacity to be rational. In other words, moral obligation is not purely a subjective matter. To say that "killing is wrong" is not on par with the statement "strawberries taste good." Instead we can rationally define the general content of our moral obligations toward others.[3] Of course, it is a separate question as to whether Christians are religiously obligated to go beyond the 'baseline' of human moral obligation

---

[3]Notable recent attempts to demonstrate this point include, Alan Donagan, The Theory of Morality (Chicago: University of Chicago Press, 1977); William Galston, Justice and the Human Good (Chicago: University of Chicago Press, 1980); Alan Gewirth, Reason and Morality (Chicago: University of Chicago Press, 1978); R. M. Hare, Freedom and Reason (Oxford: Clarendon Press, 1963); and John Rawls, A Theory of Justice (Cambridge, Mass.: Harvard University Press, 1971).

142

(i.e., to do 'supererogatory' acts).[4] But, at the very least, we are obligated to satisfy the minimum. That is why Popular Christianity needs an ethic of duty.

4. FACTORS WHICH PERPETUATE SELF-DECEPTION: (a) The therapy-orientation of contemporary American culture; and (b) The felt need to assume 'control'.

THE THERAPEUTIC SENSIBILITY. Among the social factors which have strengthened the grip of the Compart-mentalized Morality Self-Deception over Popular Chris-tianity is the therapy mania that has swept our cul-ture. Christopher Lasch emphasizes that America's civic and religious values have been replaced by what he calls the "therapeutic sensibility." Therapy, as the new salvation, promises psychic contentment and fulfillment, but only at the price of stripping life of its moral foundation.

> Even when therapists speak of the need for 'meaning' and 'love', they define love and meaning simply as the fulfillment of the patient's emotional requirements. It hardly occurs to them . . . to encourage the subject to subordinate his needs and interests to those of others, to someone or some cause or tradition outside himself. 'Love' as self-sacrifice or self-abasement, 'meaning' as submission to a higher loyalty--these sublimations strike the therapeutic sensibil-ity as intolerably oppressive, offensive to common sense and[5] injurious to personal health and well-being.

Although Popular Christians have not thrown out "self-sacrifice" as one definition of 'love' and cer-tainly find meaning in their "submission to a higher loyalty", the imprint of the "therapeutic sensibility" can be discerned throughout Popular Christianity. It is evidenced most strongly in the sentimentalization of traditional Christian ideas. Love is generally treated as a feeling word--a subjective sense of

---

[4]See Gene Outka, Agape: An Ethical Analysis (New Haven, Conn.: Yale University Press, 1972), pp. 294ff.

[5]Lasch, The Culture of Narcissism, pp. 42-43.

goodwill that we have toward others--and rarely is rendered in its biblical context as an action word (I Jn. 3:16-17). Peace is taken to mean 'the absence of conflict', a far cry from the biblical concept: 'faith in the face of conflict' (Jn. 14:27). Worship is regarded as a door to personal contentment, emotional equilibrium or ecstatic withdrawal; the biblical sense of 'worship as service' (Is. 1:17, 58:6-7; Rom. 12:1) is lost amid the frenzy to be 'spiritual'.

Popular Christianity's adoption of the 'therapeutic sensibility' is most evident in its prescription for the 'happy' home. Instead of forthrightly addressing the real role changes generated by the rising status of women, many Popular Christians have retreated to role models that characterized the 19th century frontier family. "God's order" for the family is that the wife should "submit" to her husband. The ultimate rationale for this arrangement is that it reduces household tensions and creates "peace" (i.e., the absence of conflict). Submission is good therapy. The "Christian family" is fundamentally unconcerned with the moral issue of exploitation and shows little interest in exploring alternative role models. All that matters is that a modicum of harmony is preserved.

SELF-DOMINATION. A second social factor which supports the Compartmentalized Morality Self-Deception is related to the pervasive feeling of powerlessness throughout American society. Because real social change is thought to be a forlorn cause, the 'need' to assert oneself, to attain a sense of personal power, is diverted toward the control of our own person: self-control. We may feel powerless in the marketplace, in the political forum or in our own homes . . . but we can exercise power over ourselves. Jogging, the health food craze, E.S.T., weight reduction programs, the awareness movement--all of these can be interpreted, in some respects, as attempts to gain a semblance of personal control.

In Popular Christianity the theme of personal control finds strong expression in its theology of the Holy Spirit. The Spirit, the active 'side' of God, tends to be viewed as the believer's private possession . . . the divine internalized. The Holy Spirit transforms persons, instills discipline, changes habits, and imparts inner freedom. The Spirit bestows 'gifts' to individuals and is manifest in various 'fruits' (virtues) actualized in a person's life.

The Spirit is power to accomplish what we cannot do "in our own strength."

While most of these themes can be found in biblical passages concerning the Holy Spirit, Popular Christianity offers an excessively private portrait of the Spirit. Rarely is the Holy Spirit thought of as effecting social transformation (apart from indirect influence, like changing the hearts of prominent political leaders). By implication the Spirit is impotent when it comes to addressing unjust social structures. Of course, there is ample reason to believe that the Holy Spirit is just as involved in a movement for social justice, like the Civil Rights movement, as in Joe Christian's 'cosmic' struggles with anger, stress and lust.

5. THE UNINTENDED CONSEQUENCE: A privatized form of Christian commitment that is blind to areas of public moral responsibility.

The myopic pursuit of virtue, which allegedly testifies to God, says more about the narcissistic propensities of the human spirit than anything else. A nearsighted view of Christian moral responsibility only helps to confirm the skepticism that "God really doesn't make any difference after all." Participation in self-deception affords us the comfort of becoming "connoisseurs" of our own virtue, but only at the immense cost of ignoring our mandate to be "the salt of the earth" (Mt. 5:13). A three-year-old in East Africa starves while someone is perfecting their patience; a poor family in the ghetto is evicted while suburbanites "get high on Jesus" . . . Rome burns while its citizens revel in orgies.

Now that all five components of the Compartmentalized Morality Self-Deception have been discussed, we are ready to explore a dominant religious theme within Popular Christianity that gives religious legitimation to this particular self-deception.

THE GOSPEL OF PERFECTIONISM

"You, therefore, must be perfect, as your heavenly Father is perfect" (Mt. 5:48). The verse has inspired many an aspiring perfectionist. Some have succumbed to the delusion that Jesus believed that sinlessness--absolute perfection--is an actual human possibility

145

this side of the grave. Most stop short of claiming to be sinless but interpret the words to mean that Christians should strive to cultivate their private virtues. In fact, though, the verse concludes a paragraph in which Jesus enjoins his disciples to love not only their neighbors, but their enemies also. The kind of perfection spoken of here is relational, dynamic and other-oriented . . . not the Greek idea of 'a standard of excellence' but the Hebraic notion of 'completion' and 'wholeness'.

All who adhere to the Gospel of Perfectionism have one idea in common: the Kingdom of God is within. The perfectionist longs to internalize the Kingdom. But, in so doing, he reduces the 'New Order' to a disembodied set of "do's and don'ts" . . . usually more "don'ts" than "do's." Whereas the prophet sees the Kingdom as a holistic social concept, the perfectionist understands the Kingdom only in terms of his inner life and his mini-representations of the New Order (e.g., monastic enclaves, communes, cell groups, etc.). It is interesting that at no time did Jesus refer to the Kingdom of God as an internal spiritual reality.[6]

Because the perfectionist makes the Kingdom an internal reality, he is faced with a primary dilemma: What moral values best 'model' the Kingdom? Unfortunately, the question is usually never asked, and the perfectionist makes his selection unreflectively. Usually the perfectionist's interior Kingdom is represented by the things he abstains from: "Christians don't do X, Y, Z." When the perfectionist does rise above this 'negative' moral framework, he tends to restrict his 'positive' moral obligations to his immediate environment: "The Christian should be a patient parent, a loving spouse and a faithful church member."

The perfectionist rarely has the opportunity

---

[6] In the context of Jesus' message, Luke 17:21 should definitely be translated: ". . . behold, the kingdom of God is in the midst of you." While it is grammatically possible to translate this verse as "the kingdom of God is within you," this understanding does fit Jesus' teachings about the Kingdom. See Joachim Jeremias, New Testament Theology (New York: Charles Scribner's Sons, 1971), p. 101; and Norman Perrin, Rediscovering the Teachings of Jesus (New York: Harper and Row, 1967), p. 74.

to "love your enemies and pray for those who persecute you" (Mt. 5:44), because he never 'makes waves'. His message of liberation is confined to the 'inner life'. His privatized version of the Kingdom of God rarely challenges the social order. Jesus' bold cry for justice is transmuted into the faint whimper: be a 'good' spouse, be a 'caring' parent, be an 'obedient' citizen . . . be a 'nice' girl and a 'good' boy.

Invariably the perfectionist makes his own values God's values. As a consequence, Jesus was a good capitalist (an Adam Smith before his time), a tee-totaler (it was really grape juice), and strongly backs American interests throughout the world (and why shouldn't God bless 'his people'). Rarely does the perfectionist realize how culture-bound his particular value system actually is. Usually his vision of the Kingdom God is idiosyncratic and unimaginative.

When the perfectionist decides to leave his comfortable enclave and enter the political arena (to make his 'statement'), his unreflective disposition is 'writ large'. Instead of first meditating on how the Christian faith informs one's social ethics, the politically active perfectionist jumps into the fray with 'both arms swinging'. Unfortunately, his unreflective enthusiasm results in the 'baptism' of his <u>own</u> political convictions in the name of Christianity. Hence we have the spectacle of 'moral majority' types who argue that Jesus wants us to build more nuclear weapons and cut welfare programs, while they lobby school boards to dismiss homosexual teachers (because they might corrupt the youth of America while teaching Shakespeare or trigonometry). The perfectionist's 'Kingdom from within' often betrays his prejudice 'from within'.

DUTY AND THE DEFINITION OF CHARACTER

It is a truism that "virtues without principles are blind, as principles without virtues are impotent."[7] Our actions both shape our moral characters

---

[7]William Frankena, "The Ethics of Love Conceived as an Ethics of Virtue" (<u>Journal of Religious Ethics</u> 1/1:21-36, 1973), p. 32; see also his <u>Ethics</u>, 2nd

and result from them. We do not become virtuous in isolation from everyday life, as if we could develop our characters through enough prayer, meditation or reading. An "ethics of virtue" must be informed by an "ethics of duty."

An "ethics of duty" perspective helps to expand our moral vision by heightening our awareness of how individual moral acts fit into the "total picture." Since the seminal work of Immanuel Kant, many ethicists have held the position that moral obligations to one-self and others should be capable of universal application. Essentially the "criterion of universalizability" poses the familiar question: What would happen if everyone decided to do such and such an act?

The usefulness of the criterion of universalizability in helping us to define our moral obligations to others can be seen in the following hypothetical situation. Let us say a man is walking by a pond in a deserted city park and suddenly notices that a child is drowning in the middle of the pond. Assuming that the man can swim and will not drown in the process of rescuing the child, nearly everyone would say that the man was morally obligated to save the child. But, let's imagine that the man ignored the child's plea for help--for one reason or another--and nonchalantly continued his stroll. No doubt, we would be greatly appalled at the man's indifference to the child's desperate situation.

Now let's assume that by some supernatural means we learned of the event and had the opportunity to interview the man in order to find out why he let the child drown. In the course of the interview we discovered that the man placed "a high aesthetic value" on always wearing a "neatly pressed suit" and, therefore, did not want to get his clothes wet. Moreover he had a "constitutional" dislike for children, considering them "a nuisance," and felt that "the child got what he was asking for" by wading into an unsupervised pond. Also, during the interview, we learned that the man had "very strong religious convictions" which led him to believe that "nothing happens to anyone by accident." Hence he felt that "God must have called the child home"; and, of course, he did not want "to interfere with God's plans." Furthermore,

---

ed. (Englewood Cliffs, N.J.: Prentice-Hall, 1973), pp. 62ff.

the man carefully noticed that no one else was around. Therefore, he reasoned, "I did not offend any bystander by my inaction." And, finally, the man pointed out that he was a law-abiding citizen and did "nothing against the law" by taking his regular afternoon stroll.

What would we say to this man? Could we legitimately criticize his particular religious beliefs and values? Do we have the right to impose our moral values upon him?

I think most of us would say that the man's indifference to the child was highly immoral. One way of defending this 'opinion' is that we could not conceive of anything like 'human society' if everyone were to take this attitude. In other words, the man's action could not be universalized. A more precise way of accomplishing the same thing would be to specify certain universal prerequisites for human action (e.g., life, food, adequate health care, shelter, etc.) and, then, to show why a person cannot deny another of these necessary goods without rationally contradicting his own claims to these goods.[8]

It should be noted, though, that while an "ethics of duty" is a necessary aspect of a proper moral framework, it is not complete in itself. The development of moral character is not only a composite of a person's acts, but also his motivations and disposition. For example, if the man did save the drowning child, but only because he feared that God would punish him or that people would look down on him if he let the child drown, we would still not hold the man in high esteem.

The imaginary story about the man and the drowning child fills us with moral revulsion because we can easily empathize with the helpless child. Yet the same type of moral dilemma confronts each of us daily, but on a far larger scale. For instance, let's take the problem of world hunger. Millions of children die needlessly each year because they (or their

---

[8] See Alan Gewirth, Reason and Morality (Chicago: University of Chicago Press, 1978); _____, "Starvation and Human Rights," in Ethics and Problems of the 21st Century, ed. by Kenneth Sayre (Notre Dame, Ind.: University of Notre Dame Press, 1979).

mothers) did not receive a calorie intake sufficient to nourish their developing bodies. The World Bank estimates that if only 2% of the world's grain output was redirected to the mouths that needed it, the scourge of malnutrition could be wiped from the face of the earth.[9]

Moving from the imaginary to the real, consider the following interview with another man who behaved indifferently toward a <u>real</u> child in acute need, whose cry for help could not be heard.

> I did not feel God leading me to become involved with the problem. Each of us has our special ministries in the Body of Christ, and my gift happens to be evangelism. I love telling others about Jesus. Also I doubt seriously whether the problem can really be solved apart from a personal encounter with Christ. And that's what really matters. To preserve the body and then neglect the soul is certainly not God's will. And, really, let's be practical. If Christians were to give most of their money to relief agencies, we would not have enough to build churches and get the Gospel out. It's a matter of getting your priorities straight.

The only difference between this interview and the imaginary one with the man who failed to save the drowning child is that geographic distance and the scale of the problem helped to create the illusion that it was 'right' or, at least, 'permissible' to ignore the starving child. In point of fact, though, it is as if the drowning child's shrieks filled our ears, but we just kept walking . . . hoping that no one would see our indifference . . . neglecting our duty in the pursuit of virtue.

WHAT IS CHRISTIAN GROWTH?

What does it mean to be a mature Christian? Perhaps the first thing that comes to mind is a certain constellation of religious activities: the mature

---

[9]World Bank. <u>World Development Report, 1980</u> (New York: Oxford University Press, 1980), p. 61.

Christian regularly reads her Bible, prays, attends church, shares her faith and is involved in some kind of 'ministry'. To this list of activities we might add certain character traits, like: the mature Christian is a patient parent, a caring spouse, she manifests the "fruits of the Spirit" (Gal. 5:22-23) and she is "stable" in her faith.

The image of Christian maturity within Popular Christianity sets a high standard for those who aspire to "grow in Christ." It is not surprising that we admire the mature Christian--her quality of life and her depth of religious commitment. Yet, in spite of this appealing image, there seems to be something missing.

The portrait of the mature Christian is painted with vivid hues of virtue and highlighted with vigorous brush strokes of 'spiritual' activity. But, like all portraits, Popular Christianity's depiction of the "mature Christian" gives exclusive attention to the person being painted; the background serves only to emphasize the subject. But is the backdrop really that unimportant?

Christian growth must be something more than striving after an ideal image, a well-defined portrait. Christian growth should be a profoundly other-oriented process, intensely focused on the backdrop of shared human existence. That backdrop must consist of something more than isolated microcosms of the Kingdom of God: "Christian communities."

The proving ground for Christian character is not in the congregation of the 'like-minded'; it is in the community of need, the community of all of God's children: the human community. Jesus' face is no longer transfigured on mountain tops. We now behold him in the eyes of our neighbor.

How can a Christian aspire to embody God's love unless his arms are outstretched? What does it mean to "grow in faith" unless we are transforming belief into action? How can we engage God in prayer without being engaged with the needs of another?

Whatever it means to "grow in Christ," by whatever traits we select to describe "the mature Christian," we should not be content with a definition of Christian growth which produces paragons of virtue from the dust of a disintegrating humanity. Like James and

John, who sought to purchase preferred positions in the Kingdom of God with their courage to suffer, all seekers of virtue would do well to heed the counsel of Jesus:

> . . . whoever would be great among you must be your servant, and whoever would be first among you must be the slave of all." (Mk. 10: 43b-44)

CHAPTER 7

INERRANCY: QUEST FOR CERTAINTY

THE BOOK OF BOOKS

The Bible. The term comes from a Greek word
meaning "a collection of writings." The sixty-six
books which comprise the Hebrew-Christian scriptures
have influenced the history of Western civilization
more than any other body of literature. Parts of
the Bible have been integral elements of three world
religions--Judaism, Christianity and Islam. Biblical
themes have inspired great works of literature, and
the 'world view' of the Bible facilitated the development of philosophy and natural science in the West.
We must stand in awe when we consider the historical
and cultural significance of these ancient texts.
Truly the Bible is deserving of the appellation:
"the Book of Books."

The Bible has occupied a pre-eminent place of
authority for the Christian faith. The majority of
Christians throughout history have viewed the Bible
as _an_ authoritative source for their knowledge of
God, a fount of inspiration. But the Bible's authority
stood alongside other important guides to Christian
truth: the writings of the early 'church fathers',
the edicts of church councils, Canon Law, the works
of Christian theologians and papal encyclicals.

With the Reformation principle of _sola_ _Scriptura_
(Scripture alone), the relative authority of the Bible
was enhanced; however, Martin Luther himself did not
view the Bible as being uniformly inspired. For instance, he assigned a subordinate position to Esther,

Hebrews, James, Jude and Revelation, as he did not find them to be valuable resources for the Christian. It was only at a much later date--when the combined force of the Enlightenment, the development of evolutionary biology and the onset of biblical criticism began to erode traditional Christian beliefs--that the formal belief in biblical inerrancy was born.

In an attempt to defend the Bible's authority, some construed the Bible as an objective scientific document--which could refute the challenges posed by natural science on equal footing--by claiming that the Bible was uniformly infallible, a divine memorandum composed by the Almighty himself. Many Christians viewed the claim as an extravagant and regressive response to the challenges posed by the modern age. Others went on to codify and canonize the belief in biblical inerrancy as a truth integral to Christianity. For example, a recent apology for the concept went as far as equating the defense of inerrancy with The Battle for the Bible.[1]

THE SELF-DECEPTION

The self-deception under consideration concerns how people view the Bible in terms of their overall faith structure. I will call it the Inerrancy Self-Deception. It has the following five components:

1. The Deception: The Bible is without error.

2. The Intended Objective: To uphold the authority of the teachings contained in the canonical scriptures.

3. The Defense Mechanism: Overcompensation.

4. Factors Which Perpetuate Self-Deception: (a) Social anomie; and (b) Stabilization at a "law and order" stage of moral development.

5. The Unintended Consequence: The credibility of the Hebrew-Christian scriptures is undermined by factually untrue claims.

---

[1]Harold Lindsell, Battle for the Bible (Grand Rapids, Mich.: Zondervan, 1976).

Now let's take a look at each of the five elements of the Inerrancy Self-Deception.

1. THE DECEPTION: The Bible is without error.

A recent Gallup Poll indicates that 47% of the Protestant religious public believes that "the Bible is the actual Word of God and is to be taken literally, word for word." Of those who fit into Gallup's classification of the "very highly spiritually committed," 75% affirmed that the Bible was the actual Word of God. Nearly a full 100% of those respondents who were classed as "evangelical" understood the Bible as the direct Word of God.[2]

It is fair to say that the doctrine of inerrancy is not a well-defined dogma, but a more-or-less 'assumed' belief, in the minds of most Popular Christians. The operating assumption of most Popular Christians is that the Bible is a direct communication from God. From this proposition, it is easy to see how the concept of biblical inerrancy follows. Consider the following syllogistic argument:

First Premise: The Bible is God's Word.

Second Premise: God is without error.

Conclusion: The Bible is without error.

Of course, infallibility is the strongest possible truth claim that could be ascribed to any collection of writings. It only takes <u>one</u> errant statement to invalidate the entire condition of inerrancy. For example, let's assume that it was possible to reduce the historical material within the Bible to 10,000 propositions about historical places, personages or events. If we could verify or disprove one-half of those historical statements (through archaeology, inscriptions, royal annals and letters, and various ancient Near Eastern texts), it would only take a single fallacious statement to prove that the Bible was not inerrant.

---

[2]George Gallup and Associates, <u>Religion in America: The Gallup Report</u>, Nos. 201-202 (June-July, 1982), pp. 73-74, 174-175.

Given the historical rigors entailed in the inerrancy condition, it is understandable why its advocates are constrained to advance the claim entirely on theological grounds. In fact, it is remarkable that the biblical justification for the belief hinges on only one verse in the Bible: "All Scripture is inspired by God and profitable for teaching, for reproof, for correction, and for training in righteousness. . ." (II Tim. 3:16).

Of course, advocates of inerrancy point to Old Testament passages which are written as first-person communication from God (e.g., prophetic oracles, divine communications with Abraham, Moses, etc.) as instances of direct inspiration. Also they note that Jesus' use of the Old Testament (as portrayed by the Gospel writers) did nothing to undermine the belief that "God spoke through the Law and the Prophets."

Yet the passages punctuated by "thus saith the Lord" probably comprise perhaps no more than 20% of the Bible--not enough to sustain the claim that all of the Bible is "God-breathed." Hence the doctrine of biblical inerrancy rests upon one particular interpretation of one verse (a rather 'thin' theological justification). Moreover, the condition of inerrancy also assumes that the councils of Jamnia (90 CE) and Carthage (397 CE) were inspired by God when they fixed the Old Testament and New Testament canons, respectively.

2. THE INTENDED OBJECTIVE: To uphold the authority of the teachings contained in the canonical scripture.

Even the most ardent proponents of inerrancy are interested in something more than defending a particular theory about the Bible's origins. Their ultimate concern rests with preserving the authority of the Scriptures for the Christian Church.

The most common perspective on biblical inspiration among Popular Christians is the superintendent interpretation. This approach tries to preserve the individuality of the Bible's authors while attempting to set forth an intelligible framework for verbal (word for word) inspiration. Proponents of the superintendent interpretation believe that the Holy Spirit 'moved' each of the biblical authors to write exactly what God wanted them to write. It is thought that the Holy Spirit oversaw this whole process with such meticulous care that every word of the Bible met with divine approval, as if God himself had dictated the Scriptures. Of course, the problem of how the author's autonomy can be genuinely maintained in the face of such strict divine supervision is rarely given serious consideration.

A second approach to verbal inspiration is used infrequently and has fallen into disrepute. It is the dictation interpretation. This view portrays the Bible's writers more or less as secretaries who transcribed the Scriptures from a divine dictaphone. The approach has the obvious weakness of lacking any notion of the author's autonomy.

It should be emphasized that the concept of verbal inspiration is only one approach to the problem of biblical authority. The Bible does not need to be verbally inspired or inerrant to be authoritative. In fact, the idea of biblical authority can be viewed from at least two perspectives: (1) the top-down approach; and (2) the intrinsic-worth approach.

The top-down approach views authority in terms of directives from some higher power (e.g., God, the state, a business manager, etc.). Because authority emanates expressly from the office of the higher power (and not from the directives themselves), the top-down approach is intensely interested in establishing the origin of the directives. This approach to authority was predominant in the Ancient Near East. The famous Babylonian law code, "the Law of Hammurabi", was prefaced with a scene in which Hammurabi received a commission to write a lawbook from the sun-god, Shamash, the god of justice. Similarly, Moses received the Ten Commandments directly from Yahweh, on Mt. Sinai, and the Bible portrays the entire Israelite law code as issuing directly from the mouth of Yahweh.

The concept of inerrancy assumes that the Bible's authority must be founded on a top-down approach. Popular Christianity's exclusive reliance on the top-down approach to biblical authority is evidenced in the familiar statement: "If the Bible is not completely true, then the whole thing is worthless." Unfortunately the top-down assumption leads many Popular Christians to rest their entire faith on a fragile theory about the Bible's origins which offers a pat solution to a difficult problem.

A second interpretation of biblical authority is the intrinsic-worth approach. In contrast to the top-down approach, this perspective focuses on the directives themselves . . . on their intrinsic value, as opposed to the source of the directives. Authority resides with the moral and religious content of the directives. Obviously the intrinsic-worth approach to authority is not as simple and unambiguous as the top-down approach. Spiritual discernment is a necessary ingredient.

Those who follow the intrinsic-worth approach feel no need to place the Golden Rule on equal footing with the ancient Israelite concept of herem (i.e., the holy war practice of killing all men, women, children and animals when a town was conquered). Both the practice of herem and the Golden Rule appear in the Bible. Yet, of course, there is an obvious difference between a directive to utterly annihilate "every man, woman and child" (Deut. 7:2, 13:15, 20:17, Jos. 6:21, 8:2, I Sam. 15:3) and a directive to "do for others just what you want them to do for you" (Lk. 6:31, TEV). In one directive man's inhumanity to man is clearly manifest. In the other directive we see something divine, an inspired idea that lifts us above our propensity for greed and arrogance.

The top-down approach to biblical authority requires a theory of verbal inspiration. It compels Christians to reduce the Bible to an undifferentiated, Koranic correspondence from heaven. By contrast, the intrinsic-worth approach is not concerned with the inspiration of vocables, but the inspiration of ideas. It permits Christians to discern God's thoughts in the pen of man, to discover what is divine in history without equating history with the revelation of the divine, and to disclaim every notion exalted against God and his creation . . . every notion seeking refuge in the abuse of religion.

3. THE DEFENSE MECHANISM: Overcompensation.

As I noted in Chapter 5, the defense mechanism of overcompensation is the exaggerated attempt to evade felt deficiencies by developing qualities or perspectives that appear to counteract or mollify those deficiencies. The person who overcompensates responds to threat by overstatement. Instead of squarely facing a challenge to his identity or his belief system, he reacts defensively, digging his heels in deeper, and sometimes he even overdraws his own convictions in the process.

An appropriate use of compensation allows us to face threatening situations intelligently by accentuating our perceived strengths to compensate for our weaknesses (e.g., leaving questions of astronomy, geology or taxonomy to the astronomers, geologists and biologists but challenging them when they leave the realm of scientific inquiry to pontificate on religion or ethics). By contrast, overcompensation responds to threat by retreating to familiar ground, being more concerned about 'building bunkers' than 'regrouping' and perceiving 'alternate strategies'.

The formal doctrine of inerrancy is a rather recent innovation in the history of Christianity. When one examines the historical milieu surrounding the doctrine's emergence, it is apparent that the dogma of biblical inerrancy was largely a reaction to formidable challenges which biblical criticism and natural science (especially evolutionary biology) posed for traditional Christian beliefs.[3] While Protestant liberals tended to respond to these new developments with an excessively accommodating spirit, the conservatives sought to overcome the subjectivity of their liberal counterparts by construing the Bible as an _objective_ revelation which had more _scientific_ credibility than Darwin's copious notes from his voyage on the H.M.S. Beagle. It seems more than a coincidence that at the time when many Protestants were declaring that the Bible was an infallible guide to religious and scientific truth, Vatican I (1869-70) declared that the Pope was infallible when he spoke _ex cathedra_.

Those who shout the battle cry of biblical inerrancy once again pit Christianity against scientific developments by insisting that _their_ opinions must be believed in spite of compelling evidence to the contrary. Like their forebears who condemned Copernicus' (1473-1543) heliocentric theory of planetary motion as heresy (because it was an _essential_ Christian truth that the sun and planets _revolve_ around the earth), modern disciples of inerrancy undermine

---

[3]For the historical context, see Winthrop Hudson, _Religion in America_, 2nd ed. (New York: Charles Scribner's Sons, 1973), pp. 263ff.; Ernest Sandeen, _The Roots of Fundamentalism_ (Chicago: University of Chicago Press, 1970), esp. chapter 5.

Christianity's credibility by canonizing their pet theories as foundational religious truths.

4. FACTORS WHICH PERPETUATE SELF-DECEPTION: (a) Social anomie; and (b) Stabilization at a "law and order" stage of moral development.

SOCIAL ANOMIE. Most people in modern industrial societies experience, to varying degrees, a loss of purpose or identity at some point in their life. The famous French sociologist, Emile Durkheim, called this condition "anomie" (normlessness).

Durkheim postulated that a society generates a certain set of "collective representations" which constitute a society's "collective conscience." These collective sentiments function to integrate individuals into the social order, in effect, creating social solidarity. Durkheim's study of primitive cultures demonstrated the important way that religion was a socially cohesive force which epitomized the society's "collective conscience."[4]

With the extensive division of labor in more complex societies, Durkheim noted that the "collective conscience" is less pervasive and social solidarity is based on the complex interdependence of functional groups to which the individual belongs. When this system of complex interdependence breaks down or when individuals no longer derive satisfaction from their social roles, the person is cast adrift without any social moorings.[5] The highly specialized roles and diminished collective conscience of modern societies create many occasions for social anomie--the feeling that life has lost its meaning or the perception of moral aimlessness.

The threat of anomie persistently hovers over

---

[4] Emile Durkheim, The Elementary Forms of Religious Life, trans. by J. Swain (New York: The Free Press, 1965, first published in 1912), pp. 255ff., 462ff.

[5] Emile Durkheim, On the Division of Labor in Society, trans. by G. Simpson (New York: Macmillan, 1933, first published in 1893), pp. 353ff.; Suicide, trans. by J. Spaulding & G. Simpson (Glencoe, Ill.: The Free Press, 1951, first published in 1897), pp. 241ff.

modern man. Those who invest a great deal of their personal identities in their social roles--their careers, marriages, families, goals, accomplishments--are particularly susceptible (e.g., the 'midlife crisis').[6] It's no wonder why we feel tremendously insecure when our pillars of purpose are shaken, and that we respond by tightly clutching our fragile moorings of meaning.

For some Christians it almost seems as if the Bible is a prop for their personal security, and the dogma of inerrancy is the thread that rescues them from the abyss of moral relativism. When confronted with the thought that the Bible is not infallible, the suggestion does more than challenge a cognitive belief about sixty-six books. The idea threatens to undo all of their religious and moral values, leading them through the valley of the shadow of anomie.

MORALITY AS LAW AND ORDER. In addition to the threat of social anomie, another factor helps perpetuate the Inerrancy Self-Deception: the tendency to approach moral decision-making from what has been called a "law and order" perspective.

Lawrence Kohlberg, an educational psychologist at Harvard, and his associates have conducted fascinating work on moral development over the past thirty years. On the basis of a primary study of 75 people over an 18 year period, along with cross-cultural supplemental studies, Kohlberg developed a cognitive typology of moral development which contains six basic stages of moral reasoning.

Kohlberg and his associates found that people

---

[6] See Gail Sheehy, Passages (New York: E. P. Dutton, 1974), pp. 246, 273.

[7] See Dwight Boyd, and Lawrence Kohlberg, "The Is-Ought Problem: A Developmental Perspective" (Zygon 8:358-372, 1973); Ronald Duska, and Mariellen Whelan, Moral Development: A Guide to Piaget and Kohlberg (Paramus, N.J.: Paulist Press, 1975); Lawrence Kohlberg, "The Child as Philosopher," in Moral Education, ed. by B. Chazan and J. Soltis (New York: Teachers College Press, 1975); _____, "Moral Stages and Moralization: The Cognitive-Developmental Approach," in Moral Development and Behavior, ed. by T. Lickona (New York: Holt, Rinehart & Winston, 1976).

ordinarily progress through four different stages
of moral development as they move through childhood
and adolescence.

The first stage of moral reasoning is "The Punishment and Obedience Orientation." At this stage the
child structures his morality around the physical
consequences of performing a certain act (e.g., I
will get spanked if I hit my sister) and defers to
anyone more powerful than himself.

Stage 2 is "The Instrumental Relativist Orientation." At this stage of moral reasoning, doing the
'right' thing is equated with whatever benefits our
own needs. Social relations are viewed in a narcissistic framework: "You scratch my back, and I'll scratch
yours."

At Stage 3 moral decision-making is viewed in
terms of gaining approval for one's actions from 'significant others'. It is "The Good Boy--Nice Girl Orientation." Whatever conforms to social expectations
is viewed as the 'right' thing to do.

The fourth stage is "The Law and Order Orientation." People who do most of their moral reasoning
at this stage perceive their moral obligations in
terms of duty and respect for authority. Ethical
dilemmas are resolved by obedience to some external
authority: the law, the government, 'the boss', or
sacred scriptures.

Kohlberg estimates that two out of every three
American adults plateau in their capacities for moral
reasoning at Stage 4 or below.[8] The remaining adults
are able to attain more comprehensive levels of moral
reasoning which attempt to define moral obligation
in a universal context . . . in terms of principles,
instead of simple obedience to social institutions
or a sacred canon.

Stage 5 is called the "Social Contract Legalistic
Orientation." At this stage of moral reasoning, an
individual is able to critically reflect upon his

---

[8]W. Conn, "Postconventional Morality: An Exposition
and Critique of Lawrence Kohlberg's Analysis of Moral
Development in the Adolescent and the Adult" (Lumen
Vitae 30:213-230, 1975), p. 215.

society. Right and wrong are defined in terms of mutually agreed upon legal/moral values. In contrast to the Stage 4 perspective, the law is made for man, not man for the law.

The highest operational stage of Kohlberg's typology is Stage 6: "The Universal Ethical Principle Orientation." At this stage right action is defined in terms of compliance to universal moral principles (e.g., the Golden Rule, Kant's Categorical Imperative). When these self-chosen moral principles conflict with social mores or legal norms, the universal ethical principles take precedence.

Kohlberg believes that the experience of "cognitive disequilibrium" is an essential ingredient to moral development. If a person is content with a particular level of moral reasoning, he will remain at that stage. However, if the person is confronted with a moral dilemma which is outside the competence of his particular level of moral reasoning, cognitive disequilibrium is induced and the possibility of stage advancement exists.

Kohlberg and his associates discovered that as people progressed from Stage 4 to Stages 5 and 6, they often "retrogressed" to an apparent Stage 2 narcissistic orientation. Some of these participated in "anticonventional acts of a more or less delinquent sort." The period of "retrogression" (e.g., the classic sophomore year of college) allowed individuals the opportunity to distance themselves from their parent's moral perspectives and to experience moral relativism (cp., the prodigal son, Lk. 15:11-32). Eventually, though, those who "retrogressed" to Stage 2 advanced to Stage 5 or 6 in their twenties.

Kohlberg's Stage 4, "law and order" perspective has great relevance to the Inerrancy Self-Deception. In seminars on Christian living (e.g., Basic Youth Conflicts), Popular Christians are told that all their

---

[9] Lawrence Kohlberg, "Continuities in Childhood and Adult Moral Development Revisited," in Life-Span Developmental Psychology, ed. by P. Baltes and K. W. Schaie (New York: Academic Press, 1973); Lawrence Kohlberg and Coral Gilligan, "The Adolescent as a Philosopher: The Discovery of the Self in a Postconventional World" (Daedalus 100:1051-1086, 1971).

decisions should be based on the "Word of God", an
admonition that is often accompanied by the assertion
that God communicates his will through a "chain of
command" to the "authorities" which surround us (e.g.,
the state, parents, religious leaders, etc.). Marital
conflicts are resolved by affirming "God's order"
for the family (i.e., the wife "submits" to her husband, allowing him to be "the authority" of the household.)

It is not an altogether unfair assumption to
suggest that the majority of Popular Christians do
most of their moral reasoning from a Stage 4 level
of moral development. Because the Bible is viewed
as the sole underpinning of their moral structure,
the one and only authority, the suggestion that the
Bible is not inerrant effectively perches them alongside a forboding chasm of moral anomie. Two choices
immediately present themselves: jump (i.e., abandon
Christianity) or cling to what you have and ignore
troublesome doubts.

Since neither of these options offers a constructive resolution of the problem, we must squarely face
the task of reconstructing our ethical framework from
a Stage 6 level of moral reasoning. In other words,
it is necessary to discern, thoughtfully and prayer-
fully, the Godlike 'inspired' principles and concepts
within the Bible (e.g., love for one's neighbor, the
Golden Rule, forgiveness) and commit ourselves to
these--leaving aside those ideas within the Bible
which are infected by greed, arrogance, malice and
cowardice (e.g., holy war, blind subservience to the
state, 'spiritual' imperialism).

5. THE UNINTENDED CONSEQUENCE: The credibility
of the Hebrew-Christian scriptures is undermined by
factually untrue claims.

Self-deception, even with the best of intentions,
is always counterproductive. This fact could not
be illustrated more clearly than with the Inerrancy
Self-Deception. The comfort and solace of self-deception is bought at the price of achieving precisely
the opposite of what Popular Christians intend.

Instead of defending the authority of the Bible,
the exaggerated and false claims of the inerrancy
dogma subvert the authority of the Scriptures and
the credibility of the Christian community. Thinking

that they are elevating the Bible's prestige, proponents of inerrancy perch the Scriptures on a steep precipice without any way down. Believing that they are instilling confidence in the Bible, they plant the seeds which precipitate a crisis of confidence, using 'faith' as a foil for incompetence. Like the secret maxim of Kafka's tireless workers on the Great Wall of China, Popular Christianity admonishes its adherents to "try with all your might to comprehend the decrees of the high command, but only up to a certain point; then avoid further meditation."[10]

It is a curious thing that the defenders of biblical inerrancy maintain that they are taking a "high view" of Scripture and interpreting the Bible "literally." But how can a 'high view' of the Bible be founded on falsehood? How can one presume to take the Bible 'literally' without taking the trouble to investigate the historical setting and composition of the Scriptures?[11] No one who feels genuine affection and respect for the Bible should tolerate deceptive claims for its authority, no matter what the desired effect may be.

Now that we have examined all five elements of the Inerrancy Self-Deception, let's turn to consider some commonly used evasions which apologists of inerrancy use to insulate their doctrine from criticism.

DEFENSE BY EVASION

Anyone who takes the time to read serious works on recent biblical scholarship will recognize how untenable the doctrine of inerrancy actually is. To say that the Bible is not inerrant is to state an irrefutable, factual truth. In the remaining sections of this chapter, I will substantiate this claim by identifying some major sources of theological and historical discrepancies within the Bible.

---

[10]Franz Kafka, "The Great Wall of China," in Franz Kafka: The Complete Stories, ed. by N. Glatzer (New York: Shocken Books, 1946), p. 240.

[11]A literal interpretation attempts to establish the meaning of a text in terms of the author's understanding and the understanding of his original audience.

In view of the overwhelming evidence against biblical inerrancy, the really interesting question is this: How can so many people adhere to such a mistaken belief about the Bible? Answer: it takes a lot of help. Without the support of respected authority figures in Popular Christian circles, without the accumulated weight of tradition and without a repertoire of handy evasions, this counter-factual belief could never be maintained. Let's examine nine evasions which are commonly used to deflect the facts against inerrancy.

1. "I HAVE FAITH THAT THE BIBLE IS INERRANT." This evasion could be called the 'faith defense' of inerrancy. It confuses faith statements with factual ones. Biblical inerrancy is a falsifiable claim which is advanced in the arena of factual data. It cannot be verified apart from historical facts. By contrast, faith claims, by definition, can neither be falsified nor verified by reference to factual data. As a consequence, this commonly used evasion boils down to a confession of ignorance: "I believe that the Bible is factually inerrant, but I have neither taken the time to investigate this opinion nor wish to entertain any evidence to the contrary." What appears to be a demonstration of faith is actually an affirmation of agnosticism. Unfortunately this weak evasion leads to a debilitating definition of faith: 'belief in the face of contradiction' instead of the biblical sense of the term, 'belief in action'.

2. "IF WE CRITICIZE THE BIBLE, WE ARE ELEVATING OURSELVES ABOVE IT." This position, along with its variants, could be termed the 'anti-intellectual defense'. The argument begins with the unstated assumption that critical thought—as opposed to blind obedience to unreflective personal or collective impressions—is a bad thing. Actually, though, any exercise of thought 'elevates' us, in some sense, above the object we are studying. For instance, rules of grammar 'elevate' us above particular communication events. Generally those who take the anti-intellectual defense are themselves unaware of the tremendous diversity within the Bible and choose to believe that their reading of the Bible is the only accurate interpretation. Otherwise they would be more sensitive to the absolute necessity of critical thought in fairly interpreting the Bible.

3. "I KNOW THAT THE BIBLE IS TRUE, FROM COVER

TO COVER, ON THE BASIS OF MY OWN EXPERIENCES." If we permit a loose use of the term 'existential', this evasion could be described as the 'existential defense'. The truth of the Bible is verified through subjective experiences. Generally this amounts to the claim that "biblical principles have worked for me" or that "my experience of God is consistent with the Bible." Of course, neither of these claims has anything to do with biblical inerrancy.

4. "HOW COULD SO MANY PEOPLE BE WRONG ABOUT THE BIBLE?" The question introduces the fourth evasion, which might be called the 'democratic defense' of biblical inerrancy. It equates truth with the opinion of the plurality, if not the majority. Of course, it does not take much to demolish this argument. At certain points in history the majority of people believed that the world was flat, that the sun and planets revolved around the earth, or that some men were born to be slaves. The chariot of truth and the bandwagon of popularity often travel separate roads.

5. "THE BIBLE IS INERRANT IN ITS ORIGINAL MANUSCRIPTS." Of all the evasions used by defenders of biblical inerrancy, this one is frankly despicable. Those who parrot the 'original manuscript defense' ought to know better. The argument is often used by conservative biblical 'scholars' (mastery of ancient languages does not necessarily make one a scholar) who claim that the Bible is inerrant in its original manuscripts (which we do not have). The claim is unfounded and does not succeed at undermining the credibility of the countless scribes who painstakingly copied the biblical texts down through ages.[12]

6. "IF THE BIBLE IS NOT THE LITERAL WORD OF GOD, THEN THERE CAN BE NO MORAL ABSOLUTES." I will call this the 'moral defense' argument for inerrancy. This is an increasing common argument for verbal inspiration which was popularized in the writings of the

---

[12]A helpful evaluation of conservative biblical scholarship appears in James Barr, Fundamentalism (Philadelphia: Westminster Press, 1977), pp. 120-159; 279-284.

late Francis Schaeffer.[13] Essentially, the argument begins with the recognition that complete moral relativism leads to dehumanization and the denigration of human rights. Once this point is established, it is recommended (not argued) that the Bible (as interpreted from the standpoint of Reformation thought) is the only way out of moral nihilism, because it provides us with a reliable set of religious and moral absolutes. The fundamental biblical affirmation which Schaeffer draws upon is the belief that a "personal-infinite" God created human beings in his own image, who each have the capacity to be free, morally responsible persons (Gen. 1-3).

Two things are especially misleading about Schaeffer's line of argument. First, it is assumed that one cannot cogently construct an adequate theory of morality and human rights on non-religious grounds.[14] This assumption is incorrect. Second, the theory of verbal inspiration is imported by Schaeffer to shore up the argument that a "personal-infinite" God created human beings in his own image. You do not need a theory of verbal inspiration to defend that claim; but, on the other hand, you cannot prove the claim either . . . it is a statement of faith.

7. "BIBLICAL CRITICS DO NOT BELIEVE IN INERRANCY BECAUSE THEY ASSUME THAT MIRACLES DO NOT EXIST." This evasion could be called the 'defense from presuppositions'. It is assumed that critics of the Bible embrace an anti-supernaturalist world view, a presupposition which determines their findings. There is some truth in the belief that anti-supernaturalist presuppositions may influence a few facets of modern biblical scholarship; but, for the most part, these

---

[13]See Francis Schaeffer, Escape From Reason (InterVarsity Press, 1968), pp. 80ff.; Francis Schaeffer and C. Everett Koop, Whatever Happened to the Human Race (Old Tappan, N.J.: Fleming H. Revell, 1979), pp. 151-152.

[14]For example, see William Galston, Justice and the Human Good (Chicago: University of Chicago Press, 1980); Alan Gewirth, Reason and Morality (Chicago: University of Chicago Press, 1978); Immanuel Kant, Groundwork of the Metaphysics of Morals (first published in 1785); and John Rawls, A Theory of Justice (Cambridge, Mass.: Harvard University Press, 1971).

presuppositions have little to do with the findings of biblical scholarship.

8. "JESUS TREATED THE OLD TESTAMENT AS GOD'S WORD; HOW COULD HE BE WRONG?" This could be called the 'Christological defense' of, at least, the inerrancy of the Old Testament. The crux of the argument is this: if Jesus was the Son of God, he would surely know whether or not the Old Testament scriptures were reliable. I have no doubt that Jesus genuinely believed that the Hebrew scriptures accurately recorded God's communications with Abraham, Moses, the prophets and other biblical figures. However, it is inappropriate to indulge in docetism by assuming that Jesus was privy to 20th century data generated by recent archaeological discoveries and advances in literary criticism. We might equally assume that Jesus' divinity implied that he knew Einstein's Theory of Relativity from the crib, but obviously such an assumption would be ridiculous. Jesus like the rest of his countrymen, had no reason to doubt the historical reliability of the Hebrew scriptures in his day. Therefore this line of argument is irrelevant to the problem which faces us today.

9. "GOD REVEALS HIMSELF IN DIFFERENT WAYS, AT VARIOUS TIMES IN HISTORY, IN ORDER TO COMMUNICATE EFFECTIVELY." This could be termed the 'progressive revelation defense' of biblical inerrancy. This approach begins by admitting that the Bible contains diverse ideas; however, these are not contradictory in the strict sense of the term. It is assumed that "God meets us where we are at." Therefore he may adjust his message to fit the times; yet, each new revelation of God builds upon previous knowledge, so that the condition of "progressive revelation" obtains. Proponents of the approach point out that Jesus used the progressive revelation motif when he was confronted with the charge that he violated Old Testament law codes (Mt. 19:7-9).

The major problem with the progressive revelation defense is that it does not appreciate the depth of the Bible's diversity. There are many instances in the Scriptures where we find truly contradictory theologies or moral values, not simply elaborations on previous 'revelations'. These diverse ideas cannot be unified in one grand scheme of dynamic self-disclosure. The concept of progressive revelation is an unsuccessful theological attempt to evade a fact that is unavoidable: the Bible contains theological

169

discrepancies and historical inaccuracies.

THE FACTS OF THE MATTER

An honest appraisal of the Bible will show that error lurks alongside some of the profound religious and moral ideas of world history. An adequate discussion of the historical, theological and textual problems of the Old and New Testaments would fill several volumes. I cannot even begin to address these issues in the remainder of the chapter; however, I will note a few problems for the sake of introduction.

The fact that the Bible has theological discrepancies and historical inaccuracies should not surprise us. We must remember that the Bible is composed of literature that spans over a thousand years! It only makes sense that people living in different historical epochs would think differently about God. Also, to state the obvious, the Bible was written and edited by human beings--usually exceptionally gifted people who lived and wrote in specific situations with certain purposes in mind. Once we come to terms with this fact, it is easy to understand how a writer's own biases could create a distorted, inaccurate perspective on history.

Unfortunately these obvious aspects of the Bible's composition are obscured by the flood of misinformation about the Bible in Popular Christian circles. People have been conditioned to expect things from the Bible that it cannot satisfy . . . expectations that the biblical writers never meant to satisfy.

At the outset, it should be noted that some of the material in the Bible which appears to be historically incorrect **may** actually not be history at all! At the present time, serious historical question marks envelop the whole of Israel's 'prehistory' (i.e., the period before Saul's kingdom). This prehistorical period includes the biblical narratives about the Patriarchs (Gen. 12-36), Joseph and the Sojourn in Egypt (Gen. 37-50), the Exodus from Egypt (Ex. 1-15), the Sojourn in the Wilderness (Ex. 16 - Deut. 34), and the Conquest of Canaan (Jos. 1-24). Some scholars recently have felt that the historical reliability of these narratives is so dubious that they have interpreted them largely as late literary creations, having no historical significance whatsoever, beyond the history of the compositions themselves.[15]

The debate over the historicity of the first six books of the Bible is far from being resolved. There is ample room for 'honest disagreement' among scholars. Nonetheless a brief listing of some of the problems demonstrates that the matter cannot be dismissed lightly.

1. All of the significant cities mentioned in the narratives about Abraham, Isaac and Jacob were occupied simultaneously only in the Early Iron Age (1200-900 BCE), a period far too late for the biblical Patriarchal Age.[16] Most scholars believe that the patriarchs lived at some time during the Middle Bronze Age II (c. 1900-1500

---

[15]Gösta W. Ahlström, "Another Moses Tradition" (Journal of Near Eastern Studies 39/1:65-69, 1980; Donald B. Redford, A Study of the Biblical Story of Joseph, Supplement to Vetus Testamentum, Vol. 20 (Leiden: E.J. Brill, 1970); Thomas L. Thompson, The Historicity of the Patriarchal Narratives (Beiheft zur Zeitschrift für die alttestamentliche Wissenschaft, Vol. 133, 1974); Thomas L. Thompson and Dorothy Irvin, "The Joseph and Moses Narratives," in Israelite and Judean History, ed. by J. H. Hayes and J. M. Miller (Philadelphia: Westminster Press, 1977), pp. 149-212; and John Van Seters, Abraham in History and Tradition (New Haven, Conn.: Yale University Press, 1975).

[16]See B. Mazar, "The Historical Background of the Book of Genesis" (Journal of Near Eastern Studies 28:73-84, 1969); Thompson, The Historicity of the Patriarchal Narratives, pp. 1-9, 144-195. It is particularly notable that the site at Beersheba has no settlement before the Iron Age [see Y. Aharoni, "Excavations at Tel Beersheba" (The Biblical Archaeologist 35:111-127, 1972); Kathleen Kenyon, Archaeology in the Holy Land, 4th ed. (New York: W. W. Norton & Co., 1979), p. 279]. Beersheba figures prominently in the patriarchal narratives. Abraham, Isaac and Jacob each constructed an altar there, and two patriarchs experienced a theophany at Beersheba. This reassessment of Palestinean archaeology dramatically revises the previous conclusions of the "Albright School" [e.g., John Bright, A History of Israel, 2nd ed. (Philadelphia: Westminster Press, 1972), p. 81].

BCE).

2. The Bible associates the patriarchs with the Aramaeans (Gen. 25:20, 28:1-5, 31:20, 47; Deut. 26:5), but the Aramaeans only became prominent after c. 1200 BCE.[17]

3. Previous attempts to date the patriarchal narratives in the second millennium BCE--by comparing the personal and place names or social customs of the narratives with extra-biblical materials (e.g., the Nuzi texts, Mari texts)--have been shown to be incorrect or inconclusive. The names and customs fit a later cultural milieu with the same or greater likelihood.[18]

4. The so-called "table of nations" in Genesis 10 assumes a perspective which is set in the late second millenium BCE and parts of it belong to later periods.[19]

5. The references to "the Philistines" (Gen. 21:32, 26:1ff.) in the patriarchal narratives are anachronistic prior to c. 1200 BCE. Also the reference to "Ur of the Chaldeans" (Gen. 11:28, 15:7) and the widespread domestication of camels described in the narratives (Gen. 12:16, 24:10ff.,

---

[17]See W. G. Dever, "The Patriarchal Tradition," in Israelite and Judean History, ed. by Hayes & Miller, p. 119; Van Seters, Abraham in History and Tradition, pp. 29-34.

[18]Thompson, The Historicity of the Patriarchal Narratives, pp. 17-51, 196-297; Van Seters, Abraham in History and Tradition, pp. 39-103. The late Fr. Roland de Vaux constructed the most thorough argument in favor of the historicity of the patriarchal narratives by means of the names and customs of the biblical patriarchs. See his The Early History of Israel, trans. by D. Smith (London: Darton, Longman & Todd, 1978), pp. 191-200, 230-256.

[19]Siegfried Herrmann, A History of Israel in Old Testament Times (Philadelphia: Fortress Press, 1975), pp. 42ff.

31:24) are only possible in the first millennium BCE.[20]

6. Attempts to link the patriarchs with an Early Bronze-Middle Bronze Age "Amorite migration"[21] or

---

[20] Many scholars interpret these references as anachronisms. However, it seems gratuitous to treat these and other late features of the patriarchal narratives as being simply anachronistic. Particularly the references to camels in Genesis 24 and 31 seem integral to the rest of the story (Van Seters, Abraham in History and Tradition, p. 17).

[21] The Amorite interpretation of the patriarchal narratives is based on the assertion that the patriarchs were part of Asiatic nomadic movements which swept down from the semi-arid fringes of the Fertile Crescent, disrupting the urban cultures of Mesopotamia, Syria, Palestine and Egypt. In Palestine, these nomadic groups--sometimes called the 'Amorites' (meaning 'Westerners' and not to be confused with the Amorites mentioned in the Bible)--created an "absolute break" in the culture of the Early Bronze Age at c. 2300 BCE. The nomadic "Dark Age" or "Intermediate Period" between the Early Bronze Age and the splendid, enduring culture of the Middle Bronze Age has been called the EB-MB period (sometimes called EB IV or MB I) and has been dated from 2300-1900 BCE [see Kathleen Kenyon, Amorites and Canaanites (London: Oxford University Press, 1966); _____, Archaeology in the Holy Land, pp. 117-147].
The association of the patriarchs with these Amorite migrations is flawed in two respects. First, the date of the EB-MB intermediate period is too early for the patriarchs. Second, the patriarchal migrations move in a direction opposite to the proposed migrations of the "Amorite hypothesis."
The 'classic' attempt to associate the patriarchs with an Amorite migration in the EB-MB period was forged by W. F. Albright in 1935 ["Palestine in the Earliest Historical Period" (Journal of the Palestine Oriental Society 15:193-234, 1935)]. Albright revised his earlier thesis in 1961 by lowering the end-date of the EB-MB period (Albright's MB I) from 1900 to 1800 BCE (a revision that has not been accepted by any other scholar in the field). Also, he associated Abraham with donkey caravaneers who were quite active in the 19th century BCE ["Abram the Hebrew: A New

173

to identify them with the ꜣApiru[22] are fraught with difficulties.

Archaeological Interpretation" (Bulletin of the American Schools of Oriental Research 168: 36-54, 1961)]. Albright claimed that prominent cities in the patriarchal narratives (Beersheba, Bethel, Gerar, Hebron and Shechem) were settled in the EB-MB period. However we now know that these sites were not occupied at this time (see Dever, "The Patriarchal Traditions," in Israelite and Judean History, ed. by Hayes and Miller, pp. 99-102).

R. de Vaux (The Early History of Israel, pp. 58-68, 263-266) rejected Albright's Middle Bronze I (MB I) thesis and associated the patriarchal migrations with a second wave of Amorites in MB IIA (c. 1950-1800 BCE). He did not make the previous Amorite migrations directly responsible for the destruction of the Early Bronze culture of Syria-Palestine. Instead he attributed the widespread destruction of this period to other nomadic groups, possibly from Anatolia or Caucasia. Although de Vaux's thesis provides a more acceptable date for the patriarchal migrations than Albright's MB I thesis, the theory has a notable weakness. De Vaux's hypothesis makes his second wave of nomadic Amorites responsible for the revival of urban settlements in MB IIA--a period of dramatic reconstruction marked by the appearance of wheel-made pottery, bronze weaponry and new burial customs. What kind of continuity can exist between a first and second wave of Amorites with the decisive change in material culture that we see in MB IIA? We know that the Amorites eventually became sedentary and 'civilized' at Ur and Mari, but this fact does not eliminate the problem of explaining how a newly migrated band of Amorites would suddenly either have the interest or expertise to introduce the imposing accomplishments in urbanization that characterized MB IIA.

In addition to the difficulty of locating the patriarchs within the chronology of an Amorite migration, another problem exists. The movement of the patriarchal migrations described in the Bible is from Ur to Haran. This is in a direction opposite to the proposed Amorite migrations of the EB-MB period (see Thompson, The Historicity of the Patriarchal Narratives, p. 87; Van Seters, Abraham in History and Tradition, pp. 23-26).

22 Documents throughout the ancient Near East attest

7. It appears that the narrative concerning Joseph in Genesis 37-50 is less acquainted with Egyptian culture than was previously thought. The Egyptian elements within the story postdate the Rameside Age (c. 1303-1200 BCE) and may suggest a date before the 7th century BCE. It seems likely that any educated Palestinean would have been familiar with the aspects of Egyptian culture contained within the story.[23]

8. The Bible is <u>completely</u> silent about the lengthy period of Israelite captivity in Egypt (400 years, Gen. 15:13; 430 years, Ex. 12:40; four

---

to the presence of a class of people known as the ꜣApiru or Ḫapiru during the second millennium (until 1200 BCE). The most notable source of information about these people comes from the Egyptian Amarna Letters (14 century BCE). Scholars who have associated the patriarchs (or, more generally, the Israelites) with the ꜣApiru have emphasized the similarity between the term ꜣApiru and the Hebrew term for the word 'Hebrew': ꜣibri. However the etymological link between the two terms is dubious, and several other factors militate against associating the patriarchs with the ꜣApiru. Among these is the fact that the ꜣApiru seem to be a general social class--on the fringe of society and deprived of normal legal protections--with no common ethnic identity. At times in the Amarna Letters the term seems to be applied to anyone who defies Egyptian authority. In contrast to the irenic, pastoral portrait of the biblical patriarchs, the Egyptian texts depict the ꜣApiru as roving mercenaries or freebooters who often 'lock horns' with the local urban authorities. For a full critique of the association of the ꜣApiru with the Hebrews, see Manfred Weippert, <u>The Settlement of the Israelite Tribes in Palestine</u>, Studies in Biblical Theology, 2/21, trans. by J. D. Martin (London: SCM Press, 1971), pp. 55-102.

[23]Redford, <u>A Study of the Biblical Story of Joseph</u>, pp. 187-243. It seems likely that the Joseph Story is a late literary composition which utilized familiar folktale motifs (see Dorothy Irvin, "The Joseph and Moses Narratives," is <u>Israelite and Judean History</u>, ed. by Hayes and Miller, pp. 180-191). A strong parallel exists between the plot-motif of the Story of Joseph in Genesis 39 and the Egyptian "Story of the Two Brothers," the Hittite "Story of Elkunirsha" and the Akkadian "Epic of Gilgamesh."

generations, Gen. 15:16, Ex. 6:13ff.). This is a truly remarkable datum. One would expect that if the Israelite sojourn in Egypt was historical, at least a few stories about Israelite heroes would have been passed down and recorded. Instead nothing has filtered down about this period and the personage of Moses abruptly appears after c. 400 years.

9. The biblical narratives concerning the Exodus from Egypt presume a high degree of ethnic identity among the Semites enslaved in Egypt. At best, this assumption is highly questionable.[24] The Israelites are said to have inhabited "the land of Goshen" (Gen. 45:10, 46:28), presumably located in the Egyptian Delta. However that name appears nowhere in Egyptian texts and the name itself is not Egyptian.[25]

10. While the name 'Moses' is genuinely Egyptian, the etymology which the Bible provides for his name (Ex. 2:10) is based on Hebrew and does not understand the Egyptian root from which the name derives.[26] Also there is a suspiciously striking similarity between the story of Moses' birth and the earlier birth story of Sargon the Great of Akkad. Like Moses, Sargon was born in secret, and his mother made a basket of rushes and sealed it with pitch. Sargon was set in the basket and placed in the river. The infant was discovered downstream and raised by a stranger named Akki. The child grew up to be a great king.[27]

---

[24]Thompson, "The Joseph and Moses Narratives," in Israelite and Judean History, ed. by Hayes and Miller, pp. 154-155.

[25]Donald B. Redford, "Exodus 1:11" (Vetus Testamentum 13:401-418, 1963), p. 412.

[26]Thompson, "The Joseph and Moses Narratives," in Israelite and Judean History, ed. by Hayes and Miller, pp. 154-155.

[27]See James Pritchard, The Ancient Near East, Vol. 1 (Princeton, NJ: Princeton University Press, 1958), pp. 85-6.

The biblical story of Moses' birth has Pharaoh's daughter bathing in the Nile when the baby Moses was discovered. Egyptologists have pointed out that the likelihood of having one of Pharaoh's daughters bathe in the Nile is practically nil, if not altogether inconceivable.[28]

11. John Bright maintains that the biblical tradition concerning Israel's enslavement to the Egyptians "a priori demands belief," because no nation would invent "the recollection of shameful servitude from which only the power of God brought deliverance."[29] At first glance this statement seems eminently reasonable, but further consideration shows that the tradition of Israel's captivity in Egypt (whatever its basis in history) actually enhanced Israel's national prestige. The Exodus account does not lament 400 years of forced servitude but celebrates Yahweh's decisive victory on Israel's behalf. Egypt was a 'superpower' in the ancient Near East, albeit a declining one at this time. For Moses to stroll into Pharaoh's court, demanding the release of his people (on threat of one plague after the next), is tantamount to having Lech Walesa march into the Kremlin to demand--on threat of force--Soviet non-interference in Polish affairs. If we could even imagine such a contemporary scene, it is easy to see why the story of Israel's incredible triumph over the Egyptians--bringing a superpower to its knees--significantly enhanced the nation's own self-concept.

12. The association of the Israelite exodus with Shasu migrations in the Egyptian Delta is a tantalizing suggestion, however too little is known about the Shasu at this time to draw any firm conclusions.[30]

---

[28] de Vaux, The Early History of Israel, p. 328.

[29] Bright, A History of Israel, p. 119.

[30] Siegfried Herrmann has identified the Israelite descent to and exodus from Egypt with the Shasu migrations of the 13th century BCE, which he interprets as part of a larger Aramaean migration (A History of Israel in Old Testament Times, pp. 58ff.). The

13. We have a notable lack of <u>archaeological</u> evidence showing that Edomite and Moabite settlements existed in the southern Transjordan during the Late Bronze Age, as the biblical account pre-sumes.[31]

Shasu are mentioned in Egyptian records from the Late Bronze Age. They are nomadic groups who periodically sought pasturage in the eastern zone of the Egyptian Delta and were allowed to inhabit the area only with Pharaoh's approval. Herrmann speculates that some Shasu groups entered Egypt and were subjected to forced servitude, while other Shasu groups remained in Palestine or settled near Kadesh. Moses, on this account, was a Shasu leader who rose to "a privileged position" in Egyptian society and subsequently "left Egyptian service" to liberate an enslaved group of his Shasu brethren and escape into the wilderness.

Herrmann's 'Shasu thesis' is based on Egyptian lists of foreign peoples and cities from the reigns of Amenophis III (1402-1364 BCE) and Ramesses II (1290-1224 BCE) which refer to t° $\check{s}h_3$ $s.w$ yhw_3 (the Shasu land of $\underline{Yhw_3}$). The Egyptian term $\underline{yhw_3}$ has the same consonants as the Hebrew word for Yahweh. In the Egyptian lists the word is used as a place name. This correspondence seems remarkable, however several problems weaken Herrmann's thesis. First, we know little about the Aramaean migrations toward the end of the second millennium BCE. Second, we have no suggestion that the Aramaeans were related to the Shasu or that Shasu groups settled in the vicinity of Kadesh. Third, the term 'Shasu' is often a generic designation in Egyptian records and is not limited to a particular ethnic group (Thompson, "The Joseph and Moses Narratives," in <u>Israelite and Judean History</u>, ed. by Hayes and Miller, pp. 158-9).

[31]Nelson Glueck's extensive surface surveys in the southern Transjordan in the 1930's revealed many settlements during Middle Bronze I (c. 2100-1900 BCE). However he found that the region was virtually deserted until the Iron Age ["Exploring Southern Palestine (the Negev)," in <u>The Biblical Archaeologist Reader</u>, ed. by G. E. Wright and D. N. Freedman (Garden City, N.Y.: Doubleday, 1961), pp. 8-9]. Glueck found only a few remains that could be dated to the Late Bronze Age (the only possible period for the biblical Wilderness Wandering). Subsequent investigations in the Transjordan have confirmed the basic outline of

14. It is a well-established fact that the legal and ceremonial regulations which the Bible attributes to Moses actually originated during late periods of Israelite history and received their final form during the Babylonian Exile or shortly thereafter.[32]

Glueck's findings, although it now seems that the onset of Edomite settlements should be dated around the 9th century BCE (see J. M. Miller, "The Israelite Occupation of Canaan," in Israelite and Judean History, ed. by Hayes and Miller, pp. 258-9).

In three isolated instances Edom and Moab are mentioned in Egyptian documents of the 13th century BCE. The reference to Edom comes from the Papyrus Anastasi VI. The two Moab references (Moab & Dibon) come from a topographical list from Ramesses II (See K. A. Kitchen, "Some New Light on the Asiatic Wars of Rameses II" (Journal of Egyptian Archaeology 50:47-70, 1964). The reference to the Moabite city of Dibon poses a special problem. The city site has been well excavated and there is no evidence that Dibon was populated prior to the mid-ninth century BCE. In view of the absence of Edomite and Moabite settlements in the 13th century BCE, it may be that the Egyptians used these terms loosely (to denote something other than the well-established settlements the biblical narrative depicts), however we cannot know for sure.

It is noteworthy that an Aramaic inscription was found at Deir ꜣAlla in the Transjordan which claims to be the "writing of Balaam, the son of Beor." The inscription has been dated to the mid-eighth century BCE [J. Naveh, "The Date of the Deir ꜣAlla Inscription in Aramaic Script" (Israel Exploration Journal 17:256-258, 1967)]. Balaam is mentioned in Numbers 22-24. It seems likely that Balaam lived not more than 100-200 years before the inscription--a period too late for the traditional dating of the biblical narratives about Balaam--but, of course, we can only speculate on the matter.

[32]For information on the development of Israelite legal and ceremonial regulations, see Roland de Vaux, Ancient Israel, trans. by J. McHugh (New York: McGraw-Hill, 1961).

15. The Book of Joshua creates the impression that the Israelites subjugated Canaan within a few years. This view of the Israelite conquest is contradicted by Judges 1, which lists 20 cities that the Israelites could not vanquish. The archaeological evidence throughout Palestine during this period does not support the notion of an Israelite conquest of Canaan and casts substantial doubt on the biblical narratives. For example, assuming that the Israelite conquest took place when Arad, Heshbon, Jericho, Ai and Gibeon were inhabited (as the biblical narratives presume), the conquest could not have taken place before the Iron Age--a period too late for the Israelite conquest described in Joshua.[33]

---

[33]We can be sure that the biblical narratives concerning the conquest of Canaan should be set in the 13th century BCE. The reference to Pithom and Raamses in Exodus 1:11 establishes a terminus a quo of the early 13th century for the Exodus from Egypt. The Merneptah stele contains the first and only Egyptian reference to 'Israel' and is dated to c. 1230 BCE. The stele mentions Israel in the context of other towns and peoples in Palestine that Merneptah claimed to have vanquished. Obviously this sets a terminus ad quem of 1230 BCE (but probably before that) for the conquest narratives.

We know that the central hill country of Palestine witnessed an increase in settlements toward the end of the 13th century, however there is no way of knowing whether these were Israelite settlements. H. J. Franken claims that "archaeologists would be totally unaware of any important ethnic change at the end of the Late Bronze Age were it not for the biblical tradition" ["Palestine in the Time of the Nineteenth Dynasty. (a) Archaeological Evidence," in Cambridge Ancient History, 2nd ed., Vol. II, fasc. 67 (1968), p. 9]. Similarly, Kenyon writes that "at no single moment in the archaeological record can one say that the Israelites have arrived" (Archaeology in the Holy Land, p. 206). She attributes this fact to the immigrant status of the Israelites, who, like other immigrants, tended to adopt the material culture of the region, carrying few implements that could survive the test of time.

Not only is the material culture of Palestine silent about an Israelite presence, but also the destruction layers of excavated cities in the region

(continuation of footnote 33)

do not confirm the biblical account of an Israelite conquest in the 13th century BCE. Some cities that figure prominently in the conquest stories of Numbers and Joshua were not occupied or significantly populated at this time (e.g., Ai, Arad, Gibeon, Heshbon, Hormah, Jarmuth and Jericho). At Beiten (Bethel) and Tell Duweir (Lachish) we have clear evidence of a 13th century destruction. Many scholars have assumed that the destruction layers at these two sites were caused by the Israelites. However, as Roland de Vaux has pointed out, one cannot easily attribute the destruction of either city to an Israelite conquest ["On the Right and Wrong Uses of Archaeology," in Near Eastern Archaeology in the Twentieth Century: Essays in Honor of Nelsen Glueck, ed. by J. A. Sanders (Garden City, N.Y.: Doubleday, 1970), p. 77]. De Vaux points out that the biblical text is silent about the destruction of these two cities. The capture of Bethel is mentioned in the Book of Judges (1:22-26), not in Joshua, and recent evidence from Lachish (a Ramesses III scarab) points to a later date for city's demise (the early 12th century BCE).

The only possible exception to the overwhelming discrepancies between the biblical account and the archaeological record is Hazor. The Book of Joshua (11:1-15) states that Hazor was destroyed by the incoming Israelites. However Judges 4 claims that an Israelite army led by Deborah and Barak fought against Jabin, the king of Hazor, after the conquest period described in Joshua (cp. I Sam. 12:9). It seems likely that the Israelite defeat of Sisera, the commander of Jabin's army, marked the beginning of Israelite control of Hazor, and that this local military incursion was read back to the Israelite blitzkreig described in Joshua [see G. W. Ahlström, "Another Moses Tradition" (Journal of Near Eastern Studies 39/1: 65-69, 1980), p. 68]. Against this view, Y. Yadin, the director of the Hazor excavations, believes that the Israelites were responsible for the city's destruction and the subsequent, under-developed Iron Age "settlement of semi-nomadic people" which was built upon the ruins of Late Bronze Hazor [Hazor: The Head of All Those Kingdoms (London: Oxford University Press, 1972), pp. 9ff., pp. 129ff.] However Yadin's proposal suffers from a major, unwarranted presupposition (apart from the difficulties of reconstructing the biblical tradition and a debate among archaeologists concerning the relative dating of small settlements in Galilee): Yadin assumes that the occupants of the poor Iron Age settlement at Hazor (Stratum XII) were themselves responsible for the complete destruction of the well-developed Late Bronze city of Stratum XIII [Miller, "The Israelite Occupation of Canaan" (in Israelite and Judean History, ed. by Hayes and Miller), pp. 261-262].

A pivotal consideration in relating archaeological discoveries to the Bible is that archaeological evidence does not provide a nuanced account of history. The destruction of a city site can be dated with reasonable accuracy; however, the charred remains of walls and buildings cannot tell us who or what caused the destruction. A destruction layer may have been caused by a natural disaster, an accidental fire, a conflict among 'traditional' enemies or the migration of belligerent peoples (see Weippert, The Settlement of the Israelite Tribes in Palestine, pp. 130-2).

We must also remember that the biblical period of the Conquest coincides with an extensive period of change and catastrophe throughout the eastern Mediterranean world that resulted from the inundation of the Sea Peoples (including the biblical 'Philistines'). Egypt under Ramesses III was able to repel their attack, but the Hittite Empire was seriously weakened by the powerful invaders and was 'finished off' by inland barbarian peoples. City sites in Cyprus and along the Syrian coast were decimated, including ancient Ugarit. Likewise, in Palestine many large cities met their demise. Tell Abu Hawam, Aphek, Ashdod, Ashkelon, Tell Beit Mirsim, Bethel, Beth-shan, Beth-shemesh, Gezer, Hazor, Jaffa and Megiddo were violently destroyed (see Miller, "The Israelite Occupation of Canaan," in Israelite and Judean History, ed. by Hayes and Miller, pp. 254ff.). The pattern of destruction throughout the region points to the influx of the Sea Peoples, not to the Israelites.

I will spend the remainder of the chapter discussing three different types of literary purposes which helped shape the Hebrew-Christian scriptures. Each of these purposes or intentions generated either historical errors or theological discrepancies. They are: (1) the author's theological purposes; (2) the author's political purposes; and (3) the author's desire to explain the origin of existing conditions. By recognizing each of these aims or intentions, we are able to see why the Bible is more than simply a _historical_ document. The Bible is also a _theological_ document, a _political_ document and an _etiological_ document.

THE BIBLE AS A THEOLOGICAL DOCUMENT

One of the central concerns of the authors and editors of the Scriptures was to present their understanding of God and religious conduct in a persuasive manner. Because the Bible is composed of materials spanning a millennium, it is understandable that the particular historical and cultural contexts of each author influenced their theological formulations, creating a substantial degree of theological diversity. Moreover, because each author was concerned about stating his case persuasively, there was a tendency to minimize the diversity within their own religious tradition, in the interest of presenting a clearly defined religious agenda which God had ordained before the beginning of time. Let's look at several examples of this theological diversity.

THE CONCEPT OF GOD AND THE AFTERLIFE. The Babylonian Exile roughly marks a theological watershed in the history of Israelite religion. The exilic and post-exilic prophets emphasized that God was a holy, righteous, transcendent being. The emphasis on God's separateness encouraged two other theological developments: post-exilic writers developed a well-defined angelology and the concept of an evil force--Satan--appeared on the scene.

A holy, transcendent God could no longer communicate _directly_ with man; he needed angelic beings to mediate his message. For instance, in late post-exilic Judaism it was believed that angels delivered the law to Moses, instead of receiving it from the hand of Yahweh (Acts 7:53; Gal. 3:19).

183

Similarly, a God who was righteous and good could not have a 'dark side'. Therefore the editor of I and II Chronicles (who lived after the Babylonian Exile) could not believe that God had incited King David to sin against him, as the editor of I and II Samuel had believed (II Sam. 24:1). Therefore he judiciously inserted that Satan had incited David to disobey God (I Chr. 21:1). This post-exilic shift in the conception of an utterly holy God represented a dramatic departure from the previous understanding that both good and evil came from God (Is. 45:7).

Since it was necessary to distance the location of evil from God, the 'logical' way out of the dilemma was to personify God's 'dark side' in the form of Satan. Only three references to "the accuser" are made in the Old Testament (Job 1:6ff.; Zech. 3:1ff; I Chr. 21:1), all of them being late passages. Two out of the three passages imply that Satan is in God's service and not an evil being. The concept of a personal devil was developed in the intertestamental period; and, by the time the New Testament was written, the belief in Satan was well established.

The theological diversity of the Bible is especially pronounced where speculation on the afterlife is concerned.

Pre-exilic perspectives on life after death were rather grim. The abode of the dead was "Sheol" or "the Pit" and strongly associated with the grave. The nether world was the fate of all men, both good and bad, and was an inhospitable place of darkness and desolation (Job 10:21-22; Ezek. 32:18; Is. 5:14, 14:9-11; Ps. 88:10-12). Occasionally we find the belief that Yahweh will deliver the faithful from the jaws of Sheol, although no concept of a resurrection is implied by this hope (Ps. 16:10, 49:15).

After the Exile a belief in the resurrection of the righteous began to develop (Is. 26:19; Dan. 12:2; II Mac. 7:9, 12:43). In the "intertestamental period" (the interim period between the Old and New Testament), it was believed that the wicked were not punished by eternal damnation; their fate was simple annihilation (II Mac. 7:14; Ps. Sol. 14:6; Test. Zeb. 10). By the time the New Testament was written, there was a full-blown concept of a general resurrection, where the righteous would receive heavenly rewards and the wicked would be damned for eternity (Mt. 5:22,

10:28; Mk. 9:43:48, 12:18-27; Lk. 16:19ff.).

THE CANAANITE COVER-UP.[34] The editors of the Deuteronomistic History (Deuteronomy through II Kings) tried to present a harmonized portrait of the way Israelite religion was supposed to be. Discrepant religious beliefs or practices were masked by either ignoring them or attributing them to some notorious figure (e.g., an 'evil' king). As we saw in the discussion on Canaanite religion in Chapter 5, the editor of I and II Samuel could not accept the fact that Saul, Jonathan and David each had named one of their sons after the Canaanite storm-god Baal, so the names were changed "to protect the innocent."[35]

Most of the time, though, the editors of the Deuteronomistic History displayed more ingenuity. They presented an ideal portrait of Israelite religion, a standard which supposedly existed since the time of Moses, and interpreted any departures from that norm as 'aberrant' religious practices . . . infections from Canaan. However, with the exception of a few short-lived 'reform' movements, it appears that the religion of Israel in pre-exilic times bears remarkable similarity to the Canaanite religious culture which the prophets so voraciously denounced.

What the Old Testament presents as religious 'reforms' are more likely religious innovations. As soon as the 'reformer' died, his successor promptly returned things to the status quo, and "did what was evil in the sight of Yahweh, according to all that his fathers had done." We know from anthropological studies that the religious institutions and practices of any culture are the most resistant to change; and, hence, we have every reason to believe that the religious institutions of Israel were just as conservative.

When Israelite religion is understood from the standpoint of religious 'aberrations' (the way things really were) instead of religious ideals (what the prophets hoped for), we discover some remarkable

---

[34] I am indebted to Professor G. W. Ahlström for introducing me to the approach to the study of Israelite religion that I used in this section.

[35] See p. 122ff.

things.

We know, for example, that Baal and Asherah--a Canaanite god and goddess--were worshiped rather consistently in the Jerusalem Temple (II Kg. 21:7, 23:4; Jer. 44:18-19), and that sacred prostitution was a regular feature of pre-exilic Israelite religion (I Kg. 14:24, 15:2; II Kg. 23:7). A more astounding fact is that human sacrifice was a routine religious rite which took place at the "roaster" (topheth) in the valley of Ben-Hinnom, near Jerusalem, up to the time of Jeremiah (II Kg. 16:3, 21:6, 23:10; Jer. 7:31; 19:5-6; Ezek. 16:21, 20:31, 23:39).[36]

This alternative portrait of Israelite religion was suppressed by most of the biblical authors and editors. They glazed over these discrepant religious practices by attributing them to the recalcitrance of God's chosen people or by selecting a few 'evil' kings as their primary scapegoats. Their attempt to revise the religious history of Israel was imaginative; but, unfortuntely, amounted to something less than an accurate portrayal of the history of Israelite religion.

THE PRESUMPTION OF MONOTHEISM. Moses is often considered history's first monotheist. Actually this is quite untrue. Monotheism, the belief in the existence of only one God, was a late arrival in the history of Israel, a belief especially pronounced in the writings of Deutero-Isaiah during the Babylonian Exile (Is. 41:29, 43:10, 44:8ff., 45:5-6, 21). If we are in search of history's first monotheist, we must turn to an enigmatic Egyptian Pharaoh named Akhenaton (14th century BCE) who worshiped the sun as a universal and beneficent deity.

For the editors of the Deuteronomistic History, the official party-line on the nature of God was strongly monotheistic: "Hear, O Israel: The Lord our God is one Lord" (Deut. 6:4). This tenet--fundamental to Judaism and known as the Sh^{e}ma--certainly does not reflect Israelite beliefs before the Babylonian Exile.

---

[36] For more information on human sacrifice in Israel, see R. de Vaux, Ancient Israel, pp. 441ff.

At best, the Israelite religion could be classified as henotheistic, that is, one god is worshiped but other gods are believed to exist (Ex. 15:11; Ps. 82:1, 89:7, 95:3, 97:9). It was thought that each country had a guardian deity, and Yahweh was Israel's god (Deut. 32:8ff). One of Israel's warrior-deliverers, Jephthah, even argued that Moab should be satisfied with the land that Chemosh (the god of Moab) gives them, just as Israelites can legitimately lay claim to land that Yahweh gives to Israel (Jg. 11:24). Yahweh was so strongly associated with the land of Palestine that Naaman, a Syrian general, believed that in order to worship Yahweh in his homeland, he had to transport some Israelite soil back to Syria (II Kg. 5:17).[37]

An interesting example of the Israelite belief in the existence of foreign gods appears in a story about a joint military campaign by Israel and Judah against the Moabites in approximately 850 BCE (II Kg. 3). Moab had been Israel's vassal; and, with the death of Ahab, the king of Moab (Mesha) saw an opportune time to gain political independence for his country.

The prophet Elisha accompanied the warring troops in their difficult approach to Moabite territory via the Dead Sea. The troops were in desperate need of water. Elisha directed the commanders to dig cisterns in a dry river bed and prophesied that a miraculous flow of water would soon occur. The water came; the troops were refreshed; and Elisha boldly prophesied that the armies of Moab would be defeated.

The Moabites launched a pre-emptive attack on the forces of Israel and Judah. However, the Moabite troops were routed, and the capital, Kir-hareseth, was besieged. Mesha, the king of Moab, realized that he was in desperate straits and took a drastic measure to save the country from defeat. The king sacrificed his elder son, presumably to the national god Chemosh, on top of the city wall.

The biblical account assumes that this extreme

---

[37] For a concise discussion of the concept of God in early Israelite religion, see Helmer Ringgren, _Israelite Religion_, trans. by D. Green (Philadelphia: Fortress Press, 1966), pp. 66-88.

act of piety unleashed the power of Chemosh, so that "there came great wrath upon Israel." The troops suddenly withdrew and left Moab. Elisha's prophecy of victory was foiled, apparently because the armies of Israel and Judah were "off their own turf."

PROPHECY AND FULFILLMENT.[38] Most Popular Christians assume that many events in Jesus' life, as reported by the Gospels, were prophesied in the Old Testament. It is thought that these predictions are so unambiguous that the inability of the Jewish people to recognize Jesus as their Messiah can only be attributed to their 'spiritual blindness', 'legalism', or 'hardness of heart'. In point of fact, though, many of the Old Testament passages which the New Testament writers adduced as 'proofs' of Jesus' messiahship were taken out of their original context and were radically reinterpreted to build their case.

The Jews of Jesus' time interpreted the Old Testament by means of highly subjective principles of interpretation which made liberal use of typology, allegory and loose paraphrase. From the standpoint of modern observers, this method of exegesis "played fast and free" with the text, in a way that obscured its original meaning. Understandably the New Testament writers adopted this method of "rabbinic interpretation" in their references to the Old Testament. It was a perfectly acceptable way of constructing an argument at that time. Nowadays this way of interpreting the Bible seems obviously deficient.

The New Testament authors were anxious to demonstrate that Jesus was, in fact, the Anointed One, who was anticipated by the Scriptures. Their task was certainly not easy. Behind the New Testament rationalization that Jesus came not to destroy the Law but to fulfill it, the Jesus of history actually undermined a great deal of the Mosaic Law. Jesus declared all foods clean (Mk. 7:15). In so doing, he annulled much of the ritual law of the Old Testament. He showed disrespect for the Mosaic legislation concerning the Sabbath (Mk. 2:23-28, 3:1-6; Lk. 13:10-17, 14:1-6; cp. Deut. 5:12ff.; Num. 15:32ff.). Jesus

---

[38] I have based this section on material provided by James D. G. Dunn, _Unity and Diversity in the New Testament_ (London: SCM Press, 1977), pp. 81ff.

repealed the Mosaic principle of "an eye for an eye, and a tooth for a tooth" and insisted that love and forgiveness should prevail (Mt. 5:38ff.; cp. Lev. 24: 20; Deut. 19:21). He dispensed with the Old Testament custom of taking divine oaths (Mt. 5:33; cp. Num. 30:2; Deut. 23: 21) and abolished the Mosaic law for divorce (Mt. 19:3-9; Mk. 10:2ff., cp. Deut. 24:1). In short, by some Jewish canons of theological propriety, Jesus was a heretic!

The writers of the New Testament were consumed by the theological purpose of presenting Jesus as the Messiah--the Deliverer-Redeemer who was expected since the time of the Babylonian Exile. To defend this conviction, it was necessary to marshall as much support as possible from the Hebrew scriptures. Given this strong theological intention, along with the loose method of biblical interpretation that was prac-ticed in that day, the New Testament authors often used the Old Testament in a highly selective, 'mislead-ing' manner. At times they actually created prophecies by claiming that a prediction was fulfilled when the scripture they quoted cannot even be found in the Old Testament (Mt. 2:23; Lk. 11:49; Jn. 7:38; I. Cor. 2:9; Jas. 4:5). On other occasions, the New Testament writers constructed prophecies by combining two or more different Old Testament passages into one (Mt. 21:5, 13; 27:9-10; Rom. 9:33; 11:8; II Cor. 6:16-18; Gal. 3:8; Heb. 10:37ff., 13:5).

Sometimes the New Testament authors altered an Old Testament passage to fit their purposes. For example, Paul referred to Psalm 68:18 in his discussion of the resurrection and spiritual gifts (Eph. 4:8ff.). The Psalm portrays Yahweh ascending Mt. Zion, the Temple mount, with a host of captives who pay tribute to him. Paul changed the Psalm to read "he gave gifts to men" instead of the original: "receiving gifts among men."

On another occasion, Paul argued that the promise of Christ was contained in God's covenant with Abraham (Gal. 3:16ff.). The covenant promised that Abraham and his "seed" (i.e., his descendants) would possess the land of Canaan (Gen. 12:7). The Greek translation of the Old Testament--the Septuagint--translated the Hebrew word for 'seed' (zera^c) with the word sperma, a collective singular. Paul used that translation to press his point that Christ was foreshadowed in the promise of Abraham, as Abraham's seed (singular). Of course, it makes absolutely no sense to understand the original promise in this way, as the promise clearly refers to 'seed' in the plural sense (i.e., Abraham's descendants).

Often passages were referred to Jesus that bear no relation to his messianic vocation. For example, some New Testament authors appropriated Psalm 2:7 in their understanding of Jesus' relationship with God: "You are my son, today I have begotten you." The Psalm was composed for the coronation and enthronement ceremony for one of Judah's kings. Throughout the ancient Near East it was commonly believed that the king was the viceroy of god. In Egyptian religion, during the Old Kingdom period, this belief was taken to the extreme in the idea that Pharoah was the incarnation of Horus. Of course, most Israelites did not believe that the king was God incarnate, although Psalm 45:6, taken literally, addresses the king as God. In any event, the king was embued with sacred authority and viewed as God's very son.[39] The New Testament writers used this royal song in two different ways. In the Synoptic Gospels the passage was applied to Jesus' baptism at the Jordan (Mt. 3:16; Mk. 1:11; Lk. 3:22). By contrast, Paul and the writer of Hebrews thought that the royal song referred to Jesus' resurrection (Acts 13:33; Heb. 1:5, 5:5).

A famous example of a prophecy taken out of context concerns the tradition that Jesus was born of a virgin. Only Matthew and Luke are familiar with the idea of a virgin birth; Mark, John and Paul seem to be unacquainted with the concept. Matthew (1:23) portrays Jesus' miraculous birth from a virgin as the fulfillment of a prophecy by Isaiah (7:14). Isaiah predicted that a child would be born to Ahaz, the king of Judah, who would succeed Ahaz and usher in an era of prosperity and national prestige. The child would be born to a young woman (ᵓalemah), and the prophecy understands the birth as a natural event. The Septuagint translated the Hebrew term for "young woman" with a Greek term (parthenos) which sometimes means 'virgin'. Matthew followed this translation and seized an opportunity to relate the tradition

---

[39] See Johannes C. de Moor, New Year with Canaanites and Israelites, Vol. 1 (Kampen, Netherlands: Kok, 1972), pp. 26ff.; Ringgren, Israelite Religion, pp. 220ff.

about Jesus' miraculous birth to an Old Testament prophecy, by applying the prophecy to Jesus.

In a few instances it seems that certain details of Jesus' life--as portrayed by the Gospels--were themselves shaped by messianic prophecies. For example, Micah 5:2 was an important messianic prophecy which indicated that God's anointed ruler would come from Bethlehem, the home of David. It was believed that this ideal king would be of David's lineage. Matthew and Luke were especially concerned with portraying Jesus as coming from the line of David. Both writers include elaborate genealogies within their gospels which present Jesus as a blood relative of David (Mt. 1:1ff.; Lk. 3:23ff.); however, the genealogies are different and their details cannot be reconciled.

We can be fairly sure that Jesus' family came from Nazareth (Lk. 2:4), and it seems reasonable to assume that he was also born there. Apparently Jesus' contemporaries doubted that he could be the Messiah because he was a Galilean, not born of the house of David (Mk. 12:35-37).

Faced with the dilemma of reconciling the details of Jesus' life with the prophecy of Micah 5:2, Luke presented Jesus' birth as taking place in Bethlehem, during a historically dubious Roman census[40] which took place before the death of Herod the Great (Lk. 2:1ff.). Matthew was less artful in solving the dilemma. According to him, Jesus' family always lived in Bethlehem but eventually emigrated to Nazareth in order to escape the long arm of Herod (Mt. 2:1ff.). Matthew claims that the trek to Nazareth was providential because the prophets had stated that the Messiah "will be called a Nazarene" (Mt. 2:23). In point of fact, though, the Old Testament knows of no such prophecy.

THE EMPTY TOMB. The theological purposes of the Gospel writers can be discerned in their depiction of an event that was enshrouded in historical

---

[40] For a discussion of the historical problems, see Joseph A. Fitzmyer, S.J., The Gospel According to Luke (I-IX), The Anchor Bible, Vol. 28 (Garden City, New York: Doubleday, 1981), pp. 400-405.

obscurity: the resurrection of Jesus. The reports of Jesus' resurrection, as they filtered out of Jesus' small band of disciples, were charged with emotion and wrapt in wonderment. Could it be true that Jesus was no longer dead? Who was the first to see the risen Lord? Was the promised Kingdom of God now at hand?

It has long been recognized that the Gospel accounts of the empty tomb and Jesus' resurrection appearances differ from one another in their essential details. The discrepancies are real and cannot be harmonized by the argument that each account was colored by each writer's perception of the event. This fact has led some to believe that the resurrection was never a historical actuality. Others, like myself, believe that a historical core lies behind the discrepant accounts of the empty tomb and Jesus' appearances to his disciples, a kernel of truth which makes belief in the resurrected Christ far more than a capricious theological preference. Nonetheless the confusion of the Gospel accounts of Jesus' resurrection highlights the centrality of faith to mature Christian commitment.

The Gospel narratives of the empty tomb show disagreement on nearly every detail (Mt. 28:1-10; Mk. 16:1-8; Lk. 24:1-11; Jn. 20:1-18). In Mark the women purchased spices to embalm Jesus' body after the Sabbath, whereas Luke 23:56 reports that the spices were acquired before the Sabbath. In John's account, Joseph of Arimathea and Nicodemus prepared Jesus body for burial and there is no mention of the women's involvement (19:38-40).

All of the Gospel narratives mention that a large stone sealed the tomb after Jesus' body was placed in it. Mark, Luke and John report that the stone was rolled away when the tomb was visited on Sunday morning. By contrast, Matthew's account states that the stone was in place when Mary Magdalene and her party arrived at the tomb. An earthquake occurred; an angel appeared and removed the stone; and the Roman guards were terrified. Apparently Matthew was interested in repudiating the idea that Jesus' disciples had stolen his body (28:15). Therefore he added a section which had the chief priests lobbying Pilate for a contingent of Roman troops to guard the tomb (27:62-66) and a story about the bribing of the guards after the tomb was found empty (28:11-15).

192

Divine messengers were involved in all four Gospel narratives. In Mark a "young man" sat calmly inside the tomb, whereas Matthew's account has an angel rolling away the massive stone that blocked the tomb. By contrast, the accounts in Luke and John involve two divine messengers.

All of the Gospel accounts agree that Mary Magdalene was among the first to see the empty tomb. In Matthew, Mark and Luke, Mary is in the company of other women (bringing spices and ointments to prepare Jesus' body). In John, Mary is alone, as Joseph of Arimathea and Nicodemus had prepared the body for burial earlier. Also John's account has Mary leaving the tomb before she saw the two angels in order to summon Simon Peter and "the one whom Jesus loved." Peter and the "other disciple" ran, beheld the empty tomb and departed for their homes.

The accounts in Matthew and John state that Mary Magdalene was the first to see the Risen Lord. By contrast, Luke (24:34) suggests that Peter was the first to behold the resurrected Jesus. Presumably Luke was concerned about apostolic authority or felt that Mary was not a credible witness, given her past psychological instability (Lk. 8:2).[41] Mark is silent about any resurrection appearances! In Matthew's Gospel, Mary Magdalene and the "other Mary" met Jesus as they were running to tell the disciples about the empty tomb. When they saw Jesus they "took hold of his feet and worshiped him" (28:9). John's report of the incident is much different. Mary Magdalene is alone and sees Jesus at the tomb, mistaking him for the gardener. In sharp contrast to Matthew's account, Jesus expressly warns her not to touch him.

According to Matthew, Luke and John, the women who first discovered the empty tomb quickly returned to tell the other disciples. Mark, on the other hand, reports that the women were so afraid that they kept the discovery a secret.

Discrepancies of this sort are not confined to the Gospel narratives about the empty tomb. The biblical accounts of Jesus' resurrection appearances are

---

[41]Robert M. Grant, A Historical Introduction to the New Testament (New York: Harper and Row, 1963), p. 372.

also contradictory and were shaped by the theological purpose of the Gospel writers.[42] There is also disagreement concerning other details of Jesus' life and ministry in the New Testament. Conservative scholars often try to harmonize these discrepancies by treating similar (but contradictory) accounts as representing two different events in the life of Jesus, instead of one event with two discrepant accounts. Since there was only one first encounter with the empty tomb, this approach cannot be used.

THE BIBLE AS A POLITICAL DOCUMENT

The authors and editors of the Bible were not only motivated by theological concerns but also were sometimes influenced by political biases. Given the inextricable relationship between religion and politics throughout the ancient Near East, it stands to reason that the biblical writings have strong political overtones. The ancient Israelites certainly made no rigid distinction between "church and state." Religious institutions often functioned to legitimate the policies of the king. Some material contained within the Bible is frankly little more than crass political propaganda. Most often, though, the political biases of the biblical authors are subtle and submerged beneath their overt theological intentions.

THE SIN OF JEROBOAM. The history of Israel and Judah, as the Bible presents it, was edited from a Judean (or 'southern') perspective. A cursory reading of the books of Kings and Chronicles yields the impression that the kings of Israel (the 'Northern Kingdom') exude corruption and can do no right. The biblical editors cast the history of the Northern Kingdom under the shadow of "the sin of Jeroboam."

Jeroboam was the administrator in Solomon's regime who was in charge of forced labor for the Northern Kingdom. It was a common practice in the ancient Near East for kings to conscript short-term slave labor from their own subjects for their building projects. King Solomon's immense building programs

---

[42]See Norman Perrin, The Resurrection Narratives: A New Approach (London: SCM Press, 1977).

demanded a great deal of taxes and forced labor, and it appears that the burden fell squarely on Israel's shoulders and Judah's population was exempt (I Kg. 4). When Solomon died, the people of Israel asked to be relieved of this unfair burden (I Kg. 12:4). King Rehoboam, Solomon's successor, refused to heed their complaints and a rebellion, led by Jeroboam, ensued.

The biblical writers blamed Jeroboam for splitting Israel and Judah, but actually the United Monarchy under David and Solomon was a tenuous enterprise, at best. The attitude which characterized the populace of Israel was that they had no kinship with David (II Sam. 20:1; I Kg. 12:16).

Nonetheless, in the eyes of the biblical writers, Jeroboam became the archfiend of Israelite history. He was accused of introducing foreign deities and corrupting the North's religious sensibilities.

Jeroboam established two sanctuaries at Bethel (a famous religious center) and Dan. For each of these rival temples, Jeroboam made a golden calf. Since we know that the Northern Kingdom was a bastion of traditional Yahwehism (Jerusalem, at the time, was a recently conquered Jebusite city and the Israelites were offended by Solomon's religious syncretism), it stands to reason that the bull image must have been a familiar way of depicting Yahweh at that time. The bull was a symbol of the Canaanite god El, with whom Yahweh was associated at an early date. Jeroboam could never have introduced a non-traditional iconography for Yahweh. At a later date, even Jehu's fierce tirade against Baal worship in the Northern Kingdom left the bull images untouched (II Kg. 10:28-29); hence, they were symbols of Yahweh, not Baal.

Ironically Jeroboam's attempt to bring back "the old time religion" won him a place of infamy in the 'official' history of Israel. The story about the golden calf (Ex. 32) probably originated as a polemic against Jeroboam's rival sanctuaries. The sinister "sin of Jeroboam" had absolutely nothing to do with religion . . . it was a sin of the political sort . . . a sin that ultimately stemmed from Solomon's unjust policy of taxation and Rehoboam's political ineptitude.[43]

ANTI-SEMITISM AND THE NEW TESTAMENT. Adolf Hitler's "final solution"--the extermination of the Jews--must strike every human being, who retains a thread of moral conscience, as despicable and utterly abhorrent. Nonetheless Christians must recognize that Hitler never could have executed his insane scheme without a bed of Christian anti-semitism on which to build.

The face of contemporary Christianity is pocked with a history of the persecution of the Jews. During the First Crusade of 1096, many Christians felt that the crusaders may as well take care of the "infidels at home" while they marched to wrest Palestine from Islamic control. Their religious zeal translated into the massacre of many Jews who were forced to choose between baptism or death. About one fourth to one third of the Jewish population of Germany and Northern France perished in the name of Christian love!

The Jews were even blamed for the terrible plague which ravaged Europe in the 14th century: the Black Death. Because Jewish laws concerning ritual washing checked the spread of the plague in many Jewish communities, rumors spread that the Jews had poisoned Christian wells. In blind retaliation, Christians razed Jewish communities, led massacres, and Jews everywhere were placed on trial and executed, in order to satisfy the Christian need of a scapegoat for their present misfortune.

Also, throughout Europe, for several centuries, numerous church councils, popes and civil rulers repeatedly tried to compel Jews to wear the "badge of shame"--[44] a foreboding presage of Hitler's Third Reich.

The antipathy toward the Jews was not confined to crazed mobs or corrupt civil officials. Even

---

[43]See Frank M. Cross, _Canaanite Myth and Hebrew Epic_ (Cambridge, Mass.: Harvard University Press, 1973), pp. 73-75.

[44]Edward Flannery, _The Anguish of the Jews_ (New York: Macmillan, 1965), pp. 90-2, 103, 109-110.

learned Christian theologians succumbed to the belief that the Jews were inferior, "because of their unbelief."

An extreme manifestation of Christian anti-semitism is found in a treatise that Martin Luther, the leader of the Protestant Reformation, penned later in his life. In the vituperous treatise entitled, "On the Jews and Their Lies," he warned Christians to

> be on guard against the Jews, knowing that wherever they have their synagogues, nothing is found but a den of devils in which sheer self-glory, conceit, lies, blasphemy, and defaming of God and men are practiced most maliciously and vehemently. . . .

Later in the treatise, Luther poses the rhetorical question: "What shall we Christians do with this rejected and condemned people, the Jews?" He heartily recommends the following course of action:

> First, to set fire to their synagogues or schools and to burn and cover with dirt whatever will not burn, so that no man will ever again see a stone or cinder of them.

> Second, I advise that their houses also be razed and destroyed. . . .

> Third, I advise that all their prayer books and Talmudic writings . . . be taken from them. . . .

> Fourth, I advise that their rabbis be forbidden to teach henceforth on pain of loss of limb and life. . . .

> Fifth, I advise that safe-conduct on the highways be abolished for the Jews. . . .

> Sixth, I advise that usury be prohibited to them and that all cash and treasure of silver and gold be taken from them and put

197

aside for safekeeping. . . .[45]

The battle-cry of mindless Christian persecution against the Jewish people down through the ages has been: The Jews killed Jesus! Although Christians may be loath to admit it, the seeds of later Christian anti-Semitism can be found in the New Testament itself.

Of course, technically it is incorrect to speak of anti-Semitism with reference to the New Testament, as most of the New Testament was written by people of Jewish descent. The terms 'anti-Jewish' or 'anti-Judaism' would be more precise. Nonetheless I will retain the term 'anti-Semitism' for the sake of convenience.

In the presentation of Jesus' trial and crucifixion in the Gospels, we are struck with a fundamental incongruity. On the one hand, we <u>know</u> that Jesus died from a uniquely <u>Roman</u> form of punishment (crucifixion) at the hands of <u>Roman</u> soldiers, under the direct jurisdiction of <u>Pilate</u>, the <u>Roman</u> governor. On the other hand, we are <u>told</u> that the Jewish leaders were to blame for this miscarriage of justice; that they brought Jesus to trial, orchestrated a series of false witnesses, organized the crowds, and compelled Pilate to abdicate his rightful authority by ordering an execution which he himself thought was undeserved. In short, the strong impression conveyed by the Gospels is that the Romans killed Jesus but the Jews were actually to blame.

It is widely recognized by New Testament scholarship that the Gospel accounts of Jesus' life were shaped by the personal circumstances and purposes of the writers. The earliest Gospel--Mark--was written around 70 CE, about 40 years after Jesus' crucifixion. Matthew and Luke were written in the decade or two following Mark's composition. Both books build upon Mark's presentation, freely deleting or adding material when it suited their purposes. Many scholars think that Matthew and Luke also made use of an unnamed source for Jesus' life and teachings, which for the sake of convenience, has been called 'Q' (after the German word <u>Quell</u>, meaning 'source').

---

[45]In Theodore Tappert, ed., <u>Luther's Works</u>, Vol. 47 (Philadelphia: Fortress Press, 1971), pp. 172, 268-270.

Matthew, Mark and Luke are generally called the "Synoptic Gospels" because they present Jesus' life and teachings within a similar framework and utilize parallel materials. By contrast, the Gospel of John presents an account of Jesus' life which is sharply different from synoptic accounts--in terms of both chronology and content. It seems likely that John is to be dated sometime between 90-100 CE.[46]

The Gospel writers wrote during a time when Christianity was emerging from Palestine and beginning to spread throughout the Roman Empire. Naturally, they wished to present the life of Jesus in the best possible light, in a way that would facilitate the Christian mission to the Gentiles. In a broad sense, this could be called the 'political' purpose of the Gospel writers.

We can imagine that the first Gentile Christians were somewhat embarrassed by the fact that Jesus was executed by the Roman government. What did Christianity's founder do to merit such a stern punishment? Assuming that there was some complicity on the part of Jewish officials in the Roman execution of Jesus, it was quite easy for the Gospel writers to pin the blame for Jesus' death on the Jewish leaders in Jerusalem, thereby de-emphasizing Roman involvement in the matter.

But the 'political' agenda of evangelizing the Roman Empire cannot account for the strong antipathy toward the Jews that is reflected in the Gospels of Matthew and John. Both of these writers narrate Jesus' life and teachings in such a way that their own anti-Jewish prejudice is clearly evident.

In the case of Matthew, we can surmise that he was engaged in a longstanding debate with a group of Pharisees in his own community and felt exasperated with Jewish arguments against Christian beliefs, particularly in regard to the idea that the disciples

---

[46]For further information on the composition and dating of the New Testament, see W. G. Kümmel, Introduction to the New Testament, 14th ed., trans. by A. J. Mattill, Jr. (Nashville: Abingdon Press, 1966).

stole Jesus' body and faked the resurrection.[47]
Matthew's concern to discredit "the scribes and Pharisees" reflects his desire to convert both Jew and
Gentile to Christianity, an intention that is clear
from other features of his book.

By contrast, John shows little concern for the
evangelization of the Jews and is preoccupied with
the Christian mission to the Gentile world. The "Jews"
are cast as opponents of Christianity, the outsiders
who crucified Jesus and now are condemned because
of their unbelief. The Gospel of John, written at
a later date, reflects an intensification of the conflict between Christians and Jews. Apparently, Jewish
Christians at this time were expelled from the syna-
gogues (Jn. 9:22, 16:2, cp. 9:22), a practice which
must have deterred some potential Jewish converts
to Christianity. John himself believed that soon
Jews would begin to assassinate Christians, thinking
that they were "offering service to God" (Jn. 16:2b).
His paranoia produced the most anti-Semitic passages
of the New Testament, as we shall see momentarily.[48]

The Gospel of Matthew contains several subtle
hints of the writer's anti-Jewish sentiment. For
example, in Matthew's version of the parable of the
wedding feast (22:1-14), he implicitly makes the Jews
responsible for Jesus' death. The story is about
a king who celebrated his son's marriage by inviting
a select group of his subjects to a gala feast. The
king's heralds announced the feast, but everyone ignored the invitation. In Luke's version of the parable
(14:16-24), the king interpreted the rebuff as justification for going out to the highways and byways to
"bring in the poor and maimed and blind and lame."
However, in Matthew's version, the select group of
subjects (i.e., the Jews) actually killed the king's
heralds (not simply refusing the invitation). Upon

---

[47] See Samuel Sandmel, Anti-Semitism in the New Testament? (Philadelphia: Fortress Press, 1978), pp.
49-70.

[48] See C. K. Barrett, The Gospel of John and Judaism,
trans. by D. M. Smith (Philadelphia: Fortress Press,
1975), pp. 70-2; Raymond Brown, The Community of the
Beloved Disciple (New York: Paulist Press, 1979),
pp. 40-3, 66-9; Sandmel, Anti-Semitism in the New
Testament?, pp. 101-119.

learning of the outrage, the king sent "his troops and destroyed those murderers and burned their city" (an obvious reference to the destruction of Jerusalem by the Romans in 70 CE). After the massacre, the king instructed his servants to gather all the people they could find (i.e., the Gentiles), both good and bad, and to bring them to the feast.

Two passages in Matthew are especially hostile to the Jewish people. The first is Matthew 23. The entire chapter is a lengthy, caustic invective against the Jews--placed in the mouth of Jesus--which has no parallel in the New Testament. The writer's profound bitterness toward the Jews is unleashed with unmistakable fury throughout the chapter. The "scribes and Pharisees" are called "hypocrites," "blind guides," "whitewashed tombs," "brood of vipers," "blind fools," "blind Pharisees" and "serpents." These Jews are condemned to hell and held liable for the murder of all innocent people (23:33-35). Matthew's tirade against the Jews even accuses them of crucifying the prophets of God (crucifixion was never practiced by the Jews but was a distinctly Roman punishment).

The second strongly anti-Semitic passage in Matthew appears in the account of Jesus before Pilate (27:11-26). Pilate, the Roman governor, is portrayed as a good-intentioned but weak-willed administrator who was forced to sentence Jesus to death in order to prevent a riot. In a passage without parallel in the other synoptic accounts, Matthew explicitly makes the Jews responsible for Jesus' death. The text states that Pilate took a basin of water and

> washed his hands before the crowd, saying, 'I am innocent of this man's blood; see to it yourselves'. And all the people answered, 'His blood be on us and on our children!' (27:24b-25)

Matthew's insertion of these words, inspired by his own personal bitterness, inadvertently fueled horrid mob actions against the Jews--"Christ-killers"--for centuries to come.

If Matthew occasionally lapses into anti-Semitism, the Gospel of John, relatively speaking, presents a constant barrage of anti-Jewish sentiment. Where the Synoptic Gospels refer to certain groups of Jews (e.g., the Sanhedrin, the Pharisees, the Scribes, the High Priest), John simply lumps them all into

201

the same category: "the Jews." John's use of the term was not the outcome of sloppy semantic skills. We must remember that John wrote during a period of escalating tensions between Jews and Christians. As Fr. Raymond Brown points out, "John deliberately uses the same term for the Jewish authorities of Jesus' time and for the hostile inhabitants of the synagogue in his own time."[49]

Throughout the Book of John we see a violent, exaggerated depiction of Jesus' conflict with the local Jewish authorities. On two occasions "the Jews" tried to stone Jesus (8:59, 10:31). Early in the Gospel, when Jesus healed on the Sabbath, John presents "the Jews" as beginning to plot Jesus' death (5:18). Although John does not have a lengthy discourse enumerating the faults of Judaism like Matthew 23, he does manage to place some rabid, anti-Semitic words in the mouth of Jesus. John's version of Jesus has him telling "the Jews" that they did not have Abraham as their father; instead, he says, "you are of your father the devil, and your will is to do your father's desires" (8:44).

The writer of John may have been a Jew himself, but he writes as one who has thoroughly dissociated himself from the Jewish people. As a consequence, his version of the life of Jesus sometimes borders on being comical. For example, John has Jesus--a Jew--referring to the general public as "the Jews" (13:33). When a blind man was healed on the Sabbath, the text says that his Jewish parents did not confirm their son's blindness from birth, "because they feared the Jews" (9:22). This makes about as much sense as saying that a native-born U.S. citizen "feared the Americans." Also the writer of John refers to the Mosaic Law with the same vocabulary of dissociation. The Law is referred to as "your law" or "their law" by the Jesus portrayed by John (10:34, 15:25).

Like Matthew, John lays the blame for Jesus' death squarely on the shoulders of the Jews. In fact, John conveys the impression that "the Jews" actually did the crucifying themselves (19:16)! It is interesting that an apocryphal book--the Gospel of Peter--even went beyond John's suggestive language, making the Jews explicitly responsible for carrying out Jesus'

---

[49]Brown, The Community of the Beloved Disciple, p. 41.

execution, with no mention of any Roman involvement.[50]

How much pain would have been averted, how many
lives saved, how many tears would have been unnecessary, if the Gospel writers had played it straight
with the facts? No sensitive Christian can meditate
on this question without feeling pangs of grief, some
sense of responsibility for the religious intolerance
of our forebears.

Sadly, the politics of evangelization perverted
the truth; the convert was sought at the price of
denigrating the opponent; and Jesus' proclamation
of love--ratified by his own blood--was turned into
an occasion for pointing the finger . . . an opportunity for blood-letting. What was in fact the word
of man became the Word of God, and Christians down
through the centuries went out into the world with
a tarnished image of Christ, an image marred with
the imprint of ignorance, imperialism and intolerance.

THE BIBLE AS AN ETIOLOGICAL DOCUMENT

In addition to being a theological and political
document, the Bible is also an etiological document.
In other words, certain passages in the Scriptures
arose from the need to explain the origin of some
contemporary reality, to account for some phenomenon
by identifying its causes. In this section we will
look at a few stories that had their primary raison
d'être in the need to explain the origin of some particular phenomenon.

CREATION STORIES. Since the dawn of human rationality, the Homo sapien has queried about his origins,
his place in the cosmos. Where did I come from?
How was the world created? Why was I brought into
existence?

The Bible contains not one but at least three
different creation stories! Those who ardently defend
"biblical creationism" rarely, if ever, realize that

---

[50] See E. Henneke (ed. by W. Schneemelcher), New Testament
Apocrypha, Vol. 1, trans. by R. McL. Wilson (Philadelphia: Westminster Press, 1963), pp. 183ff.

the Bible presents more than one account of the origin of the universe.

The most famous creation story appears in Genesis 1:1-2:4a. We are told that God created the universe and all creatures therein in six days and rested on the seventh. The most distinctive aspects of the story--in comparison to other creation myths in the ancient Near East--is that the account is monothe-istic,[51] it assumes that creation took place without pre-existent matter, and it accords to human beings a pre-eminent place in the created order. The content of the story may have had a long history, but the present composition is late and originated in "priestly circles" during the Exile.

Many scholars have conjectured whether Genesis 1:1-2:4a borrowed extensively from an ancient Babylo-nian creation story named the _Enūma Elish_.[52] Both the Genesis and the Babylonian accounts share the concept of a primeval darkness, the idea that creation emerged from the division of a great primeval ocean, the presence of light before luminaries were created, and both stories have man created after everything else. But the differences between the two accounts are even more prominent than the similarities. Al-though the question is moot, it seems unlikely that the Genesis account borrowed directly from the _Enūma Elish_.

A second, less majestic, creation account appears in Genesis 2:4b-25. In this story the order of

---

[51]Genesis 1:26 poses a special problem. The text states that God said, "Let us make man in our own image." Because this creation account is exilic and originated in 'priestly circles', it seems best to interpret the plural as referring to the multitude of angels that surround Yahweh [cp. I Kg. 22:19ff.; Is. 6:2; Ps. 80:1, 99:1; Ezek. 1:5ff.; Job 1; see Gerhard Von Rad, _Genesis_ (Philadelphia: Westminster Press, 1972), pp. 58-9]. It seems unlikely that we have a reference here to the earlier henotheistic idea of a heavenly council of the gods where Yahweh presides (e.g., Ps. 89:5-8).

[52]For a full discussion, see Alexander Heidel, _The Babyl-nian Genesis_, 2nd ed. (Chicago: University of Chicago Press, 1951), pp. 82ff.

creation was reversed. In contrast to the first account, a male human being was created before any plants germinated or any animals roamed the earth. The first man was formed from the dust of the earth and placed in a garden, planted by God.

Our prototypical man did not have time to lounge around in this delectable paradise. The "work ethic" made its appearance from the very start, as Adam was kept busy by the task of naming every living creature that inhabited the earth. Soon God realized that man would not be content without a companion of his own. As a consequence, God made the first woman from Adam's rib.

A third creation story, less developed than the Genesis stories, appears in Psalms 74:12-17. This poetic creation account refers to Yahweh's conquest over a primeval sea-monster named Leviathan (Is. 27:1; Ps. 104:26; Job 3:8, 41:1), who was known in Ugarit as Lotan. Yahweh's power in creation is also manifest by his domination of Prince Yam, the powerful Canaanite god of the sea (see pp. 123ff.).

> Yet God, my king, is from ancient times,
>   working salvation in the midst of the earth.
> You shattered Yam (Sea) with your might,
>   and smashed the heads of sea-monsters;
> You crushed the heads of Leviathan,
>   and gave him as food for the desert-dwellers.
> You broke open the springs and streams,
>   and dried up ever-flowing rivers.
> To you belongs the day, even also the night;
>   You have established luminaries and the sun.
> You determined all the borders of the earth;
>   You have made summer and winter.
>   (Ps. 74:12-17, my translation)

Predictably those who argue most adamantly in favor of the historicity of the Genesis creation accounts are silent when it comes to Yahweh's decisive battle with the proud Leviathan, the dragon-like sea-monster that had to be destroyed before God could establish order.

THE WALLS OF JERICHO. The story of the Israelite's destruction of the Canaanite city of Jericho is certainly the most famous of Israel's conquest stories (Jos. 5:11-6:27).

The Bible says that Joshua, the leader of the Israelites, met up with an unnamed divine visitor who identified himself as "the commander of the Lord's army." After paying homage to the angelic being, Joshua was instructed by Yahweh to march Israel's army around the impregnable city of Jericho once a day for six days. On the seventh day the Israelites were supposed to circle the city's walls seven times. During their seventh rotation, the people were to shout in unison, and God promised that the walls of Jericho would tumble down.

Joshua and the people of Israel obeyed Yahweh's instructions, and we are told that the massive walls crumbled through divine intervention. The Israelites promptly killed every man, woman, child and all the animals (except for Rahab and her father's household), but saved the precious metals for Yahweh's treasury.

With the advent of scientific archaeology, we now know that Jericho certainly was <u>not</u> a walled city during the period during which an Israelite conquest must be dated.[53] In the 14th century BCE there was a small, <u>undefended</u> village at Jericho, but the remains are scanty and the site was abandoned for 600 years thereafter.

Following the destruction of Jericho, the Bible details a conflict with a city named Ai (Jos. 7:1-8:29). The Israelites tried to destroy the city but were unable to do so, because Yahweh was punishing the people of Israel for "the sin of Achan" (he took for himself some of the booty which had been earmarked for destruction). After the Israelites killed Achan and all his family and animals, they went into battle again and won. The text reports that all of the inhabitants of Ai were killed, numbering 12,000 (Jos. 8:25).

In point of fact, though, the city was not even inhabited at this time! The biblical Ai (present day et-Tell) was a prominent city in the Early Bronze Age which was abandoned in c. 2400 BCE. The townsite remained unoccupied for over a thousand years! In the 13th century BCE a small, undefended village

---

[53]Kenyon, <u>Archaeology in the Holy Land</u>, pp. 180-2, 207-8, 331-2.

inhabited the site.[54]

The conquest stories of Jericho and Ai provided the early Israelites with an etiology of the prominent ruins at both ancient city sites. Beyond explaining the origin of these ruins, the stories have the theological purpose of underscoring the necessity of holy war (i.e., Yahweh fighting on Israel's behalf) for the nation's welfare. Also each conquest narrative has a secondary story associated with it (i.e., the story of Rahab with Jericho and Achan's sin with Ai).

While we can only speculate on the history of these compositions, we can be sure that the walls of Jericho were already rubble when the Israelites arrived on the scene and that Ai's doomed inhabitants missed their appointed day of destruction by a millennium.

WHERE DO WE GO FROM HERE?

If the Bible cannot be read as a divine memorandum from heaven, where does that leave us? Is there anything authoritative about the Scriptures that we can build our life upon? Who or what can we trust?

For many Christians the belief in verbal inspiration and biblical inerrancy provides the assurance that they have an authoritative deposit of God's truth to live by. Unfortunately, though, the solace and security offered by the doctrine of inerrancy is purchased at the price of self-deception. Instead of founding their lives on the Christian hope, Christians exchange faith in an intangible God for faith in a tangible book. It is sad that so many Christians have invested their confidence in the reliability of a collection of ancient writings, instead of placing their trust in God himself. Ink and parchment can never be a surrogate for God.

The fact that the Bible contains errors and discrepancies does not mean that the Scriptures cease to be an authoritative guide for Christian living. It simply means that we must discern God's thoughts within the Bible. Blind, uninformed trust only undermines

---

[54]Ibid., pp. 208-9, 314-5.

the Christian proclamation; it never bolsters the integrity of the Good News.

The painful process of facing reality involves the recognition of ambiguity, the realization that life has many 'gray' regions between the well-established precincts of 'black' and 'white'.

Where do we go from here? We must take the risk of becoming seekers once again!

CHAPTER 8

THE POSSIBILITIES OF FRANKNESS

THE CRISIS OF RELIGIOUS AUTHORITY

The history of the West, since the Renaissance, has witnessed the steady decline of traditional religious beliefs and institutions.

Evidences of the unremitting deterioration of religious institutions are plentiful. The Protestant Reformation segmented the one voice of the Western church and surrendered much of its ecclesiastical authority to local princes. Calvinism provided the ideological framework for the development of capitalism, but soon the capitalist system outgrew its need for religious legitimation. The Enlightenment sought through reason to break the shackles of superstition, but only at the price of withdrawing God to a distant observation-post while Newtonian physics ran the world. The phenomenal ascent of scientific inquiry gradually displaced church-sanctioned explanations of the natural world, and evolutionary biology posed serious challenges to Christian belief. Finally, the rise of expansive, modern state bureaucracies have relegated religious institutions to the periphery of the social order.

Modern Christianity faces a crisis of authority. It can no longer rely on social institutions to envelop Christian beliefs with an 'aura of plausibility'. Instead the Christian faith must be articulated in a pluralistic age, where it competes with a myriad of 'alternate religions'. Marxism, nationalism, capitalism, psychoanalyticism, scientism and numerous other 'isms' vie with Christianity for 'religious'

209

authority.

The response to this crisis by the Christian churches has been less than heartening. Instead of facing up to the challenges posed by the modern age, many Christians have retreated to their own cloistered havens of religious security. Hence, we witness a moribund state of 'religious tribalism', where great effort is expended on proving that one religious group is more doctrinally pure than 'the competition'.

How can Christians present a credible articulation of their faith--which can effectively compete with rival, secular 'religious' systems--in such a way that does not deprive Christianity of its own distinctive identity? This seems to be the primary dilemma facing Christians in an age of pluralism. On the one hand, if Christians win credibility by undermining their core beliefs, they have gained nothing. On the other hand, if Christians bask in self-deception by refusing to set aside incorrect beliefs, they forfeit their credibility and subvert what little moral authority the Christian church now commands.

The crux of this dilemma is the distinction between 'essential' and 'nonessential' Christian beliefs. Put simply, we must ask the pivotal question: What is the essence of Christianity? To respond to this question, it is necessary first to consider the central theme of Jesus' teachings: the Kingdom of God.

JESUS' PROCLAMATION OF THE KINGDOM

Critical scholarship has enabled us to reconstruct certain aspects of Jesus' original teachings from the Synoptic Gospels (Matthew, Mark, Luke).[1]

These investigations have shown that Jesus' concept of the Kingdom of God was a radically novel idea,

---

[1] The meticulous process of reconstructing Jesus' original teachings from the Gospel accounts involves, among other things, the task of determining whether a particular saying "can be shown to be dissimilar to the characteristic emphases both of ancient Judaism and of the early church."

unparallelled in comparison to the perspectives of Jesus' contemporaries. In fact, Jesus' teachings on the kingdom were so radical that sometimes the Gospel writers found it necessary to tone them down!

Even the term "kingdom of God" itself was used rarely in Jewish literature before and during Jesus' time. Jesus' frequent and varied use of the term was without precedent. Perhaps the most striking feature of Jesus' proclamation of the Kingdom is that there are no nationalistic or materialistic overtones attached to the symbol.[2] Given the current Jewish expectations of the New Age, this is a remarkable datum.

Most of Jesus' countrymen anxiously awaited the appointed moment when God would liberate Judah from Roman rule, exalting Israel above the nations and making Jerusalem the political and religious center of the world. The Essene community at Qumran expected that a Holy War was imminent and that two Messiahs--one a priest and the other a warrior--would lead them into a war that would end Israel's oppression and begin the New Age.

It was anticipated that this New Age would bring Israel unprecedented prosperity. By contrast, Jesus did not entertain his disciples with ostentatious depictions of God's coming reign. Instead he understood the consummation of the age as something unlike our earthly existence (Mk. 12:18-27), not simply as a glorious extension of worldly pursuits.

Among the various features of Jesus' proclamation of the Kingdom of God, we can identify at least six defining characteristics which underline the novelty of the concept: (1) the Kingdom has both present and future aspects; (2) the Kingdom is universally accessible; (3) the Kingdom will bring about a reversal of present conditions; (4) the Kingdom is founded on forgiveness; (5) the Kingdom is appropriated through faith; and (6) the Kingdom establishes familiarity with God.

1. THE KINGDOM HAS BOTH PRESENT AND FUTURE

---

[2]Joachim Jeremias, New Testament Theology: The Proclamation of Jesus (New York: Charles Scribner's Sons, 1971), p. 248.

211

ASPECTS. Jesus spoke of the Kingdom of God as both a present reality (Mt. 11:12; Lk. 11:20, 17:20-21) and something which lies in the immediate future (Mt. 8:11; Mk. 1:15a; Lk. 11:2, 13:28-29). He regularly used the verb 'to come' when referring to the Kingdom. With perhaps only one exception, ancient Jewish literature never refers to the New Age as 'coming'.[3] At times Jesus identified the inbreaking of the Kingdom with his ministry of exorcism (Mt. 12:28; Lk. 11:20).

Jesus was the "only Jew known to us from ancient times" who claimed "that the new age of salvation had already begun."[4] He denied that the appearance of the Kingdom would be attended with cosmic spectacles, as most of Jesus' contemporaries had anticipated (Lk. 17:20-21). Instead Jesus taught that the kingdom of God was inaugurated in obscure circumstances but would soon blossom in full view (Mt. 13:33; Mk. 4:3-9, 4:26-29, 4:30-32).

Although the point is debatable, it is likely that Jesus did not have a well-defined concept of the end of the age, beyond the general sense that God's judgment was impending.[5] Hence the apocalyptic sayings (e.g., Mt. 10:23; Mk. 9:1, 14:62; Lk. 17:23ff.) and discourses (Mt. 24; Mk. 13; Lk. 21) in the Synoptic Gospels did not originate with Jesus, but instead reflected the apocalyptic mood of the early church.

2. THE KINGDOM IS UNIVERSALLY ACCESSIBLE. It is a well-established fact that Jesus frequently ate with "tax collectors and sinners" (Mt. 11:19; Lk. 15:2). Unfortunately we cannot appreciate the revolutionary nature of this practice. According to Jewish custom, fellowship around the table had great theological significance. As Joachim Jeremias notes,

---

[3]Perrin, Rediscovering the Teachings of Jesus, (New York: Harper & Row, 1967), p. 59 (see note).

[4]D. Flusser, Jesus in Selbstzeugnissen und Bilddokumenten, Rowohlts Monographien 140 (Hamburg: Reinbeck, 1968). (Quoted in Jeremias, Theology of the New Testament, p. 108.)

[5]Perrin, Rediscovering the Teachings of Jesus, pp. 154-206.

table-fellowship means fellowship before
God, for the eating of a piece of broken
bread by everyone who shares in the meal
brings out the fact that they all have a
share in the blessing which the master of
the house had spoken over the unbroken bread.[6]

Hence Jesus' practice of inviting the outcasts of
Jewish society to dine with him was a serious affront
to common religious sensibilities.

Tax collectors and publicans (toll collectors)[7]
were despised because they were lackeys of the occupying troops from Rome and frequently exploited their
countrymen for private profit. We know that three
of Jesus' close disciples had been tax collectors
themselves (Levi, Matthew and Zacchaeus). The term
'sinners' was a designation confined to Jews who held
occupations which placed them in direct conflict with
Mosaic Law (e.g., prostitutes, robbers, usurers, money
changers, swineherds). Jesus' visible acceptance
of these dissolute and despicable traitors was understandably appalling to the Jews of his day.

It is clear that Jesus believed that no one was
excluded a priori from the Kingdom of God (Mt. 8:11;
Lk. 13: 28-29). The familiar parable of the Good
Samaritan is particularly instructive at this point
(Lk. 10:30-36). Luke presents the parable as an exemplary story which illustrates the concept of neighborliness. However, if the parable was originally an
exemplary story, we would expect that the Samaritan
would be the victim and a Jew would be the person
doing the good deed. Instead the significance of
Jesus' parable is that the story leads us to a conclusion which was literally a contradiction in terms
in the minds of his contemporaries: that a worthless
Samaritan could be called 'good'. Therefore Jesus
was challenging his audience to think the unthinkable
. . . to lay aside longstanding racial prejudice for

---

[6]Jeremias, New Testament Theology, p. 115.

[7]For the distinction between the two, see Jeremias,
New Testament Theology, pp. 110-112.

the sake of the Kingdom.[8]

3. THE KINGDOM WILL BRING ABOUT A REVERSAL OF PRESENT CONDITIONS. As Norman Perrin has observed, "the theme of eschatological reversal is one of the best-attested themes of the message of Jesus."[9] A number of Jesus' sayings (Mk. 8:35; 10:23b, 25, 31; Lk. 14:11) and parables (Lk. 14:7-11, 16:19-31, 18:10-14) warn that the coming reign of God will create a situation diametrically opposed to the status quo. By portraying the Kingdom of God as a dramatic reversal of the present age, where normal expectations about social existence are radically overturned, Jesus' audience was constrained to think critically about their life situation, rendering judgment on their own participation in exploitive relationships and institutions.

We might expect that behind the motif of reversal there lies the expectation that God will reign as a _righteous_ king. Throughout the ancient Near East, from the earliest times, kingly righteousness was understood mainly in terms of the king's power to protect the weak, the poor, the widow and the orphan (i.e., those who fell through society's 'safety net').[10] Hence God, as the righteous king, will establish just relations among men when his Kingdom comes, an event which will radically overturn present expectations.

In a sense, Jesus' message of eschatological reversal is the corollary of his intense concern for "the poor." Jesus' announcement of the good news to the poor is the "most decisive feature" of his proclamation of the Kingdom.[11] "Blessed are you poor, for yours is the kingdom of God" (Lk. 6:20). The words are familiar to us. We are unable to grasp their revolutionary import. For Jesus, the inauguration of the Kingdom was marked by the healing of human

---

[8] J. D. Crossan, "Parable and Example in the Teaching of Jesus" (_New Testament Studies_ 18:285-307, 1971/72), pp. 294-295.

[9] Perrin, _The New Testament_, p. 298.

[10] Jeremias, _New Testament Theology_, p. 98.

[11] Ibid., pp. 108ff.

suffering and the announcement that the poor are invited to sup at God's table (Lk. 7:22, cp. Mt. 8:11).

Who are the poor? The term had both material
and spiritual connotations for Jesus. The social
lepers of Jesus' day--the tax collector, the publican,
the prostitute--belonged to the company of "the poor."
More generally, the poor referred to the uneducated,
the ignorant and, of course, those who struggled
against unremitting material need.

In the context of ancient Judaism, being uneducated and being irreligious were nearly synonymous,
due to the strong emphasis placed on detailed knowledge
of the Mosaic Law. Hence Jesus' announcement that
the Kingdom of God belonged to the uneducated and
ignorant created incredible dissonance in the minds
of his listeners. Those who suffer from hunger,
thirst, exposure, illness and imprisonment are called
Jesus' brothers (Mt. 25:31-46).[12]

Unlike the sectarians at Qumran, Jesus' community
of disciples were commanded to relinquish their possessions and to give them to the poor (Mk. 10:21; Lk.
12:33), instead of pooling them for their common welfare.[13] Jesus' distrust of wealth is a distinctive
feature of his teachings. He exclaimed:

> How hard it will be for those who have riches
> to enter the kingdom of God! . . . It is
> easier for a camel to go through the eye
> of a needle than for a rich man to enter
> the kingdom of God (Mk. 10:23b, 25).

This attitude toward material wealth is decidedly
radical.

The Jews of Jesus' day--as well as most Christians
today--viewed wealth as something neutral; it could
be positive or negative, depending on how it was used.
The rabbis taught that there are two kinds of wealth:
"riches that positively harm their possessors and

---

[12]For a defense of the authenticity of this passage,
see Jeremias, _The Parables of Jesus_, 2nd ed. (New
York: Charles Scribner's Sons, 1963), pp. 207ff.

[13]Jeremias, _New Testament Theology_, p. 223.

215

other riches that stand them in good stead."[14] By
contrast, Jesus outrightly condemned all wealth in
his call to discipleship.

4. THE KINGDOM IS FOUNDED ON FORGIVENESS. Jesus
believed that God will exercise his kingly office
in the coming reign of God through the act of forgive-
ness--not by cosmic displays in the heavens or orgies
of divine wrath against the nations.[15] He enjoined
his followers to "love your enemies" (Mt. 5:44; Lk.
6:27) and expressly made forgiveness a precondition
for religious worship (Mt. 5:23-24). The central
supplication of the Lord's Prayer is "forgive us our
sins, for we ourselves forgive every one who is indebted to us" (Lk. 11:4). On two occasions it is reported
that Jesus himself forgave sins (Mk. 2:1-12; Lk. 7:36-
50). The first Christians understood that following Jesus involved a constant readiness to forgive
those who wronged them (Mt. 18:22; Lk. 17:4).

Nowhere is the Kingdom ideal of forgiveness stated
more eloquently than in the parable of the Prodigal
Son (Lk. 15:11-32). Unlike nearly all of the parables
in the New Testament, the present form and context
of this parable closely approximates the original
words of Jesus.[16]

The story is about a young man who, like many
inquisitive youths, became restless and decided to
leave the protection of home 'to see the world'.
He took his inheritance, journeyed to a foreign land,
squandered his money in debauchery and was soon penni-
less. A famine arose and he was forced to work as
a herder of pigs--an occupation despised by the Jews
of that day, which made one a 'Gentile'.

Struggling at the edge of survival, he soon came
to his senses. He decided to return to his father,
begging forgiveness, with the simple plea that he
be allowed to work as one of his father's hired hands.
When the son was approaching his home, the father

---

[14]From Midrash Exodus Rabbah 31 on Exodus 22:24 (quoted
in Perrin, Rediscovering the Teachings of Jesus, p.
143).

[15]Perrin, Rediscovering the Teachings of Jesus, p. 90.

[16]Ibid., p. 21.

recognized him and became ecstatic. He ran to his son, embracing and kissing him.

A great feast was called to celebrate the return of his wayward son. However not all shared the father's elation. The oldest son--who had been obedient and faithful to his father throughout his life--protested that he had never received the attention that was being squandered on his rebellious younger brother.

We should not interpret the protest of the eldest son as an unwarranted manifestation of sibling rivalry. Considering the values of that day, he had a perfectly legitimate point. The father responded to his son's complaint in this way: "Son, you are always with me, and all that is mine is yours. It was fitting to make merry and be glad, for your brother was dead, and is alive; he was lost, and is found."

The parable is not an allegory, where the father stands for God and the elder son represents the Pharisees. Instead it is a moving, realistic story that describes a concept which cannot be justly represented in propositional statements: the meaning of forgiveness in the Kingdom of God.[17]

5. THE KINGDOM IS APPROPRIATED THROUGH FAITH. Jesus' proclamation of God's forgiveness would have been meaningless unless it had been accompanied by a new sense of physical and psychic well-being. Suffering and sin were closely associated throughout the ancient world. Apart from his ministry of healing and exorcism, Jesus' announcement of forgiveness of sin would have seemed like a cruel joke or the product of mental derangement.

In many of the accounts of Jesus' healings and exorcisms in the Synoptic Gospels, we find a common denominator that was unique in the ancient world. Jesus often told the person being healed that their faith had made them well (Mk. 2:5, 5:34, 10:52; Lk. 7:50, 17:19). This feature, so common in the synoptic tradition, is completely absent in the Jewish and Hellenistic miracle stories which survive to this day.

Two sayings about faith, which the New Testament

---

[17]Ibid., pp. 94-98.

attributes to Jesus, seem to be authentic (Mt. 17:20; Lk. 17:6). Both sayings emphasize the powerful effect of even a shred of faith. In Matthew, Jesus declared that "if you will have faith as a grain of mustard seed, you will say to this mountain, 'Move hence to yonder place', and it will move; and nothing will be impossible to you." In Luke the mustard seed metaphor remains the same, but the power of faith is likened to the force needed to uproot a sycamore tree. Jesus' imagery was apt, as the sycamore tree in Palestine was known for its very deep root system. Also, as it is widely known, the mustard seed is extremely small; hence, only a little kernel of faith unleashes great power.

What does 'faith' mean in these sayings, as well as in the miracle stories about Jesus? We can get at the question by imagining what it must have been like to have encountered Jesus and to have heard his strange proclamation of the Kingdom of God.

For most Jews, Jesus' teachings were plainly heretical; yet, it was clear that marvelous things were happening at the hands of this Nazarene. Many could not reconcile Jesus' heretical thoughts with his miraculous works and therefore chose to believe that he was in collusion with the devil (Mk. 3:22-27). Jesus' healing touch created a dilemma of interpretation. Could God possibly be working through such a heretic; or, worse yet, could Jesus be a true spokesman of God?

Presumably those who approached Jesus, requesting healing, or those who 'tabled' their skepticism long enough to welcome his restoring hand, had the proverbial faith of a mustard seed. This faith was trust, albeit a meager amount of trust. Jesus commended those who demonstrated such trust, who gave him the benefit of the doubt. We can imagine that in many instances the restoration of health stimulated the germination, growth and blossoming of a tiny mustard seed, which is the life of complete trust and obedience to the special[18] demands of the coming New Order: the Kingdom of God.

---

[18]This section was based on a helpful analysis of faith by Perrin, Rediscovering the Teachings of Jesus, pp. 130-142.

6. THE KINGDOM ESTABLISHES FAMILIARITY WITH GOD. The primary end to which the Kingdom of God is directed is plainly friendship with God. Therefore we cannot treat Jesus' proclamation of the Kingdom in isolation from his teachings on prayer.

The seminal work of Jeremias has shown that Jesus' habit of addressing God was unequivocally unique. He frequently referred to God as "my Father." Nowhere in the Old Testament or in the Jewish writings of Palestine in the pre-Christian period do we find that God is addressed as 'father'. Moreover Jesus' habit of addressing God was unparalleled in another respect. He used the Aramaic word ᵓabba (Mk. 14:36), which was a familiar form of address used by children (of all ages) when they referred to their father. To address God with this familiar form naturally struck Jesus' contemporaries as extremely disrespectful and quite out of taste.[19]

Jesus' linguistic innovation of using ᵓabba to address God had immense theological significance. The inauguration of the Kingdom meant that people could address God plainly and confidently. At the same time, God's invitation to friendship is tempered with the recognition that we are all but children before the Creator. Therefore Jesus was able to hold familiarity and respect in a creative tension in his teachings on prayer.

Jesus believed that God's ear always harkens to sincerity, irrespective of the religious qualifications of the supplicant or the place of prayer (Mt. 6:6, 7:7; Lk. 11:5-8. 11:11-13, 18:1-5). Customary long prayers were unnecessary (Mt. 6:7; Mk. 12:40). Instead the prayers of the Kingdom are characterized by brevity and directness.

The Lord's Prayer is an authentic example of Jesus' innovative perspective on prayer. The shorter version in Luke preserves the original sense of the prayer:

Father,
Hallowed be thy name. Thy kingdom come.
Give us each day our daily bread;
and forgive us our sins,

---

[19] Jeremias, New Testament Theology, pp. 36, 61-68.

219

for we ourselves forgive everyone who
is indebted to us;
and lead us not into temptation.
(Lk. 11:2b-4)[20]

Now that six defining features of Jesus' proclamation of the Kingdom have been identified, we are ready
to return to the crucial question that faces the Christians of our day: What is the essence of Christianity?

It seems reasonable to expect that our answer
should be consistent with the main outlines of Jesus'
teachings on the Kingdom of God. Furthermore the
answer must be succinct, representing a summary of
Jesus' teachings which, in some way, reflects the
spiritual depth of his life and message.

The task before us would seem incredibly difficult, if not impossible, if it had not been for a
nameless scribe who one day posed a question to Jesus.
We are told that this learned man asked him what was
the most important idea that Jesus was trying to bring
across to his countrymen. Jesus' answer to the
scribe's probing question was to influence the Christian proclamation for centuries to come.

A CANON WITHIN THE CANON

The term 'canon' means "rule," "measuring stick"
or "standard." It is derived from the Greek word
kanōn which refers to something "made of reeds" or
"straight like reeds." The Greek and Latin church
fathers used the term to denote an authoritative list
of books of the New Testament. By 367 CE, with the
letter of Athanasius, bishop of Alexandria, there
was general agreement on what books constituted the
New Testament. As far as the Old Testament was concerned, the Christian church simply accepted the list
of authoritative books that had been ratified by the
Pharisees at Jamnia in 90 CE. Hence the term 'canon'
eventually became synonymous with the Hebrew-Christian
scriptures: the Bible.

---

[20] For further discussion on the Lord's Prayer and Jesus'
teachings on prayer in general, see Jeremias, New
Testament Theology, pp. 184-203.

To speak of a canon within the Canon means that certain texts within the Scriptures capsulize an essential religious idea which functions as an authoritative norm--a touchstone--in relation to other teachings within the Scriptures. For Christians, we might expect that this internal canon would epitomize the essence of Christianity, summarizing the salient features of Jesus' proclamation of the Kingdom.

I recommend that the internal canon of the Christian faith is remarkably simple and straightforward. Not only has this internal canon been attributed to Jesus himself, but the first Christians seized on it in their attempt to understand the meaning of Christian discipleship. Furthermore this internal canon has inspired Christians down through the ages, being recognized as an inspired idea, a standard that exudes intrinsic worth.

What is this canon within the Canon? It is Jesus' Two Great Commandments:

> The first is, 'Hear, O Israel: the Lord our God, the Lord is one; and you shall love the Lord your God with all your heart, and with all your soul, and with all your mind, and with all your strength'. The second is this, 'You shall love your neighbor as yourself'. There is no other commandment greater than these. (Mk. 12:29-31)

Both of the commandments were drawn from the Old Testament. The first is the foundational confession of Judaism, known as the Sh^{e}ma (Deut. 6:4-5). The second appears in the Book of Leviticus (19:18).

Jesus was not the first to link these two disconnected passages. Both Mark (12:32-33) and Luke (10:25) indicate that the Jewish scribe or lawyer who questioned Jesus was familiar with the association of these two passages in the Law.

What, then, was innovative about Jesus' response? In two respects Jesus' understanding of the two commandments was a departure from the views of his contemporaries.

First, Jesus radicalized the meaning of love. He claimed that true neighbor-love involved even loving your enemies (Mt. 5:43-44)!

221

Second, love was not a peripheral subject for Jesus. Instead he declared that the central feature of religious commitment was one thing, and only one thing: love for God and love for humanity. Whereas ancient Judaism--like modern Christianity--found itself torn into factions, bereft of an integrating vision and preoccupied with trivialities, Jesus' Two Great Commandments elevate us to a perspective that transcends theological hairsplitting and leads us to an active, other-oriented life of Christian discipleship.

While we should not presume that the entirety of Jesus' teachings could be distilled into two brief imperatives, it is fair to say that the Two Great Commandments provide us with a summary theology of Jesus' teachings. As a summary theology, the Two Great Commandments succinctly integrate both the 'vertical' and 'horizontal' dimensions of Jesus' proclamation of the Kingdom, in a way that is consistent with other features of his life and message.

THE INTERNAL CANON AND THE EARLY CHURCH

The first Christians recognized the centrality of agape love in their articulation of Christian commitment.[21]

Matthew believed that the Two Great Commandments were the foundation of "all the law and the prophets" (22:40).

Luke understood the Two Great Commandments as the way to receive eternal life (10:25-28).

The Apostle Paul summed up the entirety of the Law in the second commandment alone: "You shall love your neighbor as yourself" (Rom. 13:9; Gal. 5:14). Paul also wrote a hymn to agape love which is probably the most eloquent and frequently quoted passage in the New Testament (I Cor. 13).

---

[21]The 'classic' study on the Christian concept of love from the New Testament through the Protestant Reformation is Anders Nygren, Agape and Eros, trans. by P. S. Watson (New York: Harper and Row, 1969).

John rephrased Jesus' second commandment and called it "a new commandment" (Jn. 13:34-35). For John, agape love is the distinguishing mark of true Christian discipleship.

The writer of I John forcefully reiterated the centrality of love for the Christian faith when he wrote:

> If anyone says, "I love God," and hates his brother, he is a liar; for he who does not love his brother whom he has seen, cannot love God whom he has not seen. And this commandment we have from him, that he who loves God should love his brother also (4:20-21).

The Two Great Commandments enjoin us to direct our attention, our energy and our affection toward God and our fellow human beings. Of course, it is clear that our love for God is of a different nature than our love for man. As H. Richard Niebuhr has pointed out, Jesus'

> love of God and his love of neighbor are two distinct virtues that have no common quality but only a common source. Love of God is adoration of the only true good; it is gratitude to the bestower of all gifts; it is joy in Holiness; it is 'consent to Being'. But the love of man is pitiful rather than adoring; it is giving and for-giving rather than grateful; it suffers for and in their viciousness and profaneness; it does not consent to accept them as they are, but calls them to repentance . . . the love of God is passion; the love of man, compassion.[22]

PASSION FOR GOD

"You shall love the Lord your God with all your heart, and with all your soul, and with all your mind, and with all your strength."

---

[22]H. Richard Niebuhr, Christ and Culture (New York: Harper and Row, 1951), pp. 18-19.

The passion for God is simply creative, enlightened abandonment. We do not adore God because he is a means for us to resolve our identities, a bridge to span the gap between the known and the unknown, or an object of blind obedience. Instead mature love for God springs from a dynamic, unmanipulated friendship with God. Such friendship knows of no upper bound; at no moment may we declare that we have 'arrived'. Instead our journey with God constantly challenges us to new plateaus of trust and new summits of insight.

We can rightfully expect that a mature love for God will be evidenced by an active love for humanity. The overlap between the Two Great Commandments is extensive. As Søren Kierkegaard has written,

> If you want to show that your life is intended as service to God, then let it serve man, yet continually with the thought of God. God is not a part of existence in such a way that he demands his share for himself; he demands everything, but as you bring it you immediately receive, if I may put it this way, an endorsement designating where it should be forwarded, for God demands nothing for himself, although he demands everything from you.[23]

Yet, we cannot, nor should not, collapse the first commandment into the second. Our passion for God clarifies the nature of our compassion for humanity. Human compassion should never legitimate the idolatrous adoration of technological accomplishments, social achievements or heroic leaders. Our love for God does not substitute for our love of humanity; the two are necessarily complementary.

If our love for God is all-consuming, we can expect that it will shape every facet of our existence. Our trust in God helps us to assume risk when the welfare of others is at stake. Our vision of God clarifies true priorities and lifts us above the morass of petty trivialities. Our hope in God informs us that no accomplishment is beyond his transforming touch and that no disappointment can extinguish the

---

[23]S. Kierkegaard, Works of Love, trans. by Howard and Edna Hong (New York: Harper and Row, 1962), p. 159.

expectation of his Kingdom. Our acceptance of God's grace gives us the confidence to fail while beckoning us onward to uncharted realms of achievement. In short, the passion for God expands our horizons by eroding the barriers we impose to secure our parochial worlds.

COMPASSION FOR HUMANITY[24]

"You shall love your neighbor as yourself."

Compassion for humanity is simply the active recognition that every human being is a child of God, a unique pearl of precious value and the object of his all-encompassing love. Therefore acts of human compassion are intrinsically religious acts, even though they may not be understood as such. The greatest sacrilege against God is a crime against humanity, because man's inhumanity to man is a defiant insult to God himself, an affront of the highest order.

We must not confuse compassion with sympathy or empathy. There is always an element of feeling--an imaginative impulse to "walk for a day in another's moccasins"--that is integral to human compassion. But true compassion transforms feelings of concern into acts of love. Just as faith without works is dead, empathy apart from a corresponding life of service is a frivolous expenditure of energy. The neighbor-love about which Jesus spoke is the foundation of true compassion for humanity.

What does it mean to love your neighbor as yourself? We can approach the question by first inquiring what it means to love oneself. With Paul Ramsey, we would want to say that self-love involves--above all else--a recognition of our own irreducible worth.

You naturally love yourself for your own sake. You wish for your own good, and you do so even when you may have a certain distaste for the kind of person you are. Liking

24Gene Outka has written a superb analysis of Christian love which stimulated my thinking in preparing this section [Agape: An Ethical Analysis (New Haven, Conn.: Yale University Press, 1972)].

yourself or thinking yourself very nice, or not, has fundamentally nothing to do with the matter. After a failure of some sort, the will-to-live soon returns and you always lay hold expectantly on <u>another</u> possibility of attaining some good for yourself. You love yourself more than you love any good qualities or worth you may possess. . . . And regardless of differences in temperament or capacity for deep emotion, one person probably wishes his own good about as much as another person wishes for his.[25]

Even the most confirmed, self-seeking egoist is, at bottom, convinced of his own worth, irrespective of his disparaging attitude toward others. Once we generalize this common self-perception on the rest of humanity, it is easy to see that every person is at least convinced of his <u>own</u> right to flourish, his <u>own</u> sense of dignity. Hence every human being has a <u>prima facie</u> claim to be treated with respect, to be permitted to develop, to be considered as an equal among other human beings.[26]

Therefore loving others as we love ourselves means that we treat others as ends-in-themselves, instead of using them <u>merely</u> as a means to our own ends. Neighbor-love, then, presumes a baseline of human dignity which no person or institution should contravene.[27] Our worth is not determined by an amalgam of respectable qualities that are present in the

[25] Paul Ramsey, <u>Basic Christian Ethics</u> (New York: Charles Scribner's Sons, 1950), p. 100.

[26] A similar kind of argument is made by William Frankena, "The Concept of Social Justice," in <u>Social Justice</u>, edited by R. B. Brandt (Englewood Cliffs, N.J.: Prentice-Hall, 1962), pp. 19ff.

[27] My language here is self-consciously Kantian. I want to call to the reader's attention that the argument for human dignity on the basis of generalizing our own perception of self-love on the rest of humanity is weaker than other approaches. A more sure foundation for a concept of universal human dignity is human rationality, instead of the well-attested propensity of people to value their own lives. The case for

'deserving' and notably absent in the 'undeserving'.

Loving others does not mean that we give people what they want or bow to their every demand. The Christian mandate to love one another does not reduce Christians to a 'doormat' over which others may walk undeterred. Authentic Christian love often leads believers to stand up for their rights and always demands that Christians defend the human rights of others. The call of love is not an anemic invitation to exploitation; it is a potent, piercing cry for justice. At bottom, love means that we should actively seek to meet the legitimate needs of others, not their idiosyncratic preferences or insatiable wants.

The backbone of the second commandment might be called the Principle of Equal Regard: You ought to regard the needs of others on par with your own needs. In other words, the needs of my neighbor are just as compelling as my own needs. For the purposes of this discussion, I define needs as rank-ordered claims to certain material and social goods which arise from biological, psychological, and social realities.[28] Of course, the Principle of Equal Regard does not dictate that we must treat everyone identically. Instead the focus is on the fair consideration

---

human respect forged by Alan Gewirth [Reason and Morality (Chicago: University of Chicago Press, 1978)] is probably the most convincing argument for universal human dignity based on human rationality (vis-à-vis the capacity to trace logical entailments and to value logical consistency) proposed thus far. Also I refer the reader to a recent defense of Kant's concept of respecting persons as 'ends-in-themselves' [see Alan Donagan, The Theory of Morality (Chicago: University of Chicago Press, 1977), pp. 229ff].

[28] The concept of 'need' is more involved than this definition suggests. Need can be formally defined as follows:

> I need X if and only if X is a weak or strong condition for keeping, acquiring or actualizing Y which I am voluntarily disposed to keep, acquire or actualize (where Y is a commodity, a biopsychosocial attribute or a moral/religious/social idea).

This formal definition understands need-claim in terms

of another's needs.

By taking a need-based interpretation of the second commandment, we are able to see that the injunction to "love your neighbor as yourself" is a practical possibility, not a lofty, unrealistic ideal. The Principle of Equal Regard answers Freud's objection that the second commandment prescribes a social situation that would be both impossible and undesirable.[29] Clearly the strong egalitarian implications

---

of two types of goods which are set in a means-end relationship. The first-order good 'X' is the means to attain a second-order good 'Y'. For example, an adequate calorie intake (X) is a basic need, because food is essential for biological survival (Y).

Different first-order needs (X's) can be rank-ordered and weighted to a proximate degree for two reasons: (1) not all first-order needs (X's) lead to the attainment of a particular second-order good (Y) with equal probability; and (2) some second-order goods (Y's) are universally perceived as being more important than others. With respect to the first reason, it is clear that a need-claim which has an 80% probability that X_1 will lead to Y will be much more compelling than a need-claim which has only a 20% probability that X_2 will result in Y. The second reason underscores the fact that 'need' is a moral concept. Basic survival is a more essential second-order good than living a 'happy' life. Hence the first order (basic) needs of food, shelter, safe water and access to rudimentary health care and basic education have overriding priority over other 'needs' such as travel, cars, nice clothes, and innumerable other goods that we perceive as necessary elements of living a happy, satisfying life.

For further discussion on the concept of need, see William Galston, Justice and the Human Good (Chicago: University of Chicago Press, 1980), pp. 162-170.

[29]Sigmund Freud, Civilization and Its Discontents, trans. by J. Strachey (New York: W. W. Norton & Co., 1961), pp. 56-57, 90. I quote the following excerpt:

How can it [the second commandment] be possible? My love is something valuable to me which I ought not to throw away without reflection. It imposes duties on me for

of the Principle of Equal Regard are highly desirable
from the standpoint of long term social stability
and internationally recognized canons of social justice
(e.g., the U.N.'s "Universal Declaration of Human
Rights" of 1948).

LOVE AND SUPEREROGATION

Does the Principle of Equal Regard fail to grasp
the radical significance of Jesus' proclamation of
the Kingdom? Another way of framing this question
is to ask whether neighbor-love differs at all from
egalitarian justice? Does Christian love require
us to put the needs of others ahead of (not simply
on par with) our own needs?

---

whose fulfilment I must be ready to make
sacrifices. If I love someone, he must
deserve it in some way. . . . He deserves
it if he is so like me in important ways
that I can love myself in him; and he deserves it if he is so much more perfect
than myself that I can love my ideal of
my own self in him. Again, I have to love
him if he is my friend's son, since the
pain my friend would feel if any harm came
to him would be my pain too--I should have
to share it. But if he is a stranger to
me and if he cannot attract me by any worth
of his own or any significance that he may
already have acquired for my emotional life,
it will be hard for me to love him. Indeed,
I should be wrong to do so, for my love
is valued by all my own people as a sign
of my preferring them, and it is an injustice
to them if I put a stranger on par with
them. But if I am to love him (with this
universal love) merely because he, too,
is an inhabitant of this earth, like an
insect, an earthworm or a grass-snake, then
I fear that only a small modicum of love
will fall to his share--not by any possibility as much as, by the judgment of my reason,
I am entitled to retain for myself. What
is the point of a precept enunciated with
such solemnity if its fulfilment cannot
be recommended as reasonable? (56-57).

In one sense these questions are strictly academic. If Christians throughout the world actualized the Principle of Equal Regard in their daily lives, the impact in a world besieged by greed and inequality would be truly revolutionary. Think of it. About one out of every five people alive today is undernourished, deprived of access to rudimentary health care and elementary education, without a safe water source, and suffers from squalid, cramped living conditions.

Food, health care, basic literacy, safe water and adequate shelter--these are basic human needs that we take for granted in the industrialized world. If Christian communities around the world courageously drew the line between 'necessity' and 'want', sharing their abundance with others who suffer acute need, the repercussions would literally shake the moral conscience of the world. Jesus' healing touch would captivate humanity once again. Yet, technically, a bold action such as this would not be truly self-sacrificial (although it would be perceived as such), as it would involve comparatively little material loss on our part.

While the implementation of the Principle of Equal Regard would be perceived as being eminently self-sacrificial, it actually does not require true self-sacrifice or what ethicists call "supererogatory acts." These are moral actions which go beyond the pale of normal moral obligation.[30] They are acts which are praiseworthy yet, because they require extreme personal sacrifice, could never be required of a person. The defining feature of supererogatory

---

[30]The principal discussion on supererogation is J. D. Urmson, "Saints and Heroes," in Essays in Moral Philosophy, ed. by A. I. Melden (Seattle: University of Washington Press, 1958), pp. 198-216. For critiques of Urmson's position, see Yogendra Chopra, "Professor Urmson on 'Saints and Heroes'" (Philosophy 38:160-166, 1963); and Christopher New, "Saints, Heroes and Utilitarians" (Philosophy 49:179-189, 1974). Also an article by Joseph Raz has significantly advanced the discussion in my opinion ["Permissions and Supererogation" (American Philosophical Quarterly 12:161-168, 1975)].

acts is self-sacrifice.[31]

The second commandment, by itself, does not obligate Christians to do supererogatory acts. However other moral resources in the Christian tradition indicate that the highest manifestation of Christian love is true self-sacrifice (Jn. 15:13; I Jn. 3:16). Of course, Jesus' voluntary submission to the cross is, to some extent, paradigmatic for all Christians.

While supererogatory actions normally occur in extraordinary moral decision situations, usually those people who act self-sacrificially are normal, everyday people. Take the case of Atlanta bank executive Arland Williams. At 46 years his life was quite unexceptional. But when Air Florida Flight #90 plunged into the frigid Potomac River on January 13, 1982, an otherwise unexceptional man behaved nobly and heroically, in the spirit of true self-sacrificial love.

The unidentified "sixth man" in the water refused opportunity after opportunity to be brought to safety. Instead he passed on the rope to others. After all of the other survivors were rescued, the "sixth man" had disappeared from sight, beneath the icy waters. Later, in tears, the helicopter pilot exclaimed: "He could have gone on the first trip,[32] but he put everyone else ahead of himself. Everyone."

Of course, many other examples of supererogatory acts could be mentioned. Medical personnel have often risked their lives to come to the aid of victims of war or pestilence. In time of war, one hears reports of soldiers who leap on live grenades to save the lives of their fellows. Such noble human acts testify to an ideal, a standard of care and concern that exceeds our normal canons of justice and neighborliness. This ideal, for Christians, can be nothing less than agape love in the highest order.

Yet, in my opinion, such expressions of perfected Christian love are not obligatory for all Christians.

---

[31]Joel Feinberg, "Supererogation and Rules," in Doing and Deserving (Princeton, N.J.: Princeton University Press, 1970), p. 11.

[32]Claire Safran, "Hero of the Frozen River" (Readers Digest, Sept., 1982), pp. 49-53.

The second commandment does not enjoin us to extreme self-sacrifice. It only obligates us to respect the needs of others on equal footing with our own needs.[33] But, as I have suggested, if the Christian churches really followed the simple injunction of loving your neighbor as yourself, a metaphorical 'shot' would be heard around the world.

NEEDED: A NEW SPIRITUALITY

Christianity desperately needs a fresh spiritual vision. Spiritual life must no longer be confined to the familiar religious practices of prayer, Bible study and worship. This is not to suggest that these traditional habits of spirituality are unimportant; instead, the point is that they must not reinforce the religious introversion we find today.

The driving force of the new spirituality must be decidedly extroverted. As Christians assume an other-oriented posture by involving themselves in the world's struggles as God's ambassadors--advocates

---

[33] It should be noted that even the corollary to the second commandment--"love your enemies" (Mt. 5:44)--does not obligate Christians to do supererogatory acts. Instead the injunction to love your enemies underscores the fact that Christian love must be unconditional, free of meritorian criteria. The command certainly does not mean, for example, that Christians ought to forego their right to self-defense.

Jesus' sayings about resisting evil are different (Mt. 5:38-42). Taken literally, they would obligate all Christians to extreme personal sacrifice. However it seems unlikely that Jesus intended the commands to be understood as literal moral imperatives. For example, to give a demanding person both your coat and cloak would have made one stark naked, given the customary dress at that time. Similarly to 'walk the extra mile' would have led to a life of slavery, as occupying Roman troops often forced civilians temporarily into service by making them carry provisions, etc. Since these commands require practical impossibilities, we can assume that the intent of Jesus words was to stir his audience to radical questioning by overturning normal expectations, cp. Mt. 5:29-30 (see Perrin, The New Testament, p.272.

of the poor, the outcast and the defenseless--something
will take place inside of them. They will discover
new reservoirs of faith, hope and love that will deepen
the meaning of prayer and worship beyond their most
profound spiritual experience.

Obviously the present spiritual crisis will not
be remedied by ecclesiastical fiat or 'close encoun-
ters' of the spiritual kind. Instead the solution
lies within our hearts . . . within our determination
to surrender familiar moorings of religious security,
allowing ourselves to be vulnerable . . . open to
the transforming touch of Jesus of Nazareth. The
call of the Nazarene is to rediscover the meaning
of prayer, of worship, of fellowship, of service . . .
a rediscovery that will combine the ideals of passion
for God and compassion for humanity in the context
of a lively, extroverted church community. We must
be willing to lay old ideas aside, in readiness to
welcome new winds of inspiration.

Only the basic contours of this new spirituality
are presently discernable. We can expect that a diversity of religious practices and ideas will make up
its repertoire. Consequently the new spirituality
will not attempt to forge Christian unity on the basis
of liturgical or doctrinal agreement. Even though
close ecumenical relationships will be the institutional by-product of this new spiritual vision, ecclesiastical unity will be the outcome, not the source, of
this renaissance of Christian unity.

Perhaps the most distinctive feature of this
new spiritual vision will be its capacity to impart
an integrated, holistic perspective of life on earth,
where the human species becomes one human family in
the fullest sense of the term and other life forms
are accorded the respect they deserve as constituents
of God's creation. Unlike most forms of traditional
spirituality, which comprehend the holy in terms of
individual inspiration, the new spirituality will
make God's universal perspective the touchstone of
the sacred. Consequently the new spiritual vision
will comprehend the particular in terms of the whole,
that is, from the perspective of God's all-encompassing
care. If one were to search for historical antecedents
of this new spirituality, in my estimation the spirituality of St. Francis of Assisi and Albert Schweitzer
most closely approximate the ideal I have in mind.

Is the vision of a new spirituality little more

than a vague pipe dream? Perhaps. But, in the final analysis, the answer depends on us . . . on our willingness to forsake secure territory in search of new horizons of discovery. We can be assured that our mustard seed of faith will be matched with God's transforming power, but the initiative lies with us. Shall we choose to take God's hand in a venture of love? Do the risks seem too great? Let the church hear once again the calm but compelling words of Jesus: "Follow me and I will make you become fishers of men." (Mk. 1:17).

NEEDED: A NEW ACTIVISM

To complement a new, other-oriented spirituality, Christians must develop a fresh, aggressive brand of social activism. It will not do to treat social activism as the special calling of a few Christians or as a surrogate for spirituality.

The new activism will prophetically articulate the Gospel to a world tormented by injustice and ridden with inequalities. Like the new spiritual vision, we can expect that the new Christian activism will be diverse and multi-faceted. It will grapple with issues without being 'issue-oriented'; it will carry its message to the centers of power without becoming simply a special interest group. Yet, in all of its diversity, one would anticipate that two qualities will permeate the new activism: realism and hope.

The first pillar of the new activism will be a commitment to realism. By realism I do not refer to a pessimistic, cowardly, acquiescing spirit which deems that what is always will be. Instead realism means the courage to perceive things accurately, to call a spade a spade by neither exaggerating short term prospects for social change nor by depreciating the long term impact of dedicated, concerted collective action.

Hope is the second pillar of the new Christian activism. When a realistic appraisal of prospects for meaningful social change seem incredibly dim, hope steps in to urge us on. Hope, in this sense, is not a capricious fancy that a utopia lies just around the corner. Instead hope is a determinant of present action. It defines, guides and invigorates our present course of action, because the Christian hope is founded on a Kingdom which is coming . . . a Kingdom now manifest in the redeeming acts of compassion and forgiveness.

The Kingdom of God is both a promise for the future and an ideal or action-guide for the present. The promise of the Kingdom precludes the belief that injustice, cruelty and exploitation are permanent fixtures in the universe. The ideal of the Kingdom presents a hidden reality that is breaking forth, an action-guide that sparks our imagination and reproaches our apathy.[34]

---

[34]When I speak of the Kingdom of God as an 'action-guide' or 'ideal', I have in mind Immanuel Kant's understanding of theory and practice which some have called "ideal theory." Kant contends that whatever is valid in theory must have practical application. The ideal, for Kant, shapes the actual. It guides present conduct and sets goals to be striven toward. One cannot disparage moral ideals by arguing from empirical circumstances that their implementation is outside the realm of possibility: "The argument that what has not succeeded so far will therefore never succeed, does not even justify the abandonment of a pragmatic or technological intention (as that of air travel by aerostatic balloons, for instance), much less than the abandonment of a moral intention that becomes a duty unless its accomplishment is demonstrably impossible" [On the Old Saw: That May be Right in Theory but Won't Work in Practice, trans. by E. B. Ashton (Philadelphia: University of Pennsylvania Press, 1974), p. 78].
Kant's ideal theory has an interesting application in terms of the Christian concept of the Kingdom of God. Although Jesus relegated the full disclosure of the Kingdom to the immediate future, he challenged his disciples to actualize the Kingdom's ideals in their present existence. Those ideals, from the perspective of ordinary life, seem lofty and unattainable. Yet they set an agenda for Christians that ought to be striven toward.
It is interesting that Kant alludes to the concept of the Kingdom of God when he refers to "the kingdom of ends" in his moral theory (Groundwork of the Metaphysics of Morals). Certainly Kant's concept of "perpetual peace" among nations comes about as close to the full realization of the Kingdom of God on earth as any Christian visionary would dare to dream. Kant

The Kingdom is founded on both God's initiative and man's response. Because the Kingdom was inaugurated by God's unilateral offer of forgiveness, we know that the Reign of God can never be created by technological manipulation, bold political initiatives or cloistered utopias. On the other hand, the Kingdom is not some disembodied, ethereal, spiritual reality whose only ground in the present is an apocalyptic anticipation of God's self-disclosure at the end of history. Because the Kingdom is God's initiative built upon man's response, we would expect that the Kingdom that comes will be manifest in the reality that is . . . human existence . . . painful, tragic, longing for true liberation.

The Kingdom is both present and future, God's initiative and man's response. The new Christian activism must embody these creative tensions.

Unlike the woefully inadequate, vitiated form of Christian outreach that is usually associated with the term 'evangelism', the new Christian activism will address the whole spectrum of human need. The new activism will not arbitrarily choose between evangelism and social action. Jesus' proclamation of the Kingdom was not a diluted call to inner well-being. He knew of no neat dichotomies between spiritual and material need. Instead he addressed the totality of human need. Indeed if 'evangelism' is properly understood as the proclamation of the Kingdom of God, it would be conceptually impossible to define evangelism apart from a thoroughgoing concern for social justice.

---

believed that the prospect of enduring peace among nations--guaranteed by an effective international law which would protect human rights--is an attainable possibility that should guide present reforms in international relations [The Metaphysical Elements of Justice, trans. by J. Ladd (Indianapolis, Ind.: Bobbs-Merrill, 1965), pp. 125ff.; Perpetual Peace, trans. by L. W. Beck (Indianapolis: Bobbs-Merrill, 1957), pp. 35ff.]. It should be noted that Kant's breadth of vision led him to make the bold proposal of a federation of states 150 years before the charter of the United Nations [Carl Friedrich, "The Ideology of the United Nations and the Philosophy of Peace of Immanuel Kant, 1795-1945" (Journal of Politics 9:10-30, 1947)].

236

With realism as its helmet, hope as its shield and the vision of the Kingdom as its sword, the new Christian activism must carry the Good News unto the far reaches of the earth. Neither the parched earth of the African Sahel nor the monsoon drenched paddies of South Asia will be outside its purview. Its voice must be heard at the negotiating tables at Geneva, resonating the declaration that "the earth is the Lord's and the fulness thereof." Our hand is on the plow. Shall we be content to gaze wistfully into the past, or will our vision strain forward?

THE COST OF FRANKNESS

Can Popular Christianity survive without self-deception? To rephrase the question: If Popular Christianity sheds its self-deception, will it still be popular (i.e., capable of being accepted by large groups)?

Certainly part of Popular Christianity's appeal is related to its ability to offer its adherents a well-defined belief system which ameliorates the gnawing sense of moral ambiguity that afflicts modern man. Of course, the price of such certitude is self-deception; and, as I emphasized throughout the book, self-deception is a sure road to self-defeat.

Can Popular Christianity shorn of self-deception retain its sense of absolute certitude? Probably not. The cost of frankness is ambiguity. We can appreciate that ambiguity or despise it, but we cannot avoid it without resorting to self-deception. Facing a world that is not black and white can be extremely discomforting. But comfort for comfort's sake has never been a very important value for those who dared to walk in the footsteps of the Master.

Yet Christians can and must be absolutely certain about one thing: they have a mandate from God that calls them to the center of human struggle, strife and suffering with a message of reconciliation, peace and hope. They can be positive that this mandate summons them to be peacemakers, to announce forgiveness and enact justice, as ones who claim friendship with God. This is the kind of certainty that Christianity offers--a dynamic, transforming confidence that the Creator of the universe has something to say to the human condition.

Can Christianity be popular without self-deception? The answer lies with us. It will depend on the depth of our imagination, the strength of our moral fiber and the soundness of our faith.

Our generation is faced with unparalleled opportunities for doing good and unprecedented prospects for wreaking destruction. With enough moral resolve we could accomplish two goals that generations of the past hardly even dreamt of. First, we have the ability to stem and reverse the tide of thermonuclear weaponry that threatens to submerge the earth in a fiery sea of radioactivity. Second, for the first time in human history, we have the capacity to eradicate hunger and malnutrition-related diseases from the face of the earth.

The consequences of our inaction are grave. With each passing hour, the threat of nuclear war increases, either due to some accidental miscalculation or as the unintended outcome of a small-scale conflict that escalated out of control. With the serious population crisis, we can expect widespread famines and worsening deprivation in the less developed world, unless bold initiatives are taken now to avert such a crisis.

Each generation of Christians has the responsibility to articulate the prophetic spirit of their faith credibly. For our generation, the Christian's base of credibility lies in his actions. Platitudes and good intentions will not suffice. If we fail to appreciate the uniqueness of this moment in world history, cowering in self-deception, "we are of all men most to be pitied." We need not cloak our Christian commitment in falsehood. The possibilities of frankness are limitness!

Lord, make me an Instrument of your peace.
Where there is hatred, . . . let me sow love.
Where there is injury, . . . pardon.
Where there is doubt, . . . faith.
Where there is despair, . . . hope.
Where there is darkness, . . . light.
Where there is sadness, . . . joy.

O Divine Master, grant that I may not so much
     seek
To be consoled, . . . as to console,
To be understood, . . . as to understand,
To be loved, . . . as to love
     for
It is in giving, . . . that we receive,
It is in pardoning, that we are pardoned,
It is in dying, . . . that we are born to eternal
     life.

                         --St. Francis of Assisi
                           (1181/82-1226)

ABOUT THE AUTHOR

Van B. Weigel is a Ph.D. candidate at the
University of Chicago. His current work
is focused on ethics and economic development, and his doctoral dissertation is entitled: "The Basic Needs Approach to Economic
Development: Ethical Definitions." He
has a M.Div. degree from Eastern Baptist
Theological Seminary and presently teaches
in the Department of Business and Economics
at Eastern College in St. Davids, Pennsylvania.